DATE DUE

SCRAMBLE FOR THE BALKANS

MIGRATION, MINORITIES AND CITIZENSHIP

General Editors: Zig Layton-Henry, *Professor of Politics and Director of the Centre for Research in Ethnic Relations, University of Warwick*; and Danièle Joly, *Director Designate, Centre for Research in Ethnic Relations, University of Warwick*

This series has been developed to promote books on a wide range of topics concerned with migration and settlement, immigration policy, refugees, the integration and engagement of minorities, dimensions of social exclusion, racism and xenophobia, ethnic mobilisation, ethnicity and nationalism. The focus of the series is multidisciplinary and international. The series will publish both theoretical and empirical works based on original research. Priority will be given to single-authored books but edited books of high quality will be considered.

Titles include:

Naomi Carmon (*editor*)
IMMIGRATION AND INTEGRATION IN POST-INDUSTRIAL SOCIETIES

Adrian Favell
PHILOSOPHIES OF INTEGRATION

Danièle Joly
HAVEN OR HELL? Asylum Policies and Refugees in Europe

SCAPEGOATS AND SOCIAL ACTORS: The Exclusion and Integration of Minorities in Western and Eastern Europe

John Rex
ETHNIC MINORITIES IN THE MODERN NATION STATE

Steven Vertovec and Ceri Peach (*editors*)
ISLAM IN EUROPE: The Politics of Religion and Community

Migration, Minorities and Citizenship
Series Standing Order ISBN 0–333–71047–9
(*outside North America only*)

You can receive future titles in this series as they are published by placing a standing order. Please contact your bookseller or, in case of difficulty, write to us at the address below with your name and address, the title of the series and the ISBN quoted above.

Customer Services Department, Macmillan Distribution Ltd
Houndmills, Basingstoke, Hampshire RG21 6XS, England

Scramble for the Balkans

Nationalism, Globalism and the Political Economy of Reconstruction

Edited by

Carl-Ulrik Schierup
Director Centre for Studies on Migration, Ethnic Relations and Globalisation
(MERGE)
University of Umea
Sweden

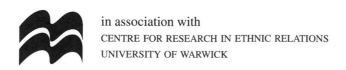

in association with
CENTRE FOR RESEARCH IN ETHNIC RELATIONS
UNIVERSITY OF WARWICK

First published in Great Britain 1999 by
MACMILLAN PRESS LTD
Houndmills, Basingstoke, Hampshire RG21 6XS and London
Companies and representatives throughout the world

A catalogue record for this book is available from the British Library.
ISBN 0–333–67902–4

 First published in the United States of America 1999 by
ST. MARTIN'S PRESS, INC.,
Scholarly and Reference Division,
175 Fifth Avenue, New York, N.Y. 10010

ISBN 0–312–21744–7

Library of Congress Cataloging-in-Publication Data
Scramble for the Balkans : nationalism, globalism and the political
economy of reconstruction / edited by Carl-Ulrik Schierup.
p.   cm. — (Migration, minorities, and citizenship)
"Published in association with the Centre for Research in Ethnic
Relations, University of Warwick."
Includes bibliographical references and index.
ISBN 0–312–21744–7 (cloth)
1. Former Yugoslav republics—Politics and government.   2. Former
Yugoslav republics—Economic conditions.   3. Former Yugoslav
republics—Ethnic relations.   4. Former Yugoslav republics—Foreign
relations.   I. Schierup, Carl-Ulrik.   II. Series.
JN9670.S38   1998
320.9497'09'049—dc21   98–23642
                                                             CIP

Selection, editorial matter and Chapters 1 and 2 © Carl-Ulrik Schierup 1999
Chapters 3–7 © Macmillan Press Ltd 1999

This book is printed on paper suitable for recycling and made from fully managed and sustained forest sources.

10   9   8   7   6   5   4   3   2   1
08   07   06   05   04   03   02   01   00   99

Printed and bound in Great Britain by
Antony Rowe Ltd, Chippenham, Wiltshire

Contents

Notes on the Contributors

Vesna Bojičić is Research Fellow at the Sussex European Institute. Publications in English include 'Bosnia-Hercegovina: an Extreme Case of Transition in the Balkans', in S. Bianchini and M. Uvalic (eds), *The Balkans and the Challenge of Economic Integration* (with M. Kaldor), *'The Political Economy of the War in Bosnia-Hercegovina,'* in M. Kaldor and B. Vashee (ed) *Restructuring the Global Military Sector: New Wars.*

Mark Duffield is Senior Researcher at the School of Public Policy at the University of Birmingham, specialising in the field of complex political emergencies, in particular comparative work on Africa and Balkans. This has included consultancy work for a number of UN agencies, donor governments and NGOs.

Ivan Iveković is Professor of Comparative Politics, School of Humanities and Social Sciences, American University, Cairo, Egypt. His publications in English include *A Political Economy of Contemporary Ethnonational Mobilization: Ethnic and Regional Conflict in Yugoslavia and Transcaucasia.*

Mary Kaldor is Jean Monnet Reader in Contemporary European Studies at the University of Sussex. Her publications include *The End of Military Fordism* (editors U. Albrecht and G. Schmeder) and *Citizenship and Democratic Control in Contemporary Europe* (with B. Einhorn and Z. Kavan).

Branka Likić-Brborić is Research Assistant at the Department of Economic History, Uppsala University. She has published a number of works in the Serbian-Croatian-Bosnian languages on the issues of reform, development, and the general theoretical problems of political economy.

Carl-Ulrik Schierup is Director for the Centre for Studies on Migration, Ethnic Relations and Globalisation (MERGE), University of Umeå, Sweden. His publications in English include *Will They Still be Dancing?*, *Migration, Socialism and the International Division of Labour*, and *Paradoxes of Multiculturalism.*

Boris Young is Fellow at the Community and Organization Research Institute (CORI) at the University of California, Santa Barbara. He is currently working on *The Great Game Redux? The Return of Caspian Oil to World Markets.*

1 The Spectre of Balkanism: Globalisation, Fragmentation and the Enigma of Reconstruction in Post-Communist Society
Carl-Ulrik Schierup

'History teaches nothing, but only punishes for not learning its lessons.'[1]

Vassily Kliuchesky

THE MALHEUR AND MISÈRE OF A TRANSITION

History Returned?

From east to west, a wave of ethnic revivalism has swept over Europe, underpinned by strivings for national and regional autonomy. The multinational Soviet empire has broken apart. Yugoslavia and Czechoslovakia are no more. A 'new world order' – or a new world *dis*order, as some prefer to call it[2] – is intimately bound to new supra-national projects, but, at the same time, the breakdown of the great ideologies and burgeoning ethnic and national conflicts. Universalist ideologies have been challenged by 'back-to-roots' movements. Transnational economic restructuring and the social and cultural crises following contemporary processes of globalisation have given rise to cosmopolitan, but also to localist or exclusionist and self-contained, identities. A fiery end of 'the short twentieth century' does not belie the ambiguous reputation it has earned for being an 'age of extremes'.[3]

In the midst of its renewal the world today seems to have turned to the past. While some have dared to proclaim the fall of the Berlin Wall 'the end of history', as incarnating an alleged ultimate victory of Western liberal democracy, others have referred to the much heralded 'new world order' as a 'new middle ages'.[4] Old empires and past national uprisings are reflected in new present-day boundaries, ethno-national conflicts and

1

hegemonic geo-political projects. Academics, journalists and politicians have spoken about the 'return' or 'rebirth' of history and of the 'clash of civilisations' epitomised in the resurfacing of old fault lines marked by religion and culture.[5]

The 'return of history' has been particularly popular as a metaphor and *Leitmotif* for students of Eastern Europe's post-communist transformation. By popular lore and by many scientists and journalists, the so-called 'rebirth of East Europe' (Roskin 1991, Gerner 1991) has come to be depicted as the reawakening of dormant but age-old cultural and national identities, suppressed, but also conserved, during a historical interlude of totalitarian and centralistic communist rule.[6] The logic of this narrative is that an unendurable pressure had been built up by new movements of civil society, progressively depriving totalitarian regimes of any sustainable legitimacy (e.g. Ramet 1991). Following this, a liberating ethnonationalist explosion blew off the heavy lid from an over-heated 'boiling cauldron'. This perspective was, for example, vividly pursued by Piotr Wandycz (1992) in *The Price of Freedom*. Others, like Misha Glenny (1993), reflecting on *The Fall of Yugoslavia*, have preferred to see the post-1989 populist eruptions as the result of mischievous efforts to 'freeze down' deeply historically embedded ethnic conflicts and hatred. And 'when the resentments were taken out of the historical deep freeze, the memory of hatred proved to be as fresh as ever after it thawed' (Glenny 1993:13). In both cases 'the revenge of the past' (Suny 1993) has been the tenet of the argument; and, whether the ethno-nationalist resurgence is seen as cultural liberation and progress or, alternatively, as a new barbarism, we meet here discourses embodying a similar primordialist logic.

The past *is*, in a certain sense, indeed still with us and is a major force behind the general development as well as the direction of local conflicts. The contemporary upsurge of nationalism in Eastern Europe is not a novel *sui generis* phenomenon (Pearson 1995:25), but part of an ongoing historical process. Nationalist agendas with a distinctive ethnic tinge have been established in this part of Europe since the beginning of the nineteenth century. Cultural, ethnic and religious fault-lines, worked out during the reign of old multi-ethnic empires (the Habsburg, the Ottoman and the Russian),[7] were subsequently stabilised through the agency of nineteenth-century nationalist movements' efforts to forge solid cultural communities by means of popular education (Jelavich 1990) and political organisation. They continue to form the basic fault-lines of contemporary ethno-national conflicts,[8] the eruptive potentials of which are quite obviously buried in the collective memories of long-since politicised ethnies (cf. Smith 1971).

Today's conflicts are nurtured and forged by yesterday's traumas. Former Yugoslavia provides a particularly good illustration of this time compression. Here, history appears indeed to have 'returned with a vengeance . . . like a film stopped for 45 years which has suddenly resumed' (Joffe 1992:25). The frustrated historical memories at stake, the political quandaries and the cruelties committed during the Balkan wars of 1991–5 are intimately linked to the great civil war staged by the Axis powers fifty years earlier (1941–5), and the imprint its massive acts of genocide left on the souls of generations. The historical experience of 1941–5, as well as the recent armed conflicts and excesses of 'ethnic cleansing' in Croatia and Bosnia-Herzegovina during 1991–5, can again be linked further back to older historical fault-lines and past ethnic and national identities and conflicts (further in Schierup 1998a and 1998b).

There are, however, many dimensions of the current transformation which demand a critical stance towards that which appears to be in what there is. Even if History is always present it does not merely repeat itself. The past in the present carries projections of the present and the future onto the past (Friedman 1992, paraphrasing Bloch 1976), whereby meaningful narratives and strategies for individuals and social collectives are constructed. Social groups and political movements in specific contexts with particular interests 'construct' themselves by making history (Friedman 1992). 'All history including modern historiography is mythology' (Friedman 1992:837) and, seen in this perspective, popular images of the 'return of history', may give evidence as to the self-fulfilling capacity of discourses tied to contemporary claims for power, more than they demonstrate the inevitable and spontaneous 'rebirth' of supposedly primordial feelings, identities and cultural values.

Former Yugoslavia and its ethnocratic successor states provide an abundance of examples of this kind of mythologies. In Serbia and Croatia, like in other parts of this former multi-ethnic, multi-national federation, charismatic leaders and regime-monitored mass media have staged chosen historical victories or traumas in exclusionary ethno-nationalist and racist dressings in order to authenticate contemporary political claims and achievements.[9] In the process, latent collectively shared and historically rooted passions and fears have been aroused and coupled with the manipulation of present anxieties and social despair.[10] Through the agency of local poets, journalists and academics an enforced cultural homogeneity has been cultivated, while an historical reality of multicultural mutuality and transethnic interpenetration has been weeded out from imagined national Gardens of Eden.

In this project of renarration, medieval empires, alleged religious traditions and nostalgic millenarian dreams have been instrumentalised in order to bring new ethnocratic regimes to power and to legitimise their particular present-day version of genocide (that is, 'ethnic cleansing'). Radicalising nineteenth century national projects, regime-monitored media[11] have presented disconcerted populations with powerful reimaginations of well-worn images of 'old national traditions', already heavily recycled across the history of the twentieth.[12] This virtual reality came to include a post-modern tinge (Dragićević-Šešić 1992), designed by IT experts to capture the minds of a younger generation with an, at most, fragmentary image of history. Bits and pieces of local historical symbolism and raw-materials from our contemporary global cultural community have become merged into new inventive fantasies of the nation.[13] A patriarchal Balkan mythology has been exploited in the post-modern genres of popular culture. In the process, 'honour and heroism' (*ćojstvo i junaštvo*) have been remoulded into an iconographic idolatry of violence and sexism (Dragićević-Šešić 1992).[14] This dramaturgy of nationalist identity politics found expression in tangible social effects. If not before, this became clear as, fashioned in the tones, tunes and fiction of a new–old Balkan '*Folk-Techno*',[15] ghetto-blasters started yelling their neo-tribal war-cries from tanks and trenches.

The Agony of Another Rebirth

Through its refashioning of 'imagined communities' (Andersson 1983) and its engineering of new–old identities insulating *Us* from *Others*, the nationalist propaganda fostered sharp ethno-national boundaries and real conflicts.[16] Next, the war itself and its inter-ethnic cruelties should come to boost self-fulfilling prophecies. Alleged 'cultural gaps' and 'ethnic distance' were now violently carved out, where they had not already been effectively construed.[17]

This is one, by now comparatively well researched, perspective on the contemporary malheur of the region of what was Yugoslavia. But the other, and closely related, side of the story is a tragedy which, beyond its regional aspects, reflects a more encompassing *misére du monde*. In this perspective the crisis and fall of Yugoslavia, as well as the contemporary depressed condition of the successor states, represent a compression of our shared contemporary traumata of poverty and unequal development in the process of globalisation, at the same time as they expose the old roots of a new world disorder. This is the common theme and perspective of the essays in this book. Taking former Yugoslavia and its successor states as their prime example, they discuss global and local contingencies of nationalism, fragmentation and the political economy of 'reconstruction' in post-communist society.

The thematic of current economic globalisation, epitomised in the neo-liberal credo of 'creative destruction',[18] relates, as it were, to a history which maybe certainly repeats itself, even if in new robes. It is of a kind, as far as it is synonymous with the triumphant advance of a so-called 'free market', connected with what Karl Polanyi (1957[1944]) once so imaginatively named 'the Great Transformation'. His critical comparative historical work still offers a potent source of inspiration, not least relating to the current complex problems and dilemmas of reconstruction in post-communist societies; that is, enigmas produced by rapid cultural change, new economic and social crises and the havoc wrought by ethnic wars. What Polanyi analysed was the Great Transformation to a capitalist market economy. He described this as a long historical process that first fully blossomed in England towards the end of the eighteenth century and which since – passing historical advances and retreats – continued to subsume a widening range of geographical localities, cultural life-worlds and institutional settings under its dominance. But social stability, and with it an environment favourable for long-term investment and economic development, has, across the history of capitalism, been intimately dependent on a 'double movement'. This implies a precarious balance between 'two organizing principles in society' (Polanyi 1957[1944]). The one is the principle of economic liberalism, aiming at the establishment of a 'self-regulating market' (Polanyi 1957[1944]), and the other, the principle of social protection aiming at the conservation of man and nature as well as productive organisation.

A *longue durée* historical experience, stretching from the late Tudors and the English Enclosure movement to the New Deal and Fordist industrialism, had demonstrated that not only human beings and natural resources, but also the organisation of capitalist production itself, had to be sheltered from the destructive effects of forms of social change driven solely by the urge for gain. A functioning capitalist economy is fundamentally dependent on political regulation and on historically established and morally sanctioned cultural institutions. Left to unbridled dominance, fundamentalist liberal principles of pure gain and market driven social self-regulation will sooner or later devour the institutional and moral ground for their own accomplishment. This was exactly, maintains Polanyi, what happened with the dramatic breakdown of the liberal world economic system in the 1930s. Deep fiscal crises in state after state led to social upheavals, to the vehement state-totalitarian reactions against liberalism represented by fascism, nazism and Stalinism, to radical nationalism and to the renewed cataclysm of global war.

The welfare state was another, more benevolent and auspicious, response to the liberal market. After the Second World War corporate state bureaucracies managed, through the vehicles of Keynesian economics and elaborate social policies, to enforce that great social compact which, in the West, was to conciliate the interests of capital with those of strong modern movements of civil society. For three decades (1945–75) this set the framework for economic expansion, relative prosperity and social stability in the dominant capitalist countries of the world. In the Soviet Union, the post-Stalinist interlude of Khrushchev's failed reforms was, in the 1960s, succeeded by Brezhnev's so-called *new social compact*; it was a recasting of the power system of actually existing socialism, institutionalising a great social compromise between the ruling bureautocratic[19] elite and a state–dependent working class (Zaslavsky 1982). Similar developments we find in other parts of the Second (communist) Europe. This less sophisticated real-socialist counterpart to the welfare state, procured – as long as it lasted – modest prosperity and relative social stability, albeit at the cost of a gradual erosion of conditions essential for its own reproduction (Piccone 1990).

Now, after the exhaustion of those two great post-Second-World-War social compacts that marked the heyday of mass industrialism in Europe – the archetypal social democratic national welfare state in the West and actually existing socialism in the East – no grand ideologically founded narratives of social solidarity, controlling the forces of a globalising capitalist market, are heard any more. 'The End of History' may indeed appear near. But, at the same time, this very silence and the dearth of alternative visions relating to broad forms of social solidarity and responsibility become increasingly alarming.

'Robbed of the protective covering of cultural institutions, human beings would perish from the effects of social exposure; they would die as the victims of acute social dislocation through vice, perversion, crime and starvation' (Polanyi (1957[1944]:73)). This gloomy scenario, painted by Polanyi towards the end of that great war which followed the breakdown of the world economy and the rise of totalitarian regimes in Europe of the 1930s, could, in fact, serve as an adequate description of the social agony that we observe today in Romania, Bulgaria, Albania and most of the new states succeeding the Soviet Union and former Yugoslavia. After five decades of bureaucratic collectivism having eradicated or fragmented whatever there was here of a genuine civil society, the post-Wall collapse of actually existing socialism left these societies devoid of protection or defence as they became exposed to the rampant commodification of an unregulated and atomising laissez-faire capitalism.

The forces of 'creative destruction' have, so far, appeared mainly in their destructive function, and today the consequences of an accelerating economic 'globalisation', as propelled by the rapid expansion of an unbound market economy after the end of the cold war, have already evolved so far that this has started to virtually terrify some of its own most powerful agents. An unrestricted contemporary neo-liberal trust in laissez-faire capitalism may lead to global social and political collapse, warns multi-milliardaire financier and philanthropist George Soros in his sensational world-wide disseminated article, 'The Capitalist Threat' (1997), echoing

Polanyi. Today, he maintains, an absolutist market-fundamentalism and the predatory capitalism it spawns in eastern Europe is a greater threat to the building of the institutions of open democratic societies than yesterday's totalitarian ideologies ever were. New forms of moral commitment, broad solidarity, and social redistribution are acutely needed. A West, indiscriminately casting universalist visions of liberal democracy in the iconography of a global market's invisible hand, will continue to invoke economic chaos, together with new, dangerous returns of the spectres of authoritarian populism and a radical and exclusive nationalism,[20] the latter nurtured by deep social injustice, inequality and poverty.

Return of the Authoritarians

In fact, Soros's dire predictions represent what has indeed already materialised, as substantial parts of post-communist Europe – with the Balkans as the most conspicuous example – find themselves in a seemingly chronic state of political crisis, institutional jeopardy, and social upheaval. The popular rebellion in Albania during the spring of 1997, provoked by a poverty-stricken population's disappointment with deceptive 'pyramid games', with the treacherous promises of corrupt political elites and with a dawning capitalist *Wirtschaftswunder*, expressed the escalating *misère* and dangerous potentials of our present Great Transformation in a dramatic and highly symbolic form. But this is only one bit of a comprehensive scenario. Less than a decade after the so-called national-liberation revolutions of 1989, popular disillusionment and desperation have, everywhere in post-communist Europe between the Adriatic coast and the Urals, given witness to the historical rebirth of authoritarian and predatory regimes.

Hence, the post-Wall 'national liberation', as we have seen it develop in, among other places, former Yugoslavia, has often – and to the unpleasant surprise for the many, among Western liberals, who expected the revolutions of 1989 to restore a much heralded 'civil society' – turned out to represent an *urge for the restoration of a strong state and paternalist protection among socially exposed population groups*. In the case of former Yugoslavia, the processes of so-called 'ethnic cleansing'[21] which this has generated have given rise to frequent analogies likening radical nationalisms of the Balkans of today with totalitarian nazi Germany of the 1930s and with the Holocaust.[22] Given the overall post-Wall situation of social crisis, poverty and radical populist upheavals, this conspicuous similarity appears to express more than a historical coincidence, which may be preempted by bringing cynical (underdog) war criminals to trial in the Hague. We are today, like in the 1930s, confronted with a dramatic second move in a 'double movement'. It is of the kind that Polanyi described as typical for the advance of a capitalist market which has abruptly outgrown established frameworks of regulation. The disintegration or indiscriminate destruction of existing cultural institutions and forms of political-economic integration, coupled with poverty, injustice and social exclusion, have, like in the case of nazism and fascism, called forth authoritarian reactions expressing strong, collectively shared emotions and tectonic social forces.

Ethnic Nationalism – Past and Present

Comparing these two periods of the twentieth century – the dark 1930s and 1940s and our present *fin de siècle* – the marked similarities of authoritarian and discriminatory regimes have been seen as condensed in the attributes of particularly virulent varieties of the form of state-building strategy named 'ethnic nationalism'.[23] It is, as argued by Robert M. Hayden (1992), a conception of the nation where citizenship is defined in narrow ethnic terms, based on assumptions of common descent. The exclusion of ethno-national minorities is, more or less explicitly, inscribed into the constitutional foundations of the state. This is, in contrast to most countries of western Europe, typical for the new Baltic States, the Transcaucasian region of the former Soviet Union, Slovakia and for the ex-Yugoslavian successor states. In ex-Yugoslavia and the Transcaucasian region ethnic nationalism has come to form the ideological justification for warfare and for a systematic and violent 'ethnic cleansing' of alleged 'national territories'.[24] Ethnic nationalism is, however, not a characteristic restricted to contemporary post-communist states. It was also a defining property of nazi Germany (and in this particular respect Germany has still not ridden itself completely of its nazi past[25]), as well as for several regimes in eastern Europe of the 1930s and 1940s. In Germany it legitimated the Holocaust and the enslavement of captives from the eastern European empire of the *Reich*[26] in the booming war industry (Cohen 1987); lesser (Slavic) breeds destined, by nature and History, to serve the '*Arian*' species, or to perish.

The exclusionism, inherently intertwined with ethnic nationalism – in extreme cases finding expression in genocide[27] or 'ethnic cleansing' – can, in general, be taken as a sign of flagging national cohesion or as the symptom of processes of state-building exposed to heavy outside pressure.[28] But wherever in today's Balkans, eastern Europe and the Transcaucasian region we find authoritarian traits and exclusionary practices based on definitions of race, culture and ethnicity, they are managed and operationalised by types of regiments and in the context of states with little *structural* affinity with the nazi state (as argued by Kaldor 1993). This is so even when, in the particularly radical case of Croatian nationalism, present-day leaders ferociously recultivate a Second-World-War-style racist and nazi-reminiscent ideology and political culture[29] (in the same instance as they revise this past, legitimising it as an integrated and dignified moment in the historical evolution of a liberal 'Western democracy'[30]). Discriminatory excesses of today are, in spite of obvious ideological affinities, in any case contingent on new constellations of cultural and social forces.

Nazi Germany was founded on the basis of a totalitarian ideology with authoritative scientific and philosophical backing, inspiring a number of prominent intellectuals across the Western world. Germany of the 1930s developed into a strong, centralised state based on a powerful financial–industrial empire and a well organised state bureaucracy monitoring efficient processes of economic reconstruction and state reorganisation. Its aggressive character emanated against the background of the specific conditions in a society devastated by war, plagued by revanchism, and tainted by the social chaos inferred by the uncompromising indemnity clauses and discriminatory conditionality inscribed into the Versailles Treaty. Nazism became, as it were, in terms of determinate state-bureaucratic intervention in crisis-ridden economies and societies, the highly unfortunate and authoritarian German counterpart to the *New Deal* and to the grand post-Wall-Street-economic-crash, state-monitored processes of economic–industrial and social reconstruction in the liberal democracies of Western Europe. The Holocaust was, as demonstrated by Zygmunt Bauman (1989), itself a masterly exercise in modern centralised state-bureaucratic planning and management and of efficient corporate industrial organisation, but with scant popular legitimacy or active participation.[31]

Our times' new nationalist regimes in the Balkans and the former Soviet Union are, in contrast, economically dependent and politically frail, marginalised by globalisation processes. Their rather nebulous imaginations of 'ethnic purity' lack a solid backing of scientifically and philosophically founded ideologies. Although seemingly strong towards the 'inside', most of these states are riven by the segmentary forces of clientilism and a neo-traditional clannishness. Their dominant élites' legitimacy is frail, and they are forced to rule through a combination of factional manipulation, bribery and threat. Their central bureaucracies are deeply corrupted by nepotist bonds, of kinship, locality and regionalism. The techniques of ethnic cleansing, as it has taken place in former Yugoslavia, have had more the character of clumsy, spuriously pre-modern forms of terror, ostracism and mob-rule[32] than of modern, rational and clinical bureaucratic operations.[33] This, of course, does not make these regimes any less perilous, or the ideologies and practices they expose less problematic. But their different quality, and their contingency on contemporary geopolitical power structures, demand different strategies than those prevalent in the historical struggle against nazism and fascism.

Global Contingencies of Balkan 'Backwardness'

Without neglecting striking historical similarities, which has made a re-visiting of the Great Transformation highly relevant today, we must take seriously the decisive qualitative differences between, even the most authoritarian, regimes in eastern Europe of today and totalitarian nazi Germany of the 1930s.[34] These differences we may attempt to comprehend and analyse alongside a synchronic (structural) axis or dimension as well as a diachronic (evolutionary) one.

Relating to the first of these dimensions, any discriminating analysis must take its point of departure in the hierarchic and asymmetric character of relations of economic, political and cultural–ideological power in the modern international system of geopolitical relationships, which has formed a constant in European history from the mercantilist period until today. Since its emergence as a cohesive national state from the later part of the nineteenth century until this day, Germany has occupied the role of one of the most forceful industrial-capitalist states within this system, with decisive power to influence the direction of global history. The latest two hundred years of Balkan history, in contrast, bear witness to the unequal struggle for constitution and survival of feeble communities on the periphery of the international system, constantly exposed to the fragmenting forces of imperial dominance and grand geopolitical projects imposed from the outside by the European great powers – among them, during this century at least, most significantly, Germany (e.g. Grenzebach 1988).

Relating to the second dimension, the evolutionary, we must build our analysis on a holistic and theoretically founded understanding of the complex dynamics inherent in the ways in which the modern system of international relations has passed several major transformations historically – transformations typically progressing through transitional periods marked by deep political, economic and cultural crises and by dramatic social upheavals. Our present process of globalisation, like other earlier periods of transition, is marked by fundamental changes in forms of production and economic organisation and by new cultural configurations worldwide.[35] But it also carries profound redefinitions of the relationships of power between societies at the powerful 'centre' and the troubled periphery of a still unequal and, maybe more than ever, polarised system of international relations (see further Duffield in this volume, Chapter 5).

What has so far emanated from the current experience of 'transition' in eastern Europe, and not least in the Balkans, is a more obstinate and ubiquitous continuity with the particular historical heritage of economic 'backwardness' (Chirot 1989), so long distinguishing a so-called 'Second Europe' from its western European first-born sibling, than most dared to imagine in 1989. This structural constant has today, however, taken on a range of features, which have as much to do with the evolution of our present condition of globalisation as with the past. It is thus the vagaries of globalisation that frame the specific political qualities marking the authoritarian regimes of our times. This is an important point of departure for a critical discussion of issues of reconstruction in the new societies, emanating from the recent fall of communist one-party rule.

State and Market in the New World Order

Beyond evident historical parallels – given by the nexus of economic and social crisis, exclusivist nationalist ideologies and authoritarian rule – the central dilemma of our current (post-communist) transformation is, following the preceding argument, no longer the deadlock between two great beasts of modernity, as Polanyi described the drama of the 1930s; the liberal market and the modern national state, equally governed by abstract rationality and bureaucratic-technocratic efficiency. In eastern Europe of the 1990s, new 'old' dilemmas emanate from the ways in which the drama of 'backwardness' is perpetuated and transformed through unequal confrontations of a new character. These confrontations are, at a general level, marked by changing relationships between market and state. Here we have, on the one side, transnational capital and the global *laissez-faire* market, which is, all over the world, increasingly cutting loose bonds of obligation to the nation state. On the other side, we have, in extended parts of eastern Europe, a feeble, a-modern state marked by authoritarian identity politics and a rampant neo-traditionalism. It is driven by informal, Mafia-like fraternal networks and the political manipulations of exclusive power cliques, all clustering around diffuse notions of the ethnic state, which functions as the legitimising tenet of their dominance. This is what lends so many instances of our times' new nationalism in the East the quality of a sustained 'abnormality' (see further Bojičić and Kaldor in this volume, Chapter 4) and extreme social and political instability.

'The new nationalism is decentralizing and fragmentative in contrast to earlier nationalisms which were unifying and centralizing,' wrote Mary Kaldor (1993). In this sense, it stands out in contrast, not only to the totalitarian experience of Germany and Italy of the 1930s and 1940s, but also (as emphasised by Suhrke 1993) to the general tendency that marked the many national liberation movements in economically underdeveloped regions of the world following after the Second World War and marking most of the Cold War period (see also, Schierup 1995a). Any proficient policy for reconstruction in the unsteady post-communist societies of the Balkans, and in particular in former Yugoslavia's successor states, must start from an understanding of this historical shift in the state formation process and of the social and political-economic forces propelling it.

ISSUES OF CRISIS AND RECONSTRUCTION

The reaction of the so-called 'international community's' and, in particular, the West, to the vagaries of the crisis in former Yugoslavia has, however, been marked by a conspicuous air of moral-political schizophrenia and by a number of short-sighted and seemingly paradoxical tactical and strategic moves (e.g. Jacobsen 1996 and Schierup 1995b). On the one hand there is the officially declared Western dedication to a general humanitarian credo of plural democracy, multiculturalism and human rights. On the other hand we have witnessed the actually existing geo-political scramble among single Western powers for spheres of influence, propping up in the process, their own favourite bastards among the new Balkan caudillos. This was, in particular, a condition that put its mark on the so-called 'peace process' up until 1995; that is, before the establishment of an overall US hegemony, iron-fistedly directing the further course of events. In this sense, the historical return (reminiscent of the Balkan Wars at the beginning of this century) of a dismal spectre of 'Balkanism' (Schierup 1995a, b), marked by fraud, manipulation and bribery, reflects also, as noted by Glenny (1994), a 'return of the great powers'.

After the signing of the Dayton Agreement – itself a contradictory construct, marked by the gap between a humanitarian rhetoric and a pragmatic *realpolitik* – great-power rivalry has retreated into the background. But it has given way to new discrepancies emanating from the prevalent approach to, and practices of, 'reconstruction', which, for the sake of *stability*, continue to effectively legitimise the local regimes that started the war and ethnic cleansing in the first place. This is rationalised as a phase in a transition to a 'normal' state of society marked by 'democracy' and a 'market economy'. But in case this proposition is skewed, and a new type of depressive *abnormality* – a state of permanent economic and social disorder, exploited, sanctioned and reproduced by the present authoritarian rulers – has become the normal and structurally embedded state of affairs on the periphery of an increasingly polarised world, then Western policy may, in effect, act to block a transition to genuine democracy as well as a proficient economic reconstruction. This is a problem, situated at the centre of the issues of crisis and reconstruction in the Balkans treated by the contributions to this volume, to which I now turn.

Globalisation as Reperipheralisation

In former socialist Yugoslavia we find the basic configuration of the kind of social (dis)order described above developing, step by step, from the beginning of the 1970s (further in Schierup 1990 and 1993). It is contingent on the exhaustion of the potentials of local bureautocratic strategies of development that, in conjunction with uncompromising global embraces of the capitalist market and the austerity strategies of international monetary organisations (e.g. Dyker 1990 and Chepulis 1994), acted to produce a protracted and deepening economic and social crisis. After conspicuous initial successes of the grand, ultra-radical, socialist modernisation project, Yugoslavia was, in effect, downgraded to its pre-Second-World-War position as a shaky, conflict-ridden community on the periphery of the world economy. This increasingly jeopardised established bureautocratic strategies for mass political and ideological integration. Contingent on this, a pervasive re-traditionalisation of society took place during the 1970s and 1980s. Most of what had, after the Second World War, been established of a modern bureaucratic accountability became exposed to the rule of an all pervading condition of political clientilism.[36] This produced – as will be discussed in Chapter 2 – an increasingly unstable and segmentary society, the cohesion of which became dependent on a fabric of primordial loyalties woven by relations of kinship, friendship, territoriality and ethnicity.

In this development, putting its stamp on every pore of Yugoslavian society during the 1970s and 1980s, there was an historical continuity with deeper roots than the socialist revolution (1941–5) and that of an 'actually existing self-management', which harboured innate segmentary and centrifugal forces. Under the shadow of economic globalisation, reperipherialisation[37] and economic retrogression, an essential characteristic of the pre-Second-World-War *ancien régime* – the reproduction of state power through clientilestic networks twined along primordial loyalties[38] – came to blend organically with the features of a fragmented (socialist) 'self-management' bureaucracy (Schierup 1990). As the economic crisis deepened during the 1980s, local political elites in the republics started to openly legitimise their rule in ethnic terms and with reference to national tradition. In the name of 'democracy', the bonds of clientilism became an effective vehicle for an authoritarian–populist political mobilisation along lines of ethnicity, nation, region and religion. These are the historical conditions that, during the late 1980s and early 1990s, gave rise to militant ethnic nationalism, political fragmentation and ethnic cleansing. And rather than becoming the harbingers of a new modern and liberal era, most of the current nationalist regimes of the successor states continue to reproduce and further deepen the wayward processes of neo-traditionalisation and the recurrent crises of legitimacy that left their distinctive mark on the later phases of actually existing socialism.

Seen in a wider perspective, this sort of condition is not confined to the space of former Yugoslavia, but is a scenario the essential features of which can be generalised concerning many spots of crisis in the contemporary world. We are confronted with a deep crisis of the legitimacy of state structures and their ability to maintain order (e.g. the critical argument by Wallerstein 1994:15). The so-called 'new barbarism',[39] belonging to a multitude of 'civil wars', 'ethnic cleansing' and to the contemporary 'neo-tribal' unrest in the world's big multiethnic cities, extends from Los Angeles to Bosnia (paraphrasing Enzensberger 1994). It is a reality contingent on encompassing structural changes in the world economy and the post-Wall breakdown of established forms of political consensus and socio-cultural integration. This does not imply that the role of the state has necessarily diminished, but that it is exposed to fundamental restructuration. This reflects a global condition in which the contemporary state is being transformed from being a buffer between external economic forces and national economies into an agency for adapting domestic economies to the exigencies of a global market (following Cox 1995, see further Iveković in this volume, Chapter 3). This transformation in function, reminiscent of a return to the nineteenth century's nightwatch state, undermines existing institutions and networks for social protection and produces recurrent crises of legitimacy for those élites who administrate the process. It is, however, in what used to be referred to as the (real-socialist) 'Second World' of a tri-partite Cold War global system (Hettne 1990) – formerly marked by elaborate systems of social protection – that the current crisis of state legitimacy is deepest and its systemic character most obvious.[40] This is expressed in the massive loss of identity, in institutional collapse, and in the moral and normative anomie on which the current breakdown of modern forms of social integration is contingent.

Predicaments of 'Fragmegration'

Seen in this perspective, the conspicuously forceful trajectories of the nationalist regimes of our times appear to be a harbinger of an actual void of sustainable authority, rather than strength; in fact, a negative inversion of Hannah Arendt's (1970) famous dictum: 'Power and violence are opposites; where the one rules absolutely, the other is absent.' Obviously, the advance of a transnational cyber-capitalism's informational society produces a contingent enfeeblement of the political authority, cultural cohesion and institutional frameworks of national states.[41] But this conflict-laden situation of our present is met by highly different strategies of elites and states located, respectively, at the core and the periphery of the contemporary international system, argues Ivan Iveković in his contribution to this volume (Chapter 3). In spite of their internal crises and all their mutual conflicts, core countries pursue their economic and political integration into powerful supra-national blocks. Peripheral regions in the former Third World, or newly peripheralised regions like those of the Second Europe, have, on the contrary, followed a course of political fragmentation, supposedly making them more easily swallowed by the global economy. This is the common development inherent in the simultaneous dissolution of the Soviet Union and former Yugoslavia and numerous similarities concerning their post-communist successor states.

This other 'double movement', of integration–fragmentation or globalisation–localisation – running parallel to the current oscillation between market liberalism and spontaneous popular reactions urging the restoration of state protectionism – has been condensed in the notion of 'fragmegration', put forward by Rosenau (1995, see further the discussion by Iveković in this volume, Chapter 3). It is the disorder of fragmegration, maintains Iveković, that shapes the 'distant proximities' (paraphrasing Rosenau 1995) of what he calls the new 'authoritarian ethnocracies' of the Balkans and Transcaucasia; two otherwise geographically, historically and culturally separate 'shatter belts' of the contemporary world disorder. They are local instances of an increasingly dominant dynamic on a world scale, marked ever more by occasions where the contradictory forces of globalisation and localisation act, in effect, as causal sources to each other. New increments of globalisation foster new increments in localisation, and vice versa, as the pace of the process increases. The effects are, supposedly, both destructive and constructive. But at the moment the destructive effects are more visible. They provoke major disturbances both at the international level (the new world disorder) and at the local level (ethnic conflicts). The disorder of 'fragmegration' fosters major shifts in the conceptions people have of themselves and of their environment, which in turn provokes shifts in their loyalties, including their identification with communities redefined in exclusionary ethno-national terms.

The Poverty of Nationalism, Promises of Transnationalism, and Imperatives of Regionalism

At a less abstract level of analysis, the Balkanisation or 'Caucasianisation' of the former multinational states of Yugoslavia and the Soviet Union can be seen as being contingent on the predominant long-term economic strategies of the international community during the 1970s and 1980s and, subsequently, during the 1990s – which is particularly visible in the case of Yugoslavia – on a geo-political scramble for spheres of influence among major Western powers.[42] But the exclusionary nationalism of the new periphery and globalising markets are, as argued by Iveković (Chapter 3 in this volume), strange bed-fellows and their temporary alliance against state socialism has now lost its initial rationale. In the long run, the course of development in the new states may well, seen from the perspective of transnational capital and Western interests in general, turn out to be highly counterproductive. A powerful, communist-ruled and authoritarian China, open to the world market and foreign investment, appears considerably more attractive than a feeble Albania wholly without rule.

The first move in Eastern Europe's post-communist transformation was, according to the Polanyian logic, indeed marked by a utopian vision of capitalism, assuming that the introduction of a self-regulating market will, all by itself, bring material affluence, welfare and, not least, the reaffirmation of 'the nation'. But a second move has been marked by a re-entry of the state, endeavouring to re-establish local control over the forces of the market. This appears to serve two inter-related purposes: to guard the interests of ruling cliques from outside interference, and to ward off crises of legitimacy of nationalist élites who feel threatened as they confront growing popular dissatisfaction with steeply deteriorating living conditions (Iveković, Chapter 3 in this volume).

However – given a global condition of ever tighter economic interdependence coupled with corrupt and disorganised local state administrations and the rule of local political élites whose shaky legitimacy builds on sustained ethno-national tensions, gangster economies and the extravagant populist inflation of expectations attached to 'national liberation' – such defensive strategies are unrealistic. They have already demonstrated a marked lack of perspective in Bulgaria, Serbia, Croatia and other parts of the Balkans, as well as in many parts of the former Soviet Union. They tend to be narrowly focused on the personal power of the new elites and not on long-term strategy, and, actively pursued, they will imply that the new nationalist regimes will soon exhaust their own legitimacy, and remain of a short-lived transitory nature.

Full integration with the European Union is a hot issue in most East European states, where it is represented as a cure for most illnesses. This option is so far, however, open only to a chosen few (among the Yugoslavian successor states it is a realistic alternative, within a nearer future, only for Slovenia), and this appears to hold true no matter how determined new states might choose to change political course and comply with the prevalent terms of conditionality. The downfall of the Second Europe was more sudden, total and destructive than anybody in the West projected, and the whole morsel much too big to swallow in one go. Already, gulping former GDR (East Germany) has given the *Bundesrepublik* protracted digestion problems. But without new openings today's prevalent condition of Balkanisation may turn into a general and widespread state of *Albanisation*, marked by the virtual collapse of the formal institutions of government.

One alternative opening – to a jeopardising national autarchy and the distant utopia of EU membership – appears in the case of the post-communist Balkans to be that of forging new regional frameworks for economic and political cooperation, outside, but in a close relationship with, the European Union. This will demand a commitment of the Union to a complex, long-term and generous policy of reconstruction – a commitment that could be imagined only as a *concerted action* recognising the 'clear correlation between the constitution of the EU as a political union and the fate of the Yugoslav regions' (Bianchini 1993:118).

The task of reconstruction requires, as it were, a profound break with the capricious geopolitical strategies that dominated the incipient stages of the involvement of the international community and certain Western European powers in the Balkan crisis. But Western Europe and the EU have good reasons – historical and moral, as well as contemporary and pragmatic – to fully accept this task. The particular responsibility of the European Union for the future of its Balkan so-called 'backyard' (see, e.g. Faber 1996) have both past and present aspects. The contemporary *malheur* of the Balkans is, to a large degree, premised on the continued replication of doubtful imperial projects imposed on it by varying European great powers across history (further, Schierup 1990), but also on the recent badly prepared and realised international recognition of new Bantustanised state entities built on crime, ethnic cleansing and social exclusion. In terms of pragmatic security reasons, the former Yugoslavia's geographical positioning in the midst of the EU geographical space itself, means that the Union has a particular interest in stability in this region. Seen in economic terms, the Balkans are, as before, Europe's most important gateway to Asia Minor, essential for the further progress of overall European economic integration.

It is of essential importance to avoid the perpetuation of political conflicts and economic crisis within this region and their possible extension to neighbouring countries, members of or associated partners of the EU. There is certainly, across the European Union, a growing awareness of this, which is crystallised in the progressive elaboration of a 'regional approach' to reconstruction (Minić 1996, Kovač 1996, Likić-Brborić in this volume, Chapter 7). There is, Jelica Minić (1996) concludes, in a review of emerging EU sponsored strategies, frameworks and instruments for regional cooperation in the Balkans and between the European Union and Balkan countries, the need for a truly comprehensive political project. This could be compared, she argues, with the 'European umbrella', which during the early 1970s assisted in bringing the countries of the European South (Greece, Spain and Portugal) beyond authoritarian rule and in setting them on the course of democratic development and auspicious economic restructuration. Today the same assistance is, obviously, necessary to the post-communist countries of the Balkans.

'Reconstruction' and the Political Economy of 'Abnormality': The Case of Bosnia-Herzegovina

A lack of a stable regional framework for peace and development in former Yugoslavia and in the Balkans in general has been a source of conflicts and backwardness throughout modern history. A proper shaping and consolidation of broader forms of economic and political co-operation is essential for long-term solutions (Zarkovic-Bookman 1994, and Likić-Brborić in Chapter 7 in this volume). EU assistance can develop into powerful instruments of pressure and for stimulating new arrangements for mutual cooperation among the countries of the region (Minić 1996).

But, when this is said, it should be noted as well that the very framework of conditionality, upon which current policies of reconstruction assistance are principled, may, as it were, turn out to reproduce or worsen that very state of 'abnormality' that has today become a distinguishing mark for most of the contemporary Balkans region as well as for many other trouble spots in the contemporary world. That means, as defined by Bojičić *et al.* (1995), a depressive state of society marked by widespread poverty and unemployment, violence and criminalisation, weak and fragmented administrations and/or legal structures. The currently dominant type of conditions for access to aid packages of the European Union relate to measurable criteria for democratisation like multi-party elections, and to certain formal criteria for macro-economic stabilisation and liberal market reforms. However, if elections are held in conditions of 'abnormality', they are likely to reproduce and legitimise current authoritarian power structures. Economic stabilisation measures and market reforms are obviously essential, but may – if guided by dogmatic propositions, and indiscriminately employed – contribute to increased poverty, inequality and unemployment. This may exacerbate the causes of violence unless complementary measures are also taken. Moreover, in many cases, stipulated conditions cannot be met without immediate and substantial assistance from the outside. If these needs are not realised, conditionality might turn out to be highly counterproductive (Bojičić *et al.* 1995). If coupled with an overall top-down approach to assistance, where assistance is mainly channelled through ruling ethnocratic elites and political change is entirely entrusted to their good will, policies for 'reconstruction' will at best be apt to sustain the status quo without open warfare, while contributions to reconciliation, sustainable peace and broad processes of political and economic 'normalisation' will remain questionable. Important aspects of this experience are discussed in Chapter 4 of this volume through Vesna Bojičić's and Mary Kaldor's case study of Bosnia-Herzegovina's post-war, post Dayton Agreement (1995) development. We are here, they argue, confronted with a *political economy of abnormality* of a particular contemporary quality. It is the result of a virulent destruction of societal institutions, giving way to the recasting of the economy in the mould of a detrimental, dualised pattern. On the one side a former public sector has been replaced by a humanitarian aid industry entirely run from the outside, but with disastrous effects seen from the perspective of local labour market development, the valuation of (what currently remains of) indigenous expertise, and the promotion of local self-confidence. On the other side there is a new criminalised economy of pillage, dominated by black market activities and the trade in arms and drugs. These two economic spheres continue to feed upon each other, and the prevailing situation of abnormality forms the basis for, and is actively perpetuated by, the political rule of a fragmenting ethnic nationalism.

It is a state of affairs that can be viewed as the result of a forced process of transition shaped by the typical reactions of a peripherilised society to contemporary forces of economic globalisation (e.g. Amin 1994). In former Yugoslavia reperipherialisation, economic regress, institutional disintegration and mounting ethno-national conflicts were, as already mentioned, to a high degree, the results of misguided market economic reforms in the 1980s, which left some of their most adverse effects on the republic of Bosnia-Herzegovina. The consequences of this inauspicious experience of transition were heavily exacerbated by the destructive effects of ethnic conflicts and the civil war among Muslims (Bosnjaks), Serbs and Croats. The basic configuration of the 'abnormal economy', following upon the civil war, Bosnia-Herzegovina shares, however, with most other parts of former Yugoslavia, with Albania which had no war, as well as with many other presently peripherilised parts of the world. An approach to 'reconstruction' that does not take its point of departure in this particular quality of presently peripherilised societies, but continues to devise technical solutions modelled on experience from other times and places (that is, the Second World War and the Marshall Plan) and according to current dogmas of transition (that is, neo-liberal conditionality) is apt to fail. The post-war experience of Bosnia and Herzegovina demonstrates that, by not realising this, the international community risks itself becoming yet another player engaged in the perpetuation of the prevailing 'abnormality'.

'DESTRUCTIVE DESTRUCTION', AND WHAT AFTER?

Technical Approach to a Political Problem: The New Aid Paradigm and Its Discrepancies

The case of Bosnia and Herzegovina illustrates in a pointed form, how different the situation in today's South-Eastern Europe is compared with that prevailing in the early 1970s, when the European Community helped to bring Southern Europe beyond the dictatorships – a development I have discussed elsewhere (Schierup 1990) in relation to the Yugoslavian experience (referring to the argument of Poulantzas, 1975). A profound structural transformation of obstructed, but auspicious, economies in Portugal, Spain and Greece was then achieved on the background of EC support for upcoming oppositional élites' mobilisation of democratic political movements and the subsequent building up of neo-corporatist state structures. What basically took place was that a number of features belonging to the established Northern European welfare states (on the eve of their decline) were extended to Southern Europe and successfully adapted to indigenous conditions (e.g. Giner 1985). This development was contingent on the growth of new economic sectors cast in the mould of Fordist mass industrialism and a consumer society (e.g. Liepitz 1987).

Such a transformation is a far cry from what is today within the horizon of the ongoing transformation of Bosnia and Herzegovina as well as that of the rest of former Yugoslavia, and even the parts of post-communist South-Eastern Europe that were not involved in war. It is partly due to the particular histories and present indigenous conditions of societies within which the effects of the prevalent transition policies were mainly destructive, and where there are scant perspectives for positive change within a nearer future. But this should not make us lose sight of the fact that the character of Western European societies themselves and the European Community has changed radically since the 1970s, and with this even the prevalent conceptions of society, economy, development and aid. This is the wider perspective of Chapter 5, in which Mark Duffield discusses the Balkan crisis as a turning point in the emergence of a new post-cold-war Western aid and security agenda.

While the dynamic economic regions of the world continue to integrate, exclusivist and fragmenting ethnic conflicts dominate in the global periphery into which large parts of the formerly socialist countries have become merged. But, today, qualified analyses of this worrying global situation, marked by global bifurcation, separate development and growing polarisation in (absolute) terms of wealth, are largely absent. The predominant approach to 'reconstruction' in former Yugoslavia reflects, argues Duffield, a more general depoliticisation of the international aid and security agenda. The formidable issue of a proliferating number of ethnic conflicts and internal wars across the world is relativised in terms of common-sense notions of 'cultural pluralism' and individualised in terms of problems of 'mental health'.

This blocks any deeper understanding of the new forms of rationality that carry up local élites' sectarian projects of economic and political survival, under those circumstances of protracted 'abnormality' that characterise an economically and socially depressed global 'South'.

The predominant international response to this new, and largely unanticipated, 'world disorder' has become to 'internalise' the solutions sought to the societies and localities in question (just as the problems and the roots of the problems are now located within these societies). This is a development which is not in itself entirely negative. But the new aid and security paradigm is operationalised through short-term, pragmatic and preferably cheap technical answers to problems that are basically of a political nature and that reflect global as well as local contingencies. This novel overall international approach to aid and reconstruction, taking off from the end of the cold war and in particular the break out of the crisis in former Yugoslavia, produces truly paradoxical results. Behind these, argues Duffield, among other facts, is that the new aid paradigm is cast within an overall, but ill-defined and diffuse ideological framework of 'cultural pluralism'. In the name of 'multiculturalism' and 'human rights', aid for building 'civil society' is channelled through local and international non-governmental organisations. These are, however, competing fiercely against each other within a tight aid market, and are induced to seek spurious technical solutions, rather than cooperating for long-term goals. Parallel to this (relatively limited) support for a fragmented NGO industry, the bulk of official reconstruction aid is channelled through local governments with whom pragmatic compromises are sought through quick fixes in the service of *realpolitik* and state partnership. This acts, in its effects, to marginalise local forces seeking genuine political and economic change – individuals, groups or movements based in civil society, state administration or in business.

Unlearned Lessons of History: International Strategies for Economic Reform, Before and After the Fall of Yugoslavia

A basic problem with the dominant Western paradigm for reconstruction is that it has, to begin with, conceptualised current problems in Eastern Europe in terms of a depoliticised notion of a preordained 'transition'; that is in terms of technical problems involved in monitoring a transition to plural democracy and market economy, the form and content of which is seen as already given. The existing state of disorder is simply supposed to form a step in this direction. The complex and conflict-ridden nature of the present transition demands, however, genuine and critical analysis and a profound re-evaluation of the strategies that at present dominate the involvement of the international community. This appears obvious, not least concerning the, so far, prevalent recipes and strategies for economic restructuration, which reveal only scant, if any, consideration for the particular histories and previous experience, cultures, and actually existing social and institutional contingencies of the societies that they endeavour to reform.

The international community, and its monetary institutions in particular, have taken little notice of the lessons of history, argues Boris Young in Chapter 6. He analyses Western policies for transition in the Yugoslav successor states within a wider comparative and historical framework, including a differential experience with economic reform policies in Latin America, East Asia and Eastern Europe. In the Balkans the present tendency is that the same economic policies that brought about the violent fragmentation of former Yugoslavia are now being thrust upon its successors; that is, the neo-liberal model for economic reform geared to the needs of international capital markets. It has, throughout the 1980s and early 1990s – in spite of the conspicuous presence of the alternative models and exceptionally successful experience of the far-eastern tigers – remained the ideology for economic restructuration of international financial institutions such as the International Monetary Fund and the World Bank. Leaving behind a mixed record in Latin America of the 1980s, it came, from 1990, to form the basis of the so-called 'shock therapy' approach, based on sudden privatisation and immediate and drastic marketisation, devised all across Eastern Europe.

Although the neo-liberal approach has, since then, proved to be a virtual economic and social disaster for most of the states adopting it in the Second Europe, argues Young, it continues, so far, to serve as the official globalisation model. Today, the Yugoslav successor states are faced with the task of integrating with the world market on terms that are considerably less favourable than those they were offered as parts of old Yugoslavia. Insisting, in this situation, on privatisation in the absence of capital, on freeing prices in the absence of working markets, and on the comparative advantages of cheap labour, when there are no jobs and no export opportunities, will lead to the perpetuation of economic crisis and to continuous social and political instability. It is therefore no wonder that, faced with the dubious demands of neo-liberal policies, major political conflicts over economic policy have evolved in each of them. But their objective possibilities for choosing an alternative cause of action, on their own account, are limited.

Privatisation: Records of a Politicised Project for Economic Recovery

For any critical review of the current enigma of transition, it is important to stress, as argued by Klaus Müller (1995:276 ff.), that the neo-liberal reforms launched in Eastern Europe from 1990 represented much more than simply a programme for economic reform. Their actual purpose was as much political as economic, aiming at divesting the old functionaries in the East of their power. They aimed at destroying existing institutions, so as to reassure political irreversibility. The top priority of privatisation was to dismantle the corporatist union between enterprise managers and workers (see further Likić-Brborić, Chapter 7 in this volume), carrying up the basic popular legitimacy of real socialism (as argued by Zaslavsky 1982).

The economic discourse of reform ranges thus way beyond economic change. 'Its aims are to reorganise the social structure, to implement new laws, and to intervene in the political process – all goals (and this is crucial) which pay no regard to politically-needed compromise, social norms or feelings of justice, but which merely create economic constraints' (Müller 1995:277). The implicit ideal is the model of the minimal nineteenth-century 'nightwatch' state. Müller (1995:277) speaks about the intellectual foundations of this approach as a 'negative sociology', built on two main assumptions. The first is that everybody will always, under any circumstances, follow his or her rationally calculated self-interest. The second represents an 'applied theory of totalitarianism', which maintains that since the old (communist) system has completely failed it must and will shortly entirely disappear. This, what is frequently named 'creative destruction' (Schumpeter), is supposed to give way to spontaneous economic activities of free and atomised individuals who will automatically cluster around newly created or transferred market-related institutions.

The abstract character of economic reform policies have called forth criticism pointing at a range of negative repercussions, which may be summarised as follows (following Müller 1995). There is no adequate capital formation from abrupt privatisation. Rapid price liberalisation does not lead to equilibrium and the effective allocation of goods, capital and labour but to stifling monopolies. Insider privatisations reproduce old or produce new malign power structures. An indiscriminate liberalisation of trade leads to the massive flight of capital and abruptly exposes industries to unequal competition. The effects are numerous closures of enterprises and the retreat of domestic capital into financial speculations and the black market. Also, the destructive effects of the attempts to transfer the neo-liberal idea of the minimal state to Eastern Europe, while abruptly dismantling existing institutions and instruments for state-monitored regulation, are now becoming increasingly exposed in the current critique.

This is manifest, for example, in the decay of infrastructure and in a poor state of previously important institutions for education and research and development (long thought to be Eastern Europe's most important comparative advantage), which are falling apart owing to the lack of public investment and organisation. This has extremely adverse effects on long-term development. A dangerous trend is manifest, as well, in the lack of conception for a welfare system and social services with the capacity to alleviate the disruptive effects of rising unemployment, the new poverty and social dislocation.

The alleged creative effects of abrupt marketisation are, in most parts of Eastern Europe, experienced so far by the majority as benefiting mainly those few that profit from a continuous state of social and institutional abnormality and the absence of legally sanctioned standards. The shaky legitimacy of leaders who are not able to demonstrate results to their peoples, supposedly to be produced by a collective willingness to suffer for the sake of the promised rapid transition to a prosperous and just society, may give way, in the worst of scenarios, to a deepening crisis of political authority in general. At the same time, the function of the West itself as an ideal model for Eastern Europe is in retreat. This is connected not only with the unfortunate effects of Western reform policies in the East, but with the decline of the universalist welfare state in the West itself, connected with the adverse longer-term effects of monetarist policies. Also, in Western European nation states, neo-liberal policies have, during the 1980s and 1990s, created an accumulated and acute need for institutional and social reform in an increasingly politically unstable society marked by sectarian cleavages and new forms of social and ethnic segregation (further, Schierup 1995c). Thus, our present transition carries with it a 'Great Deformation', as it has been phrased (Glasman 1994), of a character that we can, so far, only dimly grasp.

Prospects for an Alternative Approach to Transition: The Case of Slovenia

Facing continuous instability in the South-Eastern corner of the continent it is, as pointed out above, clearly in the interest of the European community to rapidly integrate the Balkans into new wider frameworks for economic cooperation and development. But for such an endeavour to be fortuitous local needs must necessarily take precedence over the demands of the neo-liberal model. A growing awareness of this necessity has called forth a current rethinking of the entire problem of transition to capitalism and a search for models and strategies alternative to those sustained by the neo-liberal version of neo-classical economics.

In Chapter 7, Branka Likić-Brborić takes her point of departure in an increasingly obvious crisis for neo-liberal models and policies of transition. A negative experience represented by 'destructive destruction' has, she argues, led the transition debate beyond an initially dominating, but rather technically focused, discussion between (predominantly American) adherents of 'shock therapy' and the so-called (predominantly European) 'gradualists' (that is, adherents of a more gradual transition to a liberal market economy); a debate now regarded as a sort of 'transition prehistory'. Among the most fruitful positions of the current debate is the so-called 'contingency approach', which can be seen as developing an alternative 'positive sociology' of East European societies, culture and economic history, emanating as a virtual conceptual and methodological opposite of the abstract and ahistorical neo-liberal approach. Contingency theories stress the importance of ideologies emanating from each country's unique history, which together with political, social, cultural and institutional contexts and particular types of property relations, determine strategy, goals and policies. This has shaped the global situation that we have today. It is marked not by one single model of capitalism, but by a number of qualitatively different models, ranging from US market individualism, over Western European social market economies, to the 'communitarian' model of Japan.

The direction chosen in individual Eastern European societies as to which road to capitalism to adopt, must, according to this view, be made with respect to their specific institutional settings, national histories and cultures, their citizens' preferences and the particular goals they set for economic development. Based on this argument, new recommendations for transition in Eastern European countries are emerging, taking as a point of departure an industrial democracy approach and the configurations of social market economies, all situated within the wider scenario of an extended process of European integration. The case of Slovenia, argues Likić-Brborić, which was spared from most of the destructive effects of the latest Balkan war, is especially interesting in this respect. Here the outcome of turbulent political conflicts, heated public debates and successful national consensus-making has – in spite of marked discord with the international financial institutions – become both a pragmatic and promising model for transition to capitalism. The industrial democracy model being devised demonstrates remarkable continuity with Slovenia's past affiliation with the Yugoslavian 'self-management' approach (which here had a more promising record than in the Yugoslavian federation in general). Restructured forms of decentralised and centralised so-called 'social property' function as a path-dependent alternative to overall and abrupt privatisation, together with reliance on the market mechanism. This is combined with a determined national policy, striving towards membership of the European Union.[43]

What is common for the Slovenian, and other of those few cases (the Czech Republic, Estonia, and Poland in particular) where transition economies have shown signs of catching up with past economic performance, and appear to have relatively positive prospects for leaping onto the contemporary stage of a technologically advanced global capitalism, is that each of them has had a political vision and a strategy. They have, on this basis, in spite of turbulent conflicts, been able to work out functioning compromises contingent on their particular histories and existing political, institutional and ideological premises. This is now important to emphasise, and not only in relation to a still prevalent neo-liberal, top-down approach, most resolutely backed up by the financial influence and political authority of the US. Their experience is essential to study as well, with reference to the fact that, as discussed above, integration into frameworks for cooperation monitored by the European Union become increasingly important for the future of the whole of Eastern Europe.

European Futures

In the Union today, there is, as it were, a broadening scepticism concerning the neo-liberal framework for reconstruction, among governments as well as among supra-national organisations. Alternative approaches to our present 'Great Deformation' are retrieved that may turn out to favour the development of social market economies, distinguished by principles of equitable income distribution and the development of basic social services. We may, conceivably, come to see the contours of distinctive European strategies for transition develop, which might turn out to provide a major alternative to the prevalent US-led, still predominantly neo-liberal approach to reconstruction (further Likić-Brborić in this volume, Chapter 7). In case this alternative should be translated into the framework of another centralised and bureaucratic top-down approach, however, this might block rather than stimulate a development of those local political compromises that remain an indispensable precondition for a dynamic and realistic development of any supra-national network or association for regional cooperation. No matter how essential new macro-regional projects have become for the creation of stabilising middle-range structures between the global and local levels of an incongruous process of world development, they have no realistic prospects, if social forces with the will, legitimate authority and power to carry out necessary reforms have not, in the first place, crystallised at the national level (Amin 1996, Likić-Brborić in this volume, Chapter 7).

There is no future for reforms carried out through structures abruptly installed by force from the outside. A general process of democratisation and national consensus-making, serving as a basis for developing, reforming or restructuring institutions and administrations on the basis of local premises, cannot be bypassed (Amin 1996). This does not, of course, mean that outside intervention, aid or pressure is irrelevant. On the contrary, and here the European Union must play the key part, the international community must become more conscious of its own role and of the consequences of its strategies as these are processed through the national power-struggles in each of the countries in Eastern Europe and, in particular, in the countries succeeding Yugoslavia, so heavily marked by the *malheur* of ethnic conflicts, authoritarian government and a sustained condition of economic abnormality cum social *misère*. The development of a common comprehensive, but flexible, political vision for long-term social and economic reconstruction and sustainable social integration remains a European exigency, decisive for whether we shall, as expressed by Charles Tilly (1993), succeed in pushing the condition of our part of the world away from 'malign segmentation' toward 'benign pluralism'; and this historical crossroad does not relate to the internal dilemmas and conflicts of a Balkanised Second Europe alone, but as much to those of the First.

Notes

1. Quoted in Smelev and Popov (1987:75).
2. The expression of 'new world disorder' was introduced with somewhat different connotations by Jowitt (1992) and Andersson (1992).
3. Paraphrasing the title of the fourth volume (1994a) of Eric Hobsbawm's megaopus on modern history.
4. Alludes to Fukuyama (1992) and Minc (1993), respectively.
5. Respectively, from the titles of works by Tägil (1992), Glenny (1990) and Huntington (1993).
6. This general and commonly met argument has, for example, been put forward by Lane (1992) and by Kaplan (1993).
7. A historical condition described and analysed by, among others, Cole (1985), Okey (1992), Malcolm (1994) and Schierup (1997a).
8. As described in, among other, the works on nationalism in Eastern Europe's past and present by Bremmer and Taras (1997), Banac (1992), Malcolm (1994) Cuthbertson and Leibowitz (1993).
9. See, for example, the analysis of Serbian nationalist propaganda by Ivan Čolović (1994). For general discussions of elite mobilised and transformed ethnicity see, e.g., Brass (1991) and Fishman (1980).
10. As in the case of the ghostly prelude to war, when one mass grave after another, from the time of the Second World War, was newly 'discovered', and the bones of victims of alleged Ustaša or Četnik terror exhumed in order to be 'processed' in the escalating media warfare between Serbia and Croatia. Or as in the case of Croatian president Tudman's repeated attempts to instrumentalise a reinterpretation of the memorial site of the Croatian

(Ustaša) extinction camp in Jasenovac in the service of forging a new Croatian national historical identity, cleansed from the stains of inglorious events of the past.

11. One of the most informative media studies was done by Mark Thompson for the International Centre Against Censorship (1994).

12. These well-known patterns belonging to the 'invention of national tradition have been discussed in a comparative historical perspective in Hobsbawm and Ranger (1993[1983]).

13. Different aspects of this manipulative post-modern style symbolic 'bricolage were described by Dragićević-Šešić (1992), Čolović (1994) Salecl (1994), and Bowman (1994).

14. The study of Vjeran Katunarić (1994), *Gods, Elites, and Peoples* (Croatian: *Bogovi, elite, narodi*) is an impressive attempt at deconstructing Balkan hero myths, past and present. Concerning the gender issue, see, for example, the ambitious attempt by Sofos (1996) to set up a framework for analysing contemporary processes of social construction of sexuality and gender identity within the context of ethnic conflicts and nationalist-populist politics in former Yugoslavia.

15. *Folk-Techno* is the emblem for a particular musical style that amalgamates popular kitch, so-called 'newly-composed folk-music', with techno. While *Folk-Techno* appears to have been first designed by propaganda technicians of the Yugoslav People's Army for consumption among young Serbian soldiers during the military campaign in Croatia in 1991–2, it later became a popular youth medium of expression with often critical and subversive content.

16. Consecutive sociological recordings of 'ethnic distance' in various parts of former Yugoslavia (e.g. Katunarić 1992, Miljević and Poplašen 1991, Pantić 1991) have demonstrated the constructed and conjunctural character of ethnic identities, 'distance', and boundaries. A general perspective on nationalist ideologies in former Yugoslavia, and the discourses of intellectuals and politicians as relates to a 'symbolic revival of genocide' was put forward by Denich (1994).

17. As demonstrated empirically by panel studies on 'ethnic distance' carried out during the 1980s and early 1990s by Croatian sociologists (e.g. Katunarić 1992).

18. Referring to the rapid breakdown of state led planning and management and of collective ownership rights, egalitarianist principles of redistribution, etc., in favour of the expeditious establishment of private property and the establishment of institutions needed for full marketisation. See also the contribution by Likić-Brbović (Chapter 7).

19. The neologism 'bureautocratic' is taken from Jacobsen's (1996:19) analysis of the Soviet Union. It is designed to embody the essence of all-embracing bureaucracy and autocracy as a generalised system of governance.

20. What Soros sees as an ultimate, but not too distant, threat, is an authoritarian-nationalist take-over in Russia with its enormous potential of nuclear arms.

21. Defined by the United Nations (1992) as the systematic 'elimination by the ethnic group exercising control over a given territory of members of other groups'.

22. From different angles in, for example, Meštrović (1994), Gutman (1993), and Agrell (1994).

23. Denitch (1994) uses the term as the conceptual hub in his analysis of nationalism, fragmentation and social change in the case of former Yugoslavia.

Richmond, (1987) provides a useful overview of different conceptions of 'ethnic nationalism' in the academic literature.

24. In actual politics, the distinction between exclusionary 'ethnic' definitions of the nation and citizenship and other contrasting, inclusionary and universalist ones – that is, varieties conventionally referred to, respectively, as the 'German' and the 'French' archetype – is, however (as shown by, for example, Silverman 1992, and Birnbaum 1992), complex, and often shifts surprisingly with changes in political power blocks and alliances. Among the Yugoslav successor states the case of Serbia (or the Federal Republic of Yugoslavia) is particularly interesting in this respect. It demonstrates the often floating and situational character of the ways in which nations define themselves and their political claims. Hence, at least in the beginning of the latest Balkan war, Serbia legitimated its claims concerning, allegedly Serbian, 'historical regions' in Croatia and Bosnia in terms typical for the exclusionary (German) 'ethnic' variety of nationalism, while claims designed for legitimating Serbian rule in the province of Kosovo were, predominantly, phrased in the language of an inclusionary (French-type) universalism. Still later, after serious Serbian debacles in Croatia and Bosnia and Herzegovina, and when Serbia was forced to concentrate on keeping its interior (still highly ethnically mixed) territory together, yet a third definition started to move centre stage. It was that of the tolerant and open 'multicultural state'; a conception which was particularly eagerly circulated by Mira Marković, the wife of Slobodan Milošević, and head of the orthodox, allegedly Titoist/communist, party, 'The Movement for Yugoslavia' in alliance with the ruling Socialist Party. Both 'ethnic' and 'universalist', as well as 'multiculturalist' conceptions of the nation can, however, as argued in detail by Taguieff (1991), be inherently racist in content, albeit in different ways and with different consequences.

25. This is a fact embodied in the, still (1997) valid, German nationality law, the consequences of which are most clearly exposed through the position of the large population of the Federal Republic made up of ethnic minorities of migrant origin, bereft of rights of citizenship on ethnic grounds (e.g. Birnbaum 1992, Räthzel 1997), but likewise through a contrasting treatment of the so-called 'Aussiedler' immigrants to Germany, residents of eastern European countries for generations, but allegedly of German 'blood'.

26. The development of a strong German 'informal empire in east-central Europe' during the 1930s is described in detail by Grenzebach (1988).

27. At certain times in history euphemistically called 'population transfers', as, for example, in the case of the dissection of India in 1948 or that of the eviction of the ethnic Germans from Czechoslovakia after the Second World War. On this, see the penetrating essay on discourses on genocide by Hayden (1996).

28. See, for example, Birnbaum's (1992) illuminating analysis of the meaning of ethnic nationalism across the modern histories of Germany and France. See also the argument of Schierup (1997a) discussing the meaning of ethnic nationalism in former Yugoslavia.

29. That is, that of the puppet, German-installed, Ustaša regime in the so-called 'Independent State of Croatia', 1941–5. It is in this case (following the proposition in note 34, referring to the discussion in Hobsbawm 1994a), for our present comparative purpose, more revealing to speak about 'nazism' than about 'fascism', which is a term used by some of the most influential liberal Croatian critiques of Franjo Tudman's regime. This is due to the central importance that racism occupies in the ideology of the present Croatian regime,

as well as in that of its Second World War predecessor and political ideal (the Ustaša regime).

30. As demonstrated by Franjo Tudman's recurrent renarration of the history of Jasenovac, the ill-reputed *Ustaša* extinction camp during the Second World War (see also note 12). Thus the meaning of the monument for the victims of fascism/nazism at that site has been refashioned in terms of it being a 'monument for all of those' – fascists and antifascists alike – 'fallen for the sake of the Croatian fatherland during the Second World War', with the former (that is, the Ustaša fighters) placed centre stage. At the same time, Jasenovac is being 'sold' to visiting foreign diplomats as a symbol of Croatia's historical struggle for national liberation and democracy.

31. According to Bauman (1989) the level of popular anti-Semitism in Germany of the 1930s was remarkably low, measured by average European standards. The so-called *Krystalnacht* (the Crystal Night) was a quite unique instance of spuriously spontaneous anti-Semitic terror, instigated from above. But it was, according to Bauman's analysis, without broad popular support, and subsequently the task of solving 'The Jewish Question' was almost entirely entrusted to the rational social engineering of an efficient German bureaucracy. In contrast, the ethnic cleansing taking place in Bosnia-Herzegovina, particularly during the earlier periods of the 1992–5 Bosnian war, could be characterised as a long series of localised 'Crystal Nights'. For comparative treatments of forms and contingencies of forced population movements across modern history, among them 'ethnic cleansing' during the Balkan wars of the 1990s, see Zarkovic-Bookman (1997) and Hayden (1996).

32. The particular character of the war and the present state of society in Bosnia and Herzegovina is discussed in Chapter 4 (this volume) by Bojičić and Kaldor.

33. In fact, the most well-planned, efficient and modern-looking operation of ethnic cleansing during the recent Yugoslav wars was the rapid and large-scale expulsion of the local Serbian population from the so-called Krajina area of Croatia, effected by the jointly Croatian US–German sponsored military operation 'Storm' in 1995.

34. In any such discussion, as argued by Hobsbawm (1994a), it is important to distinguish between, respectively, the historical configurations of German nazism and Italian fascism. Racism was *not* a particularly conspicuous or obvious defining characteristic of fascism, as it was of nazism. The inherently racist characteristics of the new ethnocratic regimes in the Balkans are therefore, if anything, comparable, rather, to nazism than to fascism (see also note 29).

35. A theoretical framework for analysing this complex transformation was set up by Immanuel Castells in *The Informational City* (1989).

36. For definitions and theoretical and comparative discussions of the term 'clientilism' and its relevance to and historical importance in Balkan societies, see Mouzelis (1986).

37. The term 'reperipherialisation' was introduced by Schierup (1992).

38. See the detailed empirical description by Tomasevich (1955) and the illuminating theoretical-comparative analysis by Mouzelis (1986).

39. Notion introduced by Richards (1995; see further Chapter 5). Used with ironical distance by Hobsbawm (1994b), contemplating the global contingencies of ethnic cleansing and post-modern violence in the formerly Second and Third Worlds.

40. Crisis of legitimacy in the sense as defined by Habermas (1973).

41. The most complex analysis of this development was done by Castells and Kiselyova (1995), discussing the case of the former Soviet Union.

42. These issues are discussed in detail by, among others, Schierup 1990 and 1995, Woodward (1995a+b), Jacobsen 1996, and Dallago and Uvalić (1996).
43. The odds on this path were definitely most promising in Slovenia, among all the federal units of former Yugoslavia. But given the actual existence of an overall federal project for political, social and economic reform this was, as I argued in *Migration, Socialism, and the International Division of Labour* (1990:297 ff.), a possible scenario of transition also for Yugoslavia as a whole, still open at the end of the 1980s, at the eve of its fall. Following the path of the most dynamic and democratic elements of its own post-Second-World-War political, cultural and economic and institutional trajectory, a strategy for reform which, during the 1980s, crystallised around a still actually existing trans-ethnic alliance of forces in business, administration and civil society, could have provided an alternative to the regression towards the spuriously pre-modern forms of survival strategies and ethno-nationalist haggling that came to completely take over the political scene of the 1990s. This kind of alternative development would have demanded, however, determined and broad support from the international community for overall democratic path dependent reforms, instead of the actual assistance to ethnocratic suicide that came to dominate, in particular, individual European powers' approaches to the Yugoslavian crisis (e.g. Schierup 1995a, b, Woodward 1995b, Jacobsen 1996).

2 Memorandum for Modernity? Socialist Modernisers, Retraditionalisation and the Rise of Ethnic Nationalism
Carl-Ulrik Schierup

'Upheavals take place in dead-end roads.'[1]

Bertolt Brecht

History is filled with ironic paradoxes. The annals of nationalism in Western Europe have provided us with abundant examples of how an ideological preoccupation with the past and a frenzied 'invention of tradition' (Hobsbawm and Ranger 1993[1983]) have served to legitimise the instalment of a modern social order. Following a similar logic, it is common to reason about contemporary nationalism and post-cold-war popular mobilisation in Eastern Europe by way of historical analogy. In this vein, current 'modernist' or 'constructionist' approaches to nationalism and nation-building understand the ways in which ethnicity and the nation are here, once again, constructed through the reinvention of tradition and elite manipulation of historically derived symbolism and signs, to be coterminous with a rational project of modern cultural homogenisation. This is supposed to serve an abstract bureaucratic rationality and efficient economic organisation.

This perspective was brought out most forcefully by the late Ernest Gellner (1992a), reflecting on the nature of post-cold-war ethno-nationalist revivalism in Eastern Europe. Under the specific conditions left behind by the breakup of the 'stagnant, cynical, corrupt, and inefficient order' (Gellner 1992a:248) of communism, a radical, back-to-the-roots 'ethnic nationalism' becomes, maintains Gellner, the dominant political reaction. But although the overt language of the new nationalists, typically, belongs to the romanticist rhetoric of a past 'potato age', as he expresses it, the messages and the moment's hidden logic and latent function may rather respond to the demands of the modern industrial age for shared 'high cultures' of the 'kind that can only be instilled by a disciplined, abstract-norm-observing, formal, literate, and sophistication-instilling educational system' (Gellner 1992a:251). The success of radical ethnic-nationalism, representing the dominant form of post-communist political mobilisation, is here seen as due to the fact that decades of 'resolute centralism' have destroyed alternative social platforms for independent citizens' associations. In a post-communist society where any genuine pre-modern tradition has already been effectively eradicated, there exists no serious rival ideology, nor any serious institutions rivalling the modern abstract rationality of nationalism. In this environment, once the ideology and political apparatus of communism have collapsed, 'ethnic nationalism' has few if any rivals when it comes to the effective re-establishment of a civil society. Following the shipwrecked modernisation project of communism, post-communist society represents, already, a 'structureless mass anonymous society'. In this context, ethnic nationalism serves a purely ideological function, easily instrumentalised for the effective creation of the institutional structures of a functionally fit Western modernity.

What we encounter – here in the shape of one of the still most powerful and influential interpretations of nationalism – is nothing but mainstream modernisation theory's familiar model of contemporary history as that of a grand (functionally necessary) movement from 'tradition' to 'modernity'. This is a movement bound, quite certainly, as in the case of Eastern Europe's socialist experiment, to proceed through trial and error and littered with wrecked projects. It is, nevertheless, in our age, the onc trail that wc all must walk in order to gain access to prosperity and a sustainable contemporary political community. The perspective is profoundly diachronic. Tradition belongs to the past and modernity to the present and the future. The approach rejects, with all right, alternative primordialist interpretations, for being mostly superficial and exegetic, tending merely to reproduce native ethnic-nationalist political self-understanding. But, at the same time, the modernist perspective on nationalism, tends, in line with mainstream modernisation theory in general, to provide us with another set of one-dimensional looking-glasses that hamper a sufficiently discriminating understanding of the actual complexity of the post-communist transformation.

A glance at the social reality of socialist Yugoslavia and the background to rising ethnic nationalism may provide us with historical and contemporary raw material for further discussion.

Our time's resurgent national movements in the Balkans and Eastern Europe have promised, as in the case of earlier waves of European nationalism before them, prosperity through entry into the modern age.

These promises are nowadays most often epitomised in the millenarian mirage of an all-embracing European Union into which national heralds of the east, upon the occasion of their electoral campaigns, have routinely pledged an early entry. In what was Yugoslavia, as well as in a good many other parts of what used to belong to the realm of 'actually existing socialism' (the term of Bahro 1978), there are, however, good reasons to expect that today's nationalist movements will no more easily find success in sustaining the growth of a stable modernity than their nineteenth-century predecessors. During the late nineteenth century's golden age of European nationalism – at a time when the Piedmontese champions of the Risorgimento and Prussian social engineers managed to construct strong cohesive nation-states out of culturally and politically heterogeneous city states and petty dukedoms – in the Balkans, processes of nation-state formation were still hampered by imperial domination, continued ethno-national rivalry and the nature of indigenous political and economic relations (Chirot 1989), all embedded in a structurally and geographically inferior position of the region within the international economic regime of that time (Tomasevich 1955). Following the abortive historical interlude of a modernising bureaucratic socialism, the trajectories of *our times'* national movements in the Balkans and elsewhere in The Other (post-communist) Europe are framed by a deep crisis of economy, society and cultural identity, conceivably expounding that the project of the modern national state is today questioned at a *more general* level (for example, the argument of Albrow 1996).

What emerges – beyond the collapse of programmes for modernisation through national gathering, laid out by local master minds – is a suffocating state of society. It is marked by a penetrating retraditionalisation of politics, culture, and economy. Here, 'tradition' in the European East surfaces as a contingent polarity to Western modernity, framed by our common contemporary condition of globalisation. What is reproduced – in new forms – is the ancient disparity between the societies of a First (western) and a Second (eastern) Europe. Thus, the much debated historical 'backwardness of eastern Europe' (Chirot 1989) remains a contemporary riddle. An understanding of this, in many ways paradoxical, development demands alternative perspectives that venture beyond the horizons of conventional interpretations of contemporary nationalism and the post-communist transformation.

SOCIALIST MODERNISATION AND ITS INHERENT DILEMMAS

Let the conditions for the historical emergence of real socialism, as one modernisation project between others, be our point of departure. Its original appearance within particular regions cannot be explained as being simply primordially conditioned by the character of Eastern European as opposed to Western European society; nor was its ideological surfacing structurally 'random', as we are sometimes told.[2] We are confronted with a transformation, the inner dynamics of which were, among other factors, contingent on global relationships of power.

The historical achievement of the Western European bourgeoisies was, in terms of economic modernisation, to develop an advanced industrial society based on science and technology, proletarianised labour and an increasingly sophisticated division of labour. This happened through the rupture with feudal bonds (as in France), a radical transformation of feudal social relationships (as in Britain) or through the direct physical eradication of whole peoples engaged in non-capitalist forms of production (as in the case of the genocide that destroyed the indigenous population of North America).

But, owing to the emergence of Western capitalism and imperialism as a worldwide system of domination, social revolutions in the twentieth century could never have the same agents nor the same historical, social and ideological content. The social revolutions of the twentieth century – Soviet, Chinese, Yugoslavian, Albanian and Cuban – have, without exception, taken place in societies on the periphery of an increasingly interdependent, but asymmetrically structured, global economy (cf. Skocpol 1979). Their primary problem was not to *create* new more advanced forms of economy, but to prepare their societies to command the enormous scientific–technological potential already in existence. A precondition for overcoming structurally determined economic underdevelopment was freedom from an unequal integration in the international division of labour which blocked the way (Marković 1979).

The bourgeois élites characteristic of countries like Russia, China or pre-Second-World-War Yugoslavia (based on usury capital, merchant capital and small-scale industrial entrepreneurship) were unable or disinclined to carry through a radical primitive accumulation and an effective industrial transformation. They were, typically, weak and divided (e.g. Mouzelis 1986). There were – as maintained by Robert Brenner (1989), in his illuminating analysis of the historical roots of the continued economic backwardness of Eastern Europe – important 'indigenous' reasons for this.[3] But, once inserted into world-wide structures of domination, the opportunities for action of indigenous bourgeoisies were effectively blocked by their insignificant scale, their subordinate and 'symbiotic' relationship to international large-scale capital (Marković 1974), and by a continued selfish tutoring of their peripheral societies by dominant world-political centres. The immense economic power of the West, in combination with the successful early construction of strong modern states, forcefully limited the scope of the strategies of indigenous élites in Eastern Europe and elsewhere to fight back (Chirot 1989).

Thus, historically, the ascent to power of centralised and highly disciplined communist one-party politocracies was not, seen from the perspective of 'modernisation', random. Rather, it expressed an historical necessity. There was the need for mobilising and concentrating the scattered resources of poor societies on the periphery of the capitalist world – societies dominated by strong disintegrating and centrifugal social tendencies and cultural traditionalism. There was the associated need for a forceful, centralised authority with economic bargaining power to deal with predatory great powers, discriminatory international organisations and foreign capital, the power of which underscored the convoluted development of economic underdevelopment together with political Balkanisation and corruption. All of this could hardly, under the historically prevailing circumstances, have been accomplished by any other social agent (cf. Schierup 1990).

Of course, what was in the beginning a necessity and a propelling force for a sort of 'evolutionary jump', would, in the next instance, become a stumbling block for further resource mobilisation and modernisation in both economic and political terms. But the conspicuous demise of a projected long-term revolutionary transformation of all spheres of life cannot be deduced solely from the social character or the ideological horizon of the bureaucracy itself or from the nature of an inflexible state administrative planning process as such. Soviet history, from Khrushchev to Gorbachev, as with Yugoslavian from Kidrić to Marković,[4] gives, in the face of jeopardising contradictions, witness to a will and an action to reform the economic and political system of real-socialism from within. However, the incapacity of the post-revolutionary state bureaucracies to lead their nations beyond a certain limit of modernity was politically 'overdetermined' by the types of social coalition that lay at the very root of the bureaucracy's political authority. The paralysis of almost any communist reform effort, economic as well as political, cannot be blamed simply on the bureaucracy's own taste for power 'in the last instance', nor, plainly on the propensity of an uncompromising 'moralistic centralism's' incapability of 'tolerating partial truth' and to 'absolutise everything' (Gellner 1993:2). Rather, it represents an intricate problem of transgressing certain established forms of political consensus and legitimation. This problematic has, in the case of the Soviet Union, been examined in the work of Victor Zaslavsky (1982). In Yugoslavia it took on a specific character; a problematic that has most extensively been discussed in the work of the Zagreb sociologist Josip Županov.

Actually Existing Self-Management

The way in which the new post-war Yugoslavian working class was formed, within a society that was in 1945 still overwhelmingly agrarian (extensive analysis in Schierup 1990), had important political consequences. Much of the old politically radical working class perished during the Second World War or left the ranks of the workers after the war to pass into the political and administrative structures of the new socialist state apparatus. With a massive inflow of peasants into industrial work, the working class took on a number of new features reminiscent of the south-Slav tradition of closed, corporate egalitarian village communities; it was submissive and humble towards state power to which it had always been tied as taxpayers and soldiers, but sufficiently far from the state to conserve a measure of internal autonomy (Korošić 1988:97; compare Mouzelis 1978).

Županov (1977) locates the central dilemma for Yugoslav socialist development in the contradictory relationship between a traditionalist society in the world's economic periphery and a conception of socialism that has sprung from the Western labour movement (see also, Katunarić 1988:153). Industrialism made possible, at least for some time, a compromise between the two. The mediating value was an 'egalitarianism' of a traditionalist type, which departs from the perspective of equal redistribution and an image of the limited good pertaining to the local corporate community. An extensive initial economic development, especially a rapid process of labour-intensive industrialisation, made possible, over a shorter time perspective, the seeming equalisation of the different parts of the country. At the same time it formed the basis for extensive employment, which likewise appeared to promote equal opportunities.

This model of society as a whole was realised and reinforced at the micro level in the structural unit of the working organisation. The economy was fragmented along irrational lines (of administrative and political control) into functionally disconnected and isolated 'segmentary associations' characterised by a dual power structure (Županov 1969), that is, one derived from the techno-structure and from self-management principles, and one derived from the power of informal groups. It is the latter which eventually came to predominate in the shape of an informal corporatist coalition between localised bureaucracies and the quasi-proletarians of a fragmented and traditionalist working class, crystallising around the central values of redistribution and egalitarianism (see further, Schierup 1990).

The ideological world view of the central post-revolutionary political leadership, however, was fundamentally one of modernisation. Its dominant conception of long-term development was the construction of a technically advanced society. The realisation of these visions could not continue to lean towards the egalitarianist matrix of a proto-peasant manual working class, even if this was the main political basis legitimating the bureaucracy's dominant position in society in the role of redistributing the limited good. At a certain stage, influential party-élite factions were to push forcefully for methods of economic management based on the allocative functions of the market, income differentiation, the large-scale implementation of experts and the inducement of individual entrepreneurship.

Radical, market-oriented reforms in the 1960s were staged as an attempt to realise the preconditions for a more skill- and education-intensive economic development, which, during the two preceding decades, imposing educational efforts had made possible (Schierup 1990). As such, the reforms even represented an attempt to become integrated into the international division of labour on more equal terms. In that sense, it meant a rupture with earlier extensive industrial development and with the prevalence of egalitarianist social values in a society where unskilled industrial labour occupied a central position within the established scheme of accumulation. It represented a radical rupture with state-bureaucratic hegemony and egalitarianist socio-political matrixes to the political benefit of directors of large firms, the technical intelligentsia and highly skilled and urban people in general. It meant toppling the weight of a delicate economic and socio-political rural–urban balance in favour of the advanced urban-based segments of the population, but in a society where the unskilled–semi-skilled, rural–semi-rural population segments would still represent an indispensable source of legitimacy for any stable political regime.

Bureaucratic Backlash and New–Old Liaisons

Extensive economic and political reforms of the 1960s – by certain leftist writers prematurely designated as 'the restoration of capitalism' (e.g. Carlo 1972) – were, however, to become an interim of state-bureaucratic rule.

The overall results of the reforms were disappointing. Rather than leading to the expected great leap ahead, radical reformism without an adequate institutional infrastructure was to bring economic, political and social anarchy and fragmentation. One of the adverse social consequences of the reform policy was a rapid marginalisation of large sections of the manual labour force. So-called peasant-workers, a numerically important social category, were hit from two sides in that the structural changes in industry happened simultaneously with the launching of a selective 'green revolution' in agriculture striking hard on small peasant holdings (see further, Schierup 1990:82 ff. and 158 ff.).

All of this was to undercut powerful established sources of the reforming state bureaucratic élite's legitimacy among the manual working class while, simultaneously, the élite found it increasingly difficult to control new social and cultural forces unleashed by the reforms. This appeared particularly menacing when, by the advent of the 1970s, student revolts, and numerous strikes by skilled workers, started to coalesce with the centrifugal and potentially very dangerous forces connected with resurrected nationalist claims in this overwhelmingly ethnically mixed society.

The federal élite's response became, during the early and mid-1970s, a peculiar combination of authoritarian repression, co-opting permissiveness and new pervasive reforms of the social, political and economic system from above. The proclamation and institutionalisation of a new phase in the development of 'self-management' should on the one hand act to harness popular protest and claims for social change to a common socialist cause under the guidance of the established élite. On the other hand this new reform wave was geared to curtail unwanted tendencies towards economic anarchy and so-called 'technocratic' dominance which had resulted from the haphazard manners in which the economic reforms of the 1960s had largely been conducted (Platform 1973), and which, allegedly, threatened to bring back the reign of a socially and politically disruptive peripheral capitalism, pre-Second-World-War style (see further, Schierup 1990 and 1992).

But rather than effecting the alleged new progressive era of popular democracy and efficient economic development, the reforms of the 1970s very quickly came to represent a pervasive rebureaucratisation. Actually existing self-management became equal to a flood of bureaucracy, not only in state institutions, but also in coordinating regional and local bodies for self-managers in Yugoslavian firms (Schierup 1990:226 ff and 1992). It was made possible by the fragmentation of the techno-structure in the enterprises, in particular from the mid-1970s, based on the unsuccessful launching of an ambitiously conceived, so-called 'self-management system of planning'.

This paved the way for a forceful political backlash. Writing in the 1980s – in the midst of social and economic crisis – Županov (1983b) speaks of a realignment of the old coalition between the manual working class and the political bureaucracy. This reaction was to cast Yugoslav society in a mould qualitatively different from that of the 1950s and 1960s. It meant a profound re-traditionalisation of society. Bureaucratisation during the 1970s took place mainly at the level of the republics, and became dominated by local bureaucracies without grandiose visions of internationalism, popular democracy, or economic and technological self-reliance. It exploited the opportunities that a transformed 'self-management system' offered for a pervasive bureaucratisation of all social relationships and could take on a profoundly localised form against the background of constitutional amendments that granted individual republics a large measure of political and economic autonomy (Županov 1983b).

It was a coalition of unequal partners, in which the patron (the élite) 'protects' the working class by guaranteeing existing jobs, a minimal income and extensive social privileges, while the 'protected' (the workers) – the much-hailed 'working class' of actually existing socialism – would guarantee the élite its social legitimacy (Županov 1983b). Such a coalition presupposes mutual communication: labour accepts the official ideology, while the élite accepts the values of radical egalitarianism. The élite hardly accepts egalitarianism through genuine belief, but rather because a curtailment of differentiation simplifies the social system and makes it easier to administrate (Katunarić 1988). This communication between the political élite and labour provided a solid basis for social stability in the face of a deepening economic crisis (Županov 1985). It was profoundly authoritarian in character. All that ever existed in the way of genuine workers' self-management at the enterprise level largely died out in favour of the voluntaristic regulations of a ramifying bureaucratic apparatus.

The republics' new bureaucratic élites, entrenched within what was increasingly looking like new local 'national states', were led by predominantly particularist motives, without long-term conceptions of development, and marked by a narrowing space for manoeuvre in relation to transnational capital. The new regimes had fundamental structural features in common with the political élites of pre-war Yugoslavia. Under the deepening shadow of economic subordination, essential features of a pre-war neo-colonial *ancien régime* – the reproduction of state power through political clientelism and a network of primordial loyalties (Mouzelis 1986, Tomasevich 1955) – were from the early 1970s to blend organically with the most authoritarian features of the social and political relations of real socialism. The local party élites and the increasingly 'national' working classes of the single republics and autonomous provinces were to be bound together by innumerable ties of an increasingly traditionalistic character. These were displayed in idioms such as kinship, friendship, locality and ethnicity, taking the form of a complex network of reciprocal favours, pervading the entire society (Schierup 1990; cf. Sampson 1985, discussing other socialist countries). Vertical patron–client relationships and nepotist networks of favouritism – while rooting themselves in enterprises, local communities and a widely ramified underground economy – came to penetrate every pore of society.

During the 1980s and 1990s, in a situation where national conflicts were coming to a head, such local alliances transformed themselves into broader, populist, state–people–führer-like movements. This was typical for Serbia's development, as Slobodan Milošević was (in 1987) elevated to power on the back of a radical populist 'anti-bureaucratic' movement propelled by factions within the communist party itself. But it was no less marked in Croatia where, in 1990, Franjo Tudman's right-wing nationalist so-called Croatian Democratic Alliance (HDZ) – adopting ingrained political-managerial habits belonging to that republic's remarkably hard-line orthodox-communist past, and absorbing numerous 'five minutes to twelve' converts among the old communist party cadres – inaugurated a neo-authoritarian near-to-one-party regime.

ON THE FRINGES OF THE GLOBAL SYSTEM

A Systemic Paradox

In their central theoretical work on Soviet society, *Diktatur uber die Bedürfnisse* (Dictatorship over Needs), Ferenc Féher, Agnes Heller and Geyörgy Markus (1983[1979]) point to underlying centrifugal social forces as being built into the structure and practice of Soviet state bureaucracy.

These ideas, however, were not introduced by Féher *et al*. Intellectuals in the former Yugoslavia had, although their ideas have not generally become known to an international public, exposed similar problems long ago through in-depth analyses of their own political and economic system.

In his theory of 'state capitalism' dating back to the early 1950s, the Yugoslavian politician and economist Boris Kidrić (1952 and 1969) maintains that a marked localistic and particularistic orientation was incorporated into the state planning system operating on strictly territorial principles rather than on principles of economic cost-efficiency. State socialism is a system in conflict with itself, Kidrić argued, characterised by contradictory forms of political–economic government and politicians who used doubtful strategies in order to control an inevitable crisis of legitimacy. Competing bureaucratic power-centres have endeavoured to extend administrative control within their respective territories and to create local economic monopolies. These monopolies they defended with purely political means against competition from other regional power blocks and in relation to power structures higher up in the political-administrative state elite. A one-sided policy of territoriality, and a one-sided dominance of the political over the economic, would, typically, lead to economic fragmentation, giving rise to numerous small and parallel entities with no internal division of labour, and leading to economic stagnation and to a flagrant waste of resources. Thus, an allegedly centralised management of resources would, paradoxically, give way to a divided and localised economy, governed by the shifting power-relations of factional conflicts in the bureaucracy rather than more universal criteria. In spite of the tendency towards industrial megalomania (each republic having

its own steelworks and own car factory, etc.), the real socialist society
was characterised by economic narrowness of vision and scale.

Hence, Kidrić claimed, apparently centralist, state-controlled planning
systems tended to contain strong localistic and dividing forces, which were
determined by territorial rather than functional principles in overall economic terms. Local bureaucracies competed to expand administrative control in their own territories in order to create local economic monopolies.
These monopolies were defended in the context of an ongoing political
power struggle against competition from other regions and local communities and in relation to higher-level bureaucratic power structures. The
consequences were fatal in a society which could not, at any level, integrate alternative social forces, be they functional markets, free trade unions,
political parties, or independent social movements that cut across ethnic
boundaries.

This built-in contradiction between centralism and localism was common to all the socialist countries, but in Yugoslavia factional localism
was particularly marked. Local bureaucracies knew how to take advantage of the decentralisation of the government administration that, as
early as 1950, became an integral element of the so-called workers' self-
government (Schierup 1990:210 ff.).

Prelude to the Inferno

In a historical perspective, this endeavour did not affect the underlying
state bureaucratic character of the system, but rather amplified its segmentary and potentially anarchic features. The Yugoslavian economist
Časlav Ocić (1983) builds on Kidrić's theories in his analysis of the development of local 'national economies' in the 1970s. Most pronounced,
and by far the most dangerous for the social and economic system, maintains Ocić, are the manifestations of 'bureaucratic particularism' on the
level of the republics. Wide-ranging changes in the social and economic
system and in the federal constitution (1974) made the republics' state
apparatuses the most potent vehicles for centralising political power at a
sub-federal level and for publicly legitimising local monopolies by ap-
pealing to latent ethno-national loyalties.[5] Step by step, the federal élite,
with its roots in the struggle against fascism during the Second World
War, disintegrated. The authority of the central state became increasingly challenged by a new generation of communist state bureaucracies
in the republics.

Political power accrued to the now independent communist party organisations and bureaucracies within the republics, who on the ideological platform of 'workers' self-management' formed corporate coalitions
with segments of the local working classes. This served to further com-

petition between local 'national economies' and between ethnic groups for jobs, housing and positions within local state apparatuses (see also Schierup 1990:241 ff). The eventual absence of alternative political identities rendered ethnic identity its supreme status. In this situation, an atomised federal structure, combined with continued communist party monopolies, meant that the only legitimate conflicts became those that followed ethnic lines (cf. Magnusson 1988).

The ideological legitimacy of the new 'national' élites in the republics rested on the corporative, orthodox Leninist-Stalinist idea of 'the nation'. Thus – extending a traditional ethnic-nationalist philosophy – 'nationality' was interpreted as an original ethnic-cultural collective with special rights to a certain territory. This interpretation was perfectly fitted to the efforts of the local bureaucracies to legitimise their existence and power.

During the 1970s, we can see a close interplay between economic segmentation and a corresponding disintegration of the federal political-administrative élite that had come to power after the Second World War. The common political space was divided along borders of republics and provinces (Kosovo, Vojvodina) as a new generation of élite politicians attempted to consolidate their power through protectionistic economic competition. In reality, they were striving for autonomous nation-states. In 1974, this process of consolidation into nation-states and the segmentation of the Yugoslav union was supported by the new federal constitution, created under bureaucratic tutorship and with Josip Broz Tito as its godfather. This gave the local party organisations of the republics considerable freedom to influence almost all aspects of social life: the economy, political representation, social politics and education.

Radical reforms of the education system towards the end of the 1970s were directed entirely at the level of the republics. The federal educational system had been completely dismantled. This fostered the development of separate ethnic-national identities. At the same time, higher education at the university level was given lower priority than vocational education at the high-school level. Parallel to these events, tens of thousands of highly educated people emigrated because job opportunities were scarce in an increasingly technologically backward industrial sector (see further, Schierup 1990 and 1992). It was primarily this section of the population that had embraced pan-ethnic (Yugoslavian) and cosmopolitan values (see further, Schierup 1998a). Therefore, emigration and reformation of the educational system supported the general division of the society along ethnic-national lines.

As the economic crisis deepened during the 1980s, and as the legitimacy of the dominant political elites was increasingly undermined, the tendency for the upper echelons to ethnify all social conflicts became more and more apparent. This made a disintegrating communist state bureaucracy the single most important midwife to blatantly absolutist ethnic nationalist ideologies and movements. A communist movement and a system that originally gained power primarily because it represented the only political alternative capable of uniting the population across traditional ethnic-national divides, had shown itself capable of intrinsically transforming these antagonisms whilst simultaneously elevating them to become the all pervasive issue in the political and ideological arena. An original mythology, epitomised in the pan-national–pan-ethnic slogan, 'Brotherhood and Unity', had been turned into its own inverted image.

Fed by internal bureaucratic conflicts, earlier ideas about a multi-ethnic community, mutual economic dependence and fraternal cooperation were replaced by a common, negative focus on how each group was supposedly being exploited by some Other (the Serbs by the Slovenians, Croatians and Albanians, the Slovenes and the Croatians by the Serbs and by all the less developed republics and autonomous provinces *en bloc*, etc.; see further Schierup 1990 *in passim*). This took place in wider and wider circles, from the relatively rich Slovenia in the north to the poor Kosovo in the south. Beginning in the mid-1980s, it was just such a message that was given by Slobodan Milosević and prominent Serbian intellectuals. This started the nationalist wildfire that was to turn Yugoslavia into ashes.

International Subordination and Technological Breakdown

Ocić (1983) uses the idea of intra-bureaucratic segmentation to explain the specific terms on which Yugoslavia became again, from the early 1970s onwards, a subordinate adjunct to the world economy, as this Balkan region had for so long been historically. A protracted economic and social crisis, latent during the 1970s but coming into the open during the 1980s, led, in conjunction with the centrifugal dynamics of state bureaucratic power relationships, to a growing disintegration of the economic system (see also Mihajlović 1981, Bilandžić 1981, Horvat 1985). Despite the Yugoslav constitution's emphasis on a unitary Yugoslav market, closed separate 'national' sub-economies (corresponding to territories of single republics and autonomous provinces) developed 'slowly but surely', argues Ocić (1983). This territorialisation of single autarchic economies within the federation was defended with a number of 'visible and invisible' means by competitive 'national' interest groups located in the individual republics and autonomous provinces. They produced their own legitimacy through the fabrication and management of still more openly populist–nationalist and regionally particular political ideologies (see also Bilandžić 1981; Katunarić 1988).

The fragmentation and segmentation of the market for commodities and services, of which Ocić speaks, and also of other factors of production, like capital and labour, became increasingly evident during the 1970s and 1980s, culminating in open rivalry between mutually opposed local elites mobilising around national symbols.

Republics and provinces (Kosovo and Vojvodina) developed separate power structures that favoured economic autarchy and, through a number of informal mechanisms, they would protect themselves from competition from commodities produced in other republics. They would obstruct the attempts of enterprises based in other republics, to establish plants on their territory. Capital investments would increasingly take place within single republics, while inter-republican transfers of capital dwindled.

Because of exclusiveness and an overwhelming fragmentation, the Yugoslav economy lost the effects of increasing economies of scale, and of the development of functional specialisation through republican and regional comparative advantages in resources, technology, labour and skill. As each republic endeavoured to develop its own separate 'national' economy, the Yugoslav economy as a whole took on the appearance of many undercapitalised, badly integrated, parallel, non-cooperating production units. Through informal political power structures they fiercely guarded their own 'home markets' while they fought and undercut one another trying to sell similar products on the world market (Ocić 1983; Korošić 1988). Patterns of trade were either locked inside the borders of each single republic or, increasingly, flew from each republic in the direction of the world market (Ocić 1983).

This inner political and economic disintegration should come to run parallel with an integration on unequal terms in the international division of labour. As any functioning division of labour between the federation's republics tended to disappear, new assymmetric economic ties developed in relation to transnational capital. The most important and fatal aspect of this unequal relationship became discriminatory conditions for the transfer of technology.[6] This was contingent on the collapse of any coherent development conception and policy and of any long-term efforts on technical research and development (Ðurek 1981). Promising federal institutions of technical–scientific education, research and development were dismantled in connection with the profound decentralisation of the political and institutional system during the early 1970s. The corollary of a growing autarchy of republics and autonomous provinces, and even smaller administrative divisions within former Yugoslavia, became that of single units forging individual bonds with western partners. Production equipment, industrial licences and spare parts were bought from foreign partners in haphazard manners without any coordination or cooperation at home (Mihajlović 1981; Ocić 1983:110 ff.). The existence of a multitude of different technical conceptions and systems, licences and standards acted to impede cooperation among Yugoslav partners and made Yugoslav plants increasingly dependent on foreign partners. Parallel to the disarticulation of the joint economic infrastructure in general, facilities for research and development became fragmented, weak and almost completely marginalised in an international context (see, further Ocić 1983, Đurek 1981, Schierup 1992).

RETRADITIONALISATION IN REPERIPHERIALISATION

From its position as one of the most promising newly industrialising countries in the early 1960s, Yugoslavia slipped, as it were, back to its former position as an economically stagnating and politically unstable peripheral society in the global system. The respective republics had come to constitute a framework for disconnected 'national economies', which had become extremely dependent on foreign capital, know-how and technology. While federal economic structures were being pushed into the background and the economies of the single republics got increasingly isolated from one another, Yugoslavian enterprises became unilaterally coupled to the world market as the last and most subordinate link in the transnational production chain. Simultaneously, as a result of an inflated petrodollar market following the 'oil crisis' of the 1970s and assisted by Tito's great international authority, the national debt had been allowed to grow to proportions that meant a serious threat to economic stability. The situation was further complicated by the extreme and constantly growing disparities in levels of economic development between different parts of the federation (cf. Schierup 1990:155 ff. and 189–215).

This, as we may call it, pervasive 'reperipherialisation' (Schierup 1992) of Yugoslavia in relation to the global economy acted, in its effects, to marginalise a numerous intelligentsia in relation to economy and society. It created a retrograde deterioration of the educational system, and it spawned, as will be discussed further below, a general retraditionalisation of society running along the lines of new types of social, cultural and economic interconnections between its rural and urban domains.

Marginalisation of the Intelligentsia

As expressed by Korošić (1988:147), the specific forms of articulation between a segmentary state bureaucratic management and the forces of an unequal international division of labour gave a deepening Yugoslavian economic and social crisis of the 1980s the character of a 'crisis of innovation'.

In terms of labour relationships it came to mean the continued pre-dominance of unskilled or semi-skilled manual labour in 'peripheral' labour processes structured in a growing dependency on transnational capital. At the same time, however, the development during the 1970s and 1980s represented a crisis and a marginalisation of the technical intelligentsia: a paradoxical situation where, as observed by Korošić (1988:147), a huge, but eventually largely structurally superfluous, technical intelligentsia was becoming matched by an ever-decreasing number of international patents.[7]

At the micro level this can be seen as contingent on the ways in which individual 'self-managed' enterprises operated. Following Županov's (1983a and b) model of a coalition between the bureaucracy and the working class, Yugoslav enterprises could be described as closed protectionistic enclaves employing defensive egalitarianist strategies to guard the privileges of the already employed, coupled with a reluctance to employ new skilled and technically advanced labour. New technology was frowned upon and innovators easily came into conflict with their working organisations (Korošić 1988:147; see also, Schierup 1990:141 ff).

Prevailing patterns of state bureaucratic intervention in the economy reinforced the closed character of individual enterprises (Korošić 1988). Under this system, even firms running at a deficit might even occasionally pay their workers higher wages than firms working successfully according to economic criteria. As the success of a firm came to more and more depend on administrative intervention and informal relationships with local bureaucratic power structures, so all economic and functional criteria for employing new labour tended to be eliminated. Instead, 'mechanical solidarity', centred around the primordial loyalties of family, friendship, locality and ethnic group, became the most important criterion for accepting new members, while relations of 'organic solidarity' increasingly dissolved (Županov 1981:1952; Schierup 1990:141 ff).

While earlier impressive efforts to promote large-scale research and development totally floundered and collapsed (see Đurek 1981; Horvat 1985), no new long-term conception of an integrated education of technological cadres was conceived. Flexible and functionally integrated networks of smaller-scale, high-tech and research-and-development-based enterprises and institutions, so powerful in the core industrial countries, were not within the horizon of the dominant politocratic conception of society (Korošić 1988:145). Under these conditions, the existing technical intelligentsia was most liable to be either 'exported' to the OICs, put away and pacified in some inferior administrative department, disciplined according to the static criteria of a conservative management, or remain unemployed.

A pervasive restructuration of the Yugoslavian secondary school system from the late 1970s could be seen both to reflect and to systematically reproduce this situation, setting the stage for a retraditionalisation of society.

Levelling Aspirations

Propelled by optimistic and egalitarianistic visions of a new modern and technically advanced social era, Yugoslavia witnessed in the 1960s an eruption of social and professional aspirations among young people and a mushrooming of all kinds of higher educational institutions. The historical result, under the conditions of 'reperipherialisation' from the late 1960s, was a 'hyper-production' of young 'experts' and intellectuals which a stagnating economic structure was unable to absorb (cf. Županov 1981). A long-term trend towards a new, more skilled and educated reserve army of unemployed workers during the 1970s turned into a permanent structural feature of the social stratification system in the 1980s (Davidović 1986; see also, Schierup 1990). The school system ceased to be a channel for social mobility, and people increasingly made their way by means of other (political and traditional) mechanisms for social promotion. To make a living, young people were forced into what in effect became a pervasive *re-traditionalisation of society*, embracing all facets of life. They were driven into the informal veins of an expanding, but technologically primitive, underground economy, or forced to sustain themselves as parasites in a familistic process of barter.

Not only did family and kinship groups conserve their central meaning in the life of the individual, but they also took on an increasingly important significance. The family had to find relationships and means through which the child could sign into schools for intellectual professions or get into a suitable faculty. The family itself would have to search for relationships or directly pay somebody for a young person's entry into her first job. The family would buy her an apartment or in other ways solve the young person's need for a place to live. 'Just like his peer 200 years ago', writes Županov (1981:1953) in the beginning of the 1980s, 'a young person cannot lean himself towards any other institution than his own family-background . . . Other institutions let him down – and if he has no rights to expect and realise through the institutions of society, then he must get them by barter and blackmailing; and here the family is his main support.'

An army of young, unemployed intellectuals came into conflict not only with a changing social and economic reality, but also with the prevailing political leadership's conservative view of extensive industrial development as the only strategic option (Korošić 1988:146). Such a view governed a radical reorientation of the educational system in parts of the federation during the late 1970s. Through the agency of the reforms an industrial labour force started to be formed by administrative means which would fit in with the political leadership's horizons and Yugoslavia's retrograde position in the international division of labour. This implied: a drastic reduction in the number of students accepted to higher academic education; high priority given to short-term education directed towards skilled industrial employment and other skilled occupations; the replacement of the former secondary-school system's stress on versatility and general knowledge with a system enforcing very early specialisation in extremely narrowly delimited subjects directed towards specific categories of jobs, and, finally, a marked territorialisation of the whole educational process.

The explicit goal of the first educational reform along these lines, which was undertaken in Croatia in 1978, was to curtail 'élitist tendencies' in the old school system (for documentation see Podrebarac 1985). By forcing, through political-administrative means, about 70 per cent of the primary school-leavers to enrol in schools leading to extremely narrow and specialised working-class professions, the educational system effectively ceased to provide a means of inter-generational social mobility (Županov 1981:1950). The reforms were constructed, as well, so as to systematically hamper inter-regional mobility (Županov 1981:39). An intricate system of linking contracts to employment in particular enterprises and organisations would oblige each student to work in the same local area in which they started their education. This orientation was strengthened by the clientilistic character of society in general, because, outside their own local area, without kinship and other informal relationships, it proved practically impossible to obtain such a contract (Županov 1981:39). Through this radical regionalisation of the specialised new educational system, explicitly designed to curtail 'excessive aspirations', Strpić argues, the political bureaucracy increased its administrative control over the reproduction of labour as well as its ideological control. On the one hand, the social basis for recruiting a future intelligentsia in technical and natural sciences as well as in the social sciences and the arts was drastically narrowed (Strpić 1988), as avenues towards social mobility for the majority of the population became effectively blocked (Županov 1981). But, on the other hand, the educational reforms supported the reproduction and reinforcement of the existing structure of dominance in society by narrowing the scope of higher and general education and restricting it to larger urban centres (Županov 1981; Strpić 1988). Access to a few exclusive schools with good reputations was to become the prerogative of those who commanded effective contacts in the proper networks of clientship. Thus, reproduction of the political élite was not threatened.

In its effects, Strpić (1988:39–40) concludes in a penetrating critique of the reforms, the educational reform adapted itself well to the dominant

economic and political processes in the late 1970s. In a situation where
any indigenous scientific–technological development of importance had
ceased to take place, an extensive semi-industrial and industrial production came to function as the basis for a primitive accumulation of capital
and, as long as it lasted, consolidated the rule of a primitive bureaucracy
dependent on excessive foreign loans. The reformed educational system
acted as a systemic mediator 'procuring suitable servants and subjects –
non-creative, uncritical, unfit for high-productivity, self-organisation and
social action'. This retrograde development was interlaced with a broad
re-affirmation of the rural segments of society and a 'rural–urban symbiosis' that was to remain a basic structuring feature at the heart of Yugoslavian society and the successor states during the 1980s and 1990s. It
should come to function as the political axis of those political compacts
(semi-rural manual working class and petty bureaucrats in villages and
provincial towns) that have, so far, also sustained the power of populist
tribunes like Slobodan Milošević (Serbian president), Franjo Tuđman
(Croatian president), and Alija Izetbegović (president of Bosnia-
Herzegovina).

The Rural–Urban Symbiosis

Socialist industrialisation was, in the particular case of Yugoslavia, tightly
connected with the so-called 'peasant-worker' strategy (Kostić 1955,
Cvjetičanin *et al.* 1980, Schierup 1990). This became – after the final collapse
of attempts at collectivisation in the early 1950s – the dominant socialist
policy approach to the village and the peasantry, who long remained an
abundant and strategic human capital asset for economic development.
    In a socialist society where the small peasant holding remained the all-
dominant (constitutionally and politically protected) form of property in
agriculture,[8] a decentralised strategy of labour-intensive industrialisation
brought the factories close to the villages and peasants, while cooperation between individual peasant households and a relatively small socialised sector in agriculture became the basis for a modernisation process
that generated a growing surplus of labour in peasant agriculture and
new consumers. Wages high enough to attract a growing rural surplus
population, but low enough to force the worker to keep a foothold in
the village and on the land, became the basis for a continuous process of
'primitive accumulation'[9] and 'cyclical migration' (cf. Meillassoux 1981,
Schierup 1990), and for the constitution of the peasant-workers as a major
stratum of the new industrial working class (Kostić 1955, Marković 1974,
Cvjetičanin *et al.* 1980, Puljiz 1977). Owing to the partial reproduction
of this large labour force within the framework of a rural, subsistence-
oriented economy, wages in the socialised sector of the economy could

be kept low and a 'free rent' from peasant agriculture continuously harnessed. This was, across post-Second-World-War Yugoslavian history, a powerful source of what has been called 'external accumulation'[10] (e.g. Korošić 1988) in favour of 'socialist reconstruction and development'.[11]

As pure statistics would have it, the proportion of the rural population in the total Yugoslavian population was to decrease quite dramatically (from more than two-thirds of the total in 1948 to less than a fifth in 1981), starting shortly after the Second World War (when Yugoslavia was still a country overwhelmingly dominated by a smallholding peasantry) and extending into the 1980s (Puljiz 1977, Livada 1988).[12] Also, according to official data, the proportion of 'peasant-workers' in the Yugoslav working class decreased considerably, particularly from the early 1960s onwards, after having reached a peak during a period of extensive industrialisation in the 1950s (Cvjetičanin et al. 1980:22 ff.). Nevertheless, most of the population continued to live in villages or minor urban centres. But even numerous land-owning families, their adult members employed outside the farm, and officially registered as 'workers', continued to live at the homestead, which remained an essential part of the family economy. They were the numerous village-based commuters (see Oliveira-Roca 1984 and 1988). Also, the genuinely urban population would only rarely sell their inherited agricultural plots, but stuck to them stubbornly, partly in order to be able to supplement an insufficient income (see Cvjetičanin 1988), and partly in order to conserve a defensive platform of retreat in the event of misfortune or crisis (Cvjetičanin 1980:172 ff.; Cvjetičanin 1988). This meant that both in the village and in the town a large population was found that could in fact be described in terms of 'ad-hoc' or 'situational' peasants (Korošić 1988:91). In the village there were hardly any 'genuine' peasants left, but rather a sort of proto-peasantry, for whom the land remained an indispensable source of income, often in terms of natural economy. In the urban–industrial areas, one would, conversely, find numerous forms of real dependency on this spurious but actually existing proto-peasant economy.

The intensification of Yugoslavia's economic crisis during the 1980s restored the importance of private agriculture with great force. From then onwards it was to become the most important 'shock-absorber' for the crisis, as the urban–industrial segment of the economy was being forced to wake up after having been 'doped' by so-called 'external accumulation' (that is, excessive foreign loans and migrant remittances) during the 1970s (Puljiz 1987:15). The great economic reforms and incipient prosperity for certain urban groups in the 1960s and a conspicuous petro-dollar boom (excessive foreign loans), having broad distributive effects in terms of rising living standards during the 1970s, seemed to fade out of sight as historical intermezzos, when a latent economic crisis came fully into the open by 1980. At this juncture a still fairly traditionalist peasant agriculture could once again, as during the great depression of the 1930s (see Schierup 1990), become the main bastion of retreat for substantial population groups. Thus, argues the Yugoslavian rural sociologist, Vlado Puljiz (1988:20), as 'with historical irony . . . the individual peasant holding which the agrarian policy, during the whole post-war period, has endeavoured to beat down as a survival from past times' should once again (as in the 1930s) 'become the main cushion for the crisis warding off a social misery of huge dimensions' (see Mitrany 1951 and Schierup 1990).

A cultural backlash and 'retraditionalisation' of all social relationships went hand in hand with this reaffirmation of a 'rural–urban symbiosis' embracing the major part of the population. Those who were the most exposed to dramatically decreasing living standards were those among the urban population living exclusively on their wages or pensions. As the crisis made the population rely more heavily on private land, and other supplementary sources of income, the 'mixed' agricultural household and 'peasant-worker' stratum in the villages reaffirmed itself (see Cvjetičanin 1988). Also a large part of the urban population, symbolically and economically reinforcing their social relationships with the village population, revived their interest in inherited agricultural plots, as, for example, did industrial and office workers from Zagreb, Belgrade and other large cities who returned to the villages to cultivate their inherited plots during weekends. Hence, 'a massive trend started moving in the opposite direction' of the pervasive post-war processes of industrialisation and urbanisation: 'i.e. from the non-agricultural to the agricultural sector' (Cvjetičanin 1988:128–9).

But this obvious reaffirmation of the 'peasant-worker' was now no longer about a specific type of 'primitive accumulation' directed towards a dynamic process of domestic industrialisation. Rather, 'the free rent' reaped from a subsistence-oriented agriculture was now to be *transferred directly abroad* in the context of a growing transnational domination of the whole economic process.

The most important mechanism became that of sub-contracting, where foreign companies made arrangements with Yugoslav firms for utilising existing production facilities, exploiting village-based labour in return for sub-minimal wages. Perhaps the most conspicuous example of this was the development of the textile and clothing industry during the 1980s (Chepulis 1984a), which, in effect, meant the re-establishment of a tradition for foreign dominance in that industry, first established during the period between the two world wars (as described by Chepulis 1984b; see also Schierup 1990:39–40 and 46 ff). Because of the low productivity of labour and unfavourable conditions on the world market during the 1980s, textiles were generally exported at prices way below the cost of production, and export itself became 'an economic sacrifice and necessity for maintaining production' (Chepulis 1984a:12). This was a direct effect of changing federal economic policies during the 1980s, which, through a number of measures, enforced a reorientation towards 'export at any price' (Chepulis 1984a:12) in an endeavour to cope with new austerity measures imposed by the international monetary organisations.

A comparative advantage of the Yugoslav textile industry was its proximity to European markets. Nevertheless, the crisis drove the wages down to far below the minimum level of subsistence. The Yugoslavian textile industry paid lower wages than any other industry, and became renowned for having the 'highest level of exploitation in the world' (*Ekonomska Politika* 1989:15 ff.). Thus, with an average of less than three dollars a day, Yugoslav textile workers' wages went below those of countries such as Indonesia, Taiwan and South Korea, some of Yugoslavia's main competitors on the world market (*Ekonomska Politika* 1989:15 ff). As in other NICs, unskilled female workers with close ties to the village and agriculture were to form the bulk of the labour force in the textile industry (cf. Gómez de Estrada and Reddock 1987). Most came from 'mixed' agricultural (peasant-worker) households, and their wages represented only a small supplement to the total family income.

MEMORANDUM FOR MODERNITY

It was to this dismal situation – of protracted economic and social crisis, of political fragmentation and a ramifying nepotistic clientilism, and of cultural segmentation cum retraditionalisation – that the so-called *Memorandum* of the Serbian academy of sciences reacted in 1986. The *Memorandum* (1989) is the most famous and the most ill-reputed document pertaining to the new wave of ethnic nationalism that sprouted forth in different parts of former Yugoslavia from the beginning of the 1980s. It never was more than an unfinished draft, sketched by a group of odd companions among Serbian intellectuals, and was made public by accident. It had, nevertheless, an enormous influence on public debate in the federation, contributing to a general shift of the political climate of the 1980s.

By Slovenian, Croatian and Kosovo Albanian intellectuals, as well as by many liberal Serbian intellectuals in opposition, the *Memorandum* has been habitually referred to as a sort of Miloševićean *Mein Kampf.* However, those who look here for some kind of conventional, *nazi*-style race-biology-founded denouncement of 'democracy', an open call for the brainless discipline of uniform mass movements, a Sensucht for black pedagogy or the hailing of ritualised violence and militarism, will search in vain. The first part of the *Memorandum* includes sound and skilful social science analysis of the roots of political fragmentation and authoritarian–bureaucratic misuse of power, of economic decay, educational demise, and the cultural regression into the particular neo-Stalinist version of an ethnicising traditionalism characteristic of Yugoslavia in the 1970s and 1980s. It is marked by a warm and rather liberal plea for economic reintegration among the republics and for a general course of modernisation within the framework of an advanced market economy. It praises pluralist democracy with a social dimension and opts for a broad, rationalist-style cultural renaissance in conformity with the creed and the demands of modern Europeanness.

The second, controversial and, in fact, the only publicly discussed part of the *Memorandum* is, in contrast, phrased in a rather national-chauvinist mood. It presents an ethnic nationalist alternative to the paramount grand recipe for modernisation cast in the mould of a rejuvenated pan-nationalist Yugoslavian federal project. If this paramount (federal Yugoslavian) project fails, the *Memorandum* alleges, its history and its present (1986) dismal condition justifies – in a situation where all others appear simply to follow *their* idiosyncratic ethnic-nationalist goals – that even the Serbian people may concentrate all of their cultural energy in order to define their own ethnic-nationalist trajectory into the modern age.

Déjà vu! We meet here the familiar iron-fisted logic of the modernist intellectual interpretation of nationalism, most radically expressed by Gellner (1983); the nationalist imperative of modernity cast in a functional fit (whether achieved through ethnic nationalism or via some other route to cultural homogenisation) between *one economy, one state* and *one* (modern, standardised, national) *culture*. This was the very message of the *Memorandum* captured by Slobodan Milošević, then (1987) moving to the apex (through a palace revolution) of the Serbian communist party, and translated into the infamous populist dictum: 'All Serbs in one state!' (whether a modern rational and culturally homogenised Yugoslavian project or something else).

But the *Memorandum*'s shocking repercussions cannot be inferred simply on the basis of a critique of the document in itself, as has often been tried. The *Memorandum* was scarcely more radical in its ethnic-nationalist rhetoric than the cyclically reappearing rhetoric of other nationalist intellectuals before: Croatians during the early 1970s, Slovenians and Albanians (in the Serbian province of Kosovo) from the early 1980s; and not forgetting the past Islamistic allegations of the former dissident and today's president of Bosnia-Herzegovina, Alija Izetbegović.

The *Memorandum*'s particularly explosive potential must be comprehended through an overall understanding of the social situation within which it appeared and was used. Not only did the Serbs represent by the far largest population group, dispersed all over the federation with open ethnic-nationalist claims among them, therefore representing a by far greater threat to the political stability of precarious federal arrangements than among any other nationality. Not only had the influence of the numerically dominant and traditionally politically potent Serbian heartland been forcefully put into brackets by Josip Broz Tito's bizarre confederation-like constitution of 1974; and not only did forceful Serbian irredenta outside this central homeland (in Kosovo, Bosnia-Herzegovina and Croatia) – feeling increasingly minoritised through exposure to the ethnicised political games in every republic – represent a potentially radical nationalist force. What was particularly ominous was that all of this coalesced with severe economic crisis and social depreciation from the beginning of the 1980s. It was a situation aggravated by international super-austerity measures couched in the shell of revived federal (liberal market) reform policies; the so-called 'Stabilisation Programme', which now, once again, threatened to bereave the common woman of her state-sponsored bread and salt. All of former Yugoslavia (not only the Serbs) was, at the time, moving into a state of inflammable social unrest. This was, as has during the last few years been proved again and again almost everywhere in Europe, a fertile soil for ethnic-nationalist mobilisation. This is particularly so in a situation, as in Serbia of the late 1980s, where the only existing organised political power (the local communist party) now turned openly nationalist, but without any challenge from competing political agencies or a broad and politically articulated civil society.

Slobodan Milošević's populist rhetoric proved to become the most compelling of all the competing ethnic-national trajectories entering the Yugoslavian neo-Balkanisation theatre during the late 1980s and early 1990s.[13] It held strong appeal to most social strata in Serbian society. Its tremendously mobilising effect could be attributed to its adept skill in fusing several traditionally competing political discourses and ideological perspectives. At the same time, the so-called, 'anti-bureaucratic revolution' was able to distance itself effectively from the most discrediting features of the 'old' (communist-politocratic) system and yet to integrate and forcefully reformulate its basic left-populist idioms of legitimacy. Finally, it was able to present itself as something genuinely contemporary – the agent for a transition into a brighter 'European' future – while at the same time successfully allying itself with, incorporating and merging traditional nationalism and its populist support into one over-arching ideological-political hegemony.[14] This gave Milošević, at least in the beginning, an extremely broad and powerful popular legitimacy. Serbia was to be transformed into a prosperous modern 'Switzerland of the Balkans', relying on a high-tech market economy and new spontaneous forms of (plebiscitian) democracy combined with the very best of the nearer and more distant past – the tradition of Yugoslavian 'self-management' (direct, local-level democracy) and the age-old Serbian fighting spirit (the romanticist ethnic-nationalist Kosovo-mythology).

The basic message was, however, like that of the *Memorandum*, essentially, and in the name of contemporary 'Europeanism', that of 'nationalism for modernisation'.

THE NEW NATIONALISM: ANATHEMA OF REASON?

Nationalist mobilisation among Serbs all over the federation came to be the overture to warfare and 'ethnic cleansing'; features that are definitely not in themselves foreign to the formation of modern nation-states. The Holocaust, for instance, has been interpreted as a sort of quintessence of modernity (Bauman 1989). Ethnic cleansing has been fundamental to the processes through which several European states have, in the course of recent history, constructed the essence of their more or less 'pure' modern national being, for example, the 'cleansing' of Jews and Gypsies in Germany, of Germans in Poland and former Czechoslovakia, of Serbs, Jews and Gypsies in Croatia, and of Armenians and Greeks in Turkey.[15]

During the 1980s and early 1990s 'ethnic cleansing' became, as well, one of the most conspicuous features of the so-called post-communist political transformation on the territory of former Yugoslavia; it was practised, not only by the Serbs, but, more or less arduously, by all of the parties in the current conflicts. Cynically seen, this might in light of historical experience be regarded as just another phase in the creation of modern culturally homogenised national states, taking on notably bloody features in an ethnically mixed part of the European continent marked by competing nationalist projects. But it is, as yet, difficult here on the ground to discern any fulfilment of the modern logics of nationalist master-programmes like the *Memorandum* or even Milošević's so-called 'anti-bureaucratic revolution'. At work, we meet neither the spirit of rationalist enlightenment, nor any contemporary ethics of a Weberian, Protestant-ethic type of modernity; according to Gellner (1992b),[16] the only two surviving avenues in the conquest of contemporary modernisation. Nor will the historical image of the Holocaust's rationalised and hyper-perfectionist modern mass murder do. Rather, at least on the surface, the generalised violence following ethnic-nationalist mobilisation all over former Yugoslavia appears to correspond to Hans Magnus Enzensberger's (1993) axiom of the triumph of irrationality in contemporary civil wars; a pandemonium of 'losers fighting losers' without any kind of orderly conception of the present, let alone a vision of the future. Or, as described in a similar vein by Mary Kaldor (1993), 'the new nationalism is private, anarchic, and disintegrative'.

The seemingly unbounded nature of current 'ethnic cleansing' cannot be explained with reference to an elaborate and relatively coherent ideological system as in nazism. It has to do, rather, with the particular character of the new nationalism, which, Kaldor argues, could best be identified as 'a primitive grab for power' based on an anarchic 'war economy' – 'a social formation dependent on continuous violence'. This is not a war economy in the traditional sense of sustaining strong states, but rather to 'sustain a loose coalition of petty criminals, ex-soldiers, and power-hungry anonymous politicians all of whom are bound together', under the token of ethno-nationalism, 'in a shared complicity for war crimes and a shared interest in reproducing the sources of power and wealth'. The new nationalism is decentralised and fragmenting, in contrast to earlier nationalisms which were centralising and unifying. Its ideological legitimacy has become that of trivial and *ad hoc* identitarian claims.

This is a far cry from the modernist horizon of the *Memorandum* of the Serbian Academy of Sciences or, for that matter, any other local intellectual master programme for national reconstruction in ex- or post-Yugoslavia. But the basic scenario, so conjured up, corresponds only too well to the visage of a wide range of other crisis-ridden trouble spots in the contemporary world: Cambodia, Afghanistan, Palestine, Africa's Horn, Angola, the Congo, the post-Soviet Trans-Caucasian region or, even, Nicaragua, Venezuela and Peru, to mention only a few. In other words, it keeps up with some general modern global process, marked by the return of neo-traditionalism in the contexts of 'political economies of internal war' (Duffield 1994b), rather than with the fantasies of modernist Balkan intellectuals.

We may, more productively, see neo-traditionalism as one major contemporary identitarian pole contingent on complex cultural logics of a truly paradoxical global system of modernity (cf. Friedman 1988). While – after the worldwide demise of two of the great modernist ideological paradigms and social compacts (welfare-state capitalism and state-socialism) – post-modernism has tended towards intellectual hegemony in a stagnant consumerist west and modernism moved towards a 'Confucian' East (Friedman 1988), a new traditionalism has tended to take over the hegemonic position in the identitarian space, not only of the Third World, but of the Second as well.

Like in post-modernism, neo-traditionalist movements have become the 'seekers of solid identities' in a contemporary world of contingency and flux (Peterson 1994). But, on the periphery of the transnational world-system, these ersatz neo-tribes (Maffesoli 1991, Bauman 1992, 1993) express something existentially different from the identitarian manipulation of the modern media 'image space' (Peterson 1994:6) in the post-modernist West. They express, as well, the cultural accomplice to the fabrication of new local shadow economies, structured around *a reason of survivalism and fast spoils*, woven intricately into the tissue of very real traditionalist social relationships (kin, clan, friendship, locality, ethnicity). We encounter a growth of an ethos belonging to *Mafia-like* patron–client networks and informal economies; configurations induced and made imperative by transnational relationships that have turned these parts of the world into the last link in a chain of complex interdependency, structured along the lines of political dominance and an uneven international division of labour.

Their particular background in the 'Second World' is the exposition of increasingly unequal conditions in confrontation with a global capitalist economy undergoing profound restructuration. The social and economic systems of actually existing socialism proved incapable of commanding or developing forms of organisation contingent with the demands of the third industrial revolution (micro-electronic) on increased 'just in time' flexibility, human creativity, and decentralised institutional autonomy harnessed to an intensified accumulation of capital (cf. Castells and Kiselyova 1995). At the same historical juncture, transnational capital's vastly expanded integration of selected former 'Third World' regions into their economic orbit meant that the stagnating and increasingly world-market-dependent economies of the Second Europe were rather abruptly exposed to new sources of ferocious competition. In extended parts of the 'Second World', the diacritical development became that of an incremental evacuation of intellectual and skilled labour from the accumulation scheme, an extended brain drain and the forced full or partial reproduction of the majority of the remaining labour force within informal shadow-economic networks. In Yugoslavia this was dramatically expressed through the revival of the generalised rural-urban symbiosis. In this context, a pervasive retraditionalisation functions as the elementary cultural kit of a day-to-day social life revolving around regional–local networks of self-help and clientilism: that is, society structured along networks of patron–client relationships.

The imperatives of the new transnational micro-electronic world order left modernist reformers little choice other than one of combining their efforts at economic, political and cultural change with some transformed version of habitual legitimacy policies. Hyper-radical modernisation projects – like that of Ante Marković, the last federal premier in Yugoslavia, or Jegor Gajdar's neo-liberal market absolutism – have, with unanticipated speed, been devoured by their own unwelcome offspring: social marginality, poverty, industrial closures, public sector shrinkage and threats of mass unemployment. But, once leaning towards well-worn matrixes of populist legitimacy, reminiscent of a late edition of real socialism, local regimes are easily caught in a social dynamic which they themselves are not able to control. For, in a part of the world where international super-austerity measures and isolationist containment policies make no social compromise possible whatsoever, the most obvious exit for shipwrecked élites, as well as the only immediate avenue to the boons of modernity apparently still open to the common man, appeared, in the last instance, to be that of internal war, 'ethnic cleansing' and an anarchic economy of pillage, all couched in a massive cultural exodus into a more glorious past. This is the critical historical memorandum of Yugoslavia addressed to any unilateral modernist perspective.

Notes

1. Quotation in the German original: *'Me-ti lehrte: Umwälzungen finden in Sack-gassen statt'*. (Brecht 1967:515).
2. Seemingly implicated by, for example, Gellner (1992b).
3. These were, to a large degree, premised on the particular character of tradi-tional agrarian regimes. In contrast to Western Europe, Eastern Europe was, according to Brenner's analysis, marked by strong corporate peasant com-munities and a landed class of lords inclined towards the politically effected extortion of corvé labour. This precluded a radical rupture with traditional bonds and counteracted, for a long time, any pervasive process of pro-letarianisation, and thereby also mass industrialisation and the growth of a genuine (Western-styled) bourgeoisie. See also, concerning the particular case of the Balkans, the analyses of Adanir (1989) and Lampe (1989), following similar lines of argument.
4. Borislav Kidrić was an influential post-Second-World-War Yugoslav economist and (communist) reformist. Ante Marković was a liberal reformist economist and socialist Yugoslavia's last premier.
5. From the vantage point of political science, Ramet (1992) maps in detail the complex conflicts and changing alignments between republican élites within a labile federal framework.
6. Over 90 per cent of contracts with foreign partners to import technology contained various restrictive clauses (Ocić 1983.:111ff.). In 1983, for example, 62 per cent of the contracts excluded the export of products produced with purchased technology; 44 per cent obliged the Yugoslav buyer to report any technological progress or invention connected with the use of purchased equipment to the partner with which the contract was made; and 26 per cent contained clauses that obliged the Yugoslav partners to use the purchased technology in combination with imported raw materials, materials for opera-tion and maintainance, and spare parts from sources decided by the seller. The results have became outspoken technological dependency, stagnating autonomous development of technology in Yugoslavia and decreasing com-petitive power on foreign markets (Ocić 1983; Đurek 1981).
7. While the size of its highly qualified technical intelligentsia is very large, of all the countries of Europe, Yugoslavia had, during the early 1980s, the low-est number of patents realised in relation to the number of citizens (Ocić 1983:110).

8. In Yugoslavia the socialised sector (Serbo-Croato-Bosnian: *društveni sektor*) in agriculture never came to encompass more than approximately 15 per cent of the total surface of agricultural land in the federation.

9. The concept of 'primitive accumulation' belongs to the terminology of Marxist political economy, used in Karl Marx's analysis of the rise of capitalism in England. The basic idea is that any initial capitalist takeoff needs to accumulate a substantial surplus for further investment, and that this must be drawn from forms of society and modes of production that are pre- or non-capitalist. This was, for example, according to Marx, the logic of the English enclosure movement. In socialist Yugoslavia, the notion of 'primitive accumulation' was widely used, by orthodox communist planners and liberal economists alike, as a notion describing the socialist (industrialised) economies' accumulation of resources from economic sectors that did not themselves belong to the socialist economy proper; e.g. surplus drawn petty peasant agriculture, but also via foreign loans and guest workers' remittances were described as sources of 'primitive accumulation' for the socialist economy (that is, the so-called 'social sector'/Serbian-Croatian-Bosnian: *društveni sektor*).

10. That is, harnessed from outside the mainstream framework of a modern industrialised capitalist or socialist economy.

11. This, accordingly, represents a 'socialist' version of what the French social anthropologist, Claude Meillassoux (1981) calls 'migration tournante' (that is, cyclical migration). He argues that capital realises the means of lowering the reproduction costs of labour in the periphery of its global system (in Third-World countries) via the purchase of cheap labour power belonging to migrant workers feeding themselves on the basis of peasant subsistence crops. This household-based food production never enters the capitalist market or burdens the capitalists' expenses for variable capital (that is, labour costs). It is based on unpaid household labour within a separate and qualitatively different pre-capitalist sector of production. It represents a continued primitive accumulation effected through the migration of peasant-workers oscillating back and forth between contexts dominated by two juxtaposed modes of production: that is, on the one hand, the 'rural' (pre-capitalist), so-called 'domestic mode of production' and, on the other hand, the dominant capitalist one. Therefore, at the same time as capital exploits and disintegrates them, the deliberate and organised conservation of 'pre-' or 'non-capitalist' systems of reproduction exempted from the ordinary labour market become essential for continued capital accumulation.

12. In 1948 the percentage of the population totally dependent on income from agriculture was still 67 per cent on average in the federation (47 per cent in the republic of Slovenia, 74 per cent in Bosnia and Herzegovina, and 80 per cent in the province of Kosovo).

13. Slobodan Milošević's political thinking can be found most clearly stated in his book *The Years of Disentanglement* (Milošević 1989).

14. Bowman (1994) and Salecl (1994) analyse in detail the complex strategies of hegemony embodied in populist-nationalist mobilisation in Yugoslavia in the 1980s and 1990s.

15. Most thoroughly modern 'ethnic cleansing' was cultivated in nazi ideology and a perverse industrialised practice, but was brought to a horrendous modern efficiency even in the Stalinist-Soviet ethnic deportation politics of the 1930s. As an arch-modernist and rationalist par excellence, Ernest Gellner (1992b, 1993) tends to see this as the out mostly perverted forms of a modern rationalist 'reason' running astray; aberrations, paradoxically, doomed to ruin due

to their very 'hyper-perfection'; that is, their absolutism, fanaticism and un-compromising vanity, while aspiring to bring about modernisation by strict design and rigid social engineering. The surviving and successful projects of modernisation are, rather, the pragmatic, open-minded and flexible 'muddling through' ones.

16. For Gellner (1992b) Islamism is basically the vigorous implementation of an ethos of a radical modernisation project, comparable to the Protestant ethic (à la Weber).

3 Modern Authoritarian Ethnocracy: Balkanisation and the Political Economy of International Relations

Ivan Iveković

The new economic, social and political dynamics, initiated about six years ago with the overall collapse of the 'real socialist' model of development in East Central Europe and Soviet Union, still begs for comprehensive explanations. The new configuration of forces, both at the global level and in individual countries, and the new articulations being established between the two levels, require new conceptual frameworks that go beyond mere 'transitologist' explanations of the political process and beyond 'culturologist' over-simplifications. I believe that such a perspective could be offered by the 'new' political economy, which may eventually bring us closer to an understanding of what really happened and what the meaning is of the observed transition process. As a native of the shattered European East, I was particularly interested to discover the underlying economic logic of the political process which led to state-making and unmaking. I tried to identify the common denominators for the almost simultaneous disintegration of the Yugoslav federation and the Soviet Union, and to understand why 'ethnic conflict' in the Yugoslav space and Transcaucasia took such a similar ugly turn. I analysed the topic from different angles,[1] while in what now follows the focus is narrowed to the relationships between state, domestic, economic and political developments, and global economic processes.

THE MODERN AUTHORITARIAN ETHNOCRACY

Any superficial observer of contemporary ethnic conflicts in the two geographically separated regions may confirm that the similarities are striking. They began as the élite's competition over the appropriation and redistribution of scarce resources, then took the form of ethnic homogenisation and differentiation whose outcome was mass political

62

mobilisation and confrontation, leading to clashes between exclusive ethno-nationalist projects, political violence, ethnic cleansing and wars for territories. Everything was, and still is, justified with similar stereotypical discourses and almost identical – although mutually contradictory – historic, demographic, political and cultural arguments. In both 'regional laboratories' ethnic myths were exploited and religious feelings abused in order to serve current policies of ethnocide. The regimes that emerged from this political process are clearly nationalist and may be called 'modern authoritarian ethnocracies'.

It is beyond the scope of this short chapter to reproduce the dramatic and unique narratives of these conflicts. However, it is symptomatic that they erupted almost simultaneously in two geographically separated, very specific, and yet in certain aspects, similar border-zones, and that they gave birth to a similar form of state and political system. I believe that these similarities derive from the political space where these countries are located (geopolitics) and similar internal social constraints (social times). The Balkans are currently a Western European peripheral borderland, which Yugoslav wars had temporarily transformed into a shatterbelt, but which are supposed to become the most important European continental gateway to the Middle East. On the other hand, Transcaucasia, together with Northern Caucasus and Central Asia, is for the first time in modern history a buffer-zone separating Russia from the Middle East. Additionally, this region contains huge oil and gas potentials, which may prove more important than those of the Middle East. It is relevant that Chechnya is located on the pipelines crossroads from where Caspian and Central Asian oil is dispatched towards European Russia and its Black Sea port facilities.

The common traits of the ethnocracies established in these two regions may be summarised in the following ways:

- The state is explicitly or implicitly defined as an ethnic state; ethnic minorities are *de jure* (constitutional nationalism) and/or *de facto* excluded from the system; they are typically victims of state-sponsored terror, ethnic cleansing and discrimination.
- The inaugurated political and economic systems are still in flux and transitional.
- There is a state-sponsored nationalist 'mentality' rather than a full-blown totalitarian nationalist ideology.
- In a system of one-dimensional political pluralism, the political stage is dominated by large electoral movements and fluctuating parliamentarian coalitions, typically led by a more or less charismatic leader of the 'caudillo' type; there is manipulation of the electorate, voting machines, élite bargaining, and cliques' politics.

- The leadership is operating with ill-defined but often predictable limits; there are strong autocratic tendencies, but no total control over all aspects of public life; the leader arbitrates between different cliques by co-optation, bribery and threats.
- There is state manipulation of and through the mass media, especially TV, radio and high-circulation printed press, which typically are controlled by pro-regime coteries.
- The legitimacy of the state is weak, but the regime is oppressive and appears internally 'strong'.
- Democratic institutions are not consolidated, the civil society is weak and the space for opposition activities is greatly reduced.
- The state has only a relative control over the means of armed combat, which is a specific situation characteristic only of transitional situations and countries caught up in civil wars. Once the state consolidates, its total monopoly will be re-established.
- Post-communist Croatia, the rump Yugoslavia (Serbia and Montenegro), Bosnia and Herzegovina (divided into three ethnic homelands) and Macedonia in the Balkans share the above-stated common traits. Armenia, Azerbaijan and Georgia (effectively divided into three or four homelands) are the three Transcaucasian ethnocracies. Eventually, Albania, Moldova and Slovakia could enter the same category and stand in sharp contrast to 'non-consolidated élitist democracies' that are taking shape in Slovenia, Hungary, the Czech Republic and Poland. Equally, they have to be distinguished from 'crypto-communist regimes' or 'modern post-communist autocracies' in Central Asia, although the contours of these groupings are often fluid.

BRINGING THE STATE BACK IN[2]

In the modern era a special relationship has been established between state, state coercion, economic development, social stratification and the political processes. Whether one likes it or not, the modern nation-state is not only the dominant, but also the unavoidable form of political and economic organisation of society in the contemporary world. But, until recently, this relationship has been systematically downplayed by the apologists of private enterprise and *laissez-faire* as well as Marxists. However, 'development studies', dealing with Third-World problems, brought the state back into the picture. It was understood that the state cannot be by-passed and that the 'invisible hand' of the free market is not sufficient in itself to promote development, whatever meaning is given to that term. After the collapse of the communist project in the former Soviet Union and East Central Europe, it is again the state that is called upon to play a key role in the demise of the state-command economy, in the process of privatisation and in the process of integration of the radically restructured 'national' economies into the global system.

Evidently the modern territorial state is not only 'a bordered power-container' (Giddens 1985:120) with a clearly defined territory and citizenry, but it is also an economic power container and major allocator of resources, statuses and benefits. These states are not only political units in the world states' system, which pursue their goals partly in cooperation and partly in conflict with each other, but also play an essential role in the spatial division of labour. They act as buffers and at the same time they mediate between national production and the surrounding world by controlling transborder transactions and movements of people. The type of relationships which are established with the external markets determines the domestic division of labour, which in turn shapes national political structures. As the international division of labour is antinomous, different states tend to reproduce different political structures and institutions. The status and role of individual actors in the shifting international hierarchy of states essentially depends on their role and place in the international division of labour. This somewhat simplified picture of the international division of roles is blurred by the existing system of inter-state political and/or economic alliances, by the directions of transnational capital flows and by the imperfections and contradictions of the global system itself.

The emergence of the global system, most 'statist' theories agree, was directly linked to the development of capitalism in Western Europe and its gradual spread to the rest of the world. If it is so, it should be also recognised that the terms of integration of different countries into the international (capitalist) division of labour were unequal from the beginning, if for no reason other than the simple one that the majority of peripheral countries were essentially producers and exporters of raw material, while only a few core countries monopolised modern technologies and were producing and exporting manufactured goods. This axial division of labour on a world scale tends to reproduce inequalities. By adopting 'open-door' policies, states may speed up the process of integration of their economies into the global system, or by pursuing autarchic policies they may hinder the same process. Between the two extremes there were always a number of medium-range and transitional formulas of 'import substitution' and protection tariffs policies. Beyond the conflict of ideologies which masked more important economic contradictions, the Cold War was essentially a conflict of two concepts of development, one autarchic, masked with 'socialist', anti-imperialist and/or populist rhetoric, and another one advocating 'free trade' and open borders for the circulation of capital, commodities and know-how. Participation and democracy were not really the primary concerns on either side of this divide-line, and ruthless dictatorships could be found on both sides of the barricades.

Max Weber gave much more weight to the state, both in the process of capital accumulation and in the shaping of the social structure, than was suggested by Talcott Parsons in his interpretation of Weber's *The Protestant Ethic*, which is largely responsible for the vagaries of Anglo-Saxon social sciences.[3] A new reading of Weber confirms that he believed that 'it was a question of competing national states in a condition of perpetual struggle and war ... Out of this alliance of the state with capital, dictated by necessity, arose the national citizen class, the bourgeoisie in the modern sense of the word. Hence it is the closed national state which afforded to capitalism its chance for development' (Weber 1981:339). According to Tom Nairn,

> [A]s capitalism spread, and smashed the ancient social formations surrounding it, they always tended to fall apart along the fault-lines contained inside them. It is a matter of elementary truth that these lines were nearly always ones of nationality (although in certain well-known cases deeply established religious divisions could perform the same function). (Nairn 1977:353).

Recent interpretations seek to bring the state back as a major factor of economic, social and political change and development. State intervention is again viewed as vital, not only for 'developing' Third World countries and ex-colonies, but also for post-communist societies. According to Friedrich List, the last century's forgotten champion of the protectionist nation-state, state intervention is the indispensable precondition for successful economic (capitalist) development.[4] On a world scale the processes of capitalist integration and reproduction cannot spread to the periphery without the active role and cooperation of the same peripheral state. In the following pages I try to explain why.

The central role of the modern state, capitalist and/or communist alike, is to assure a balanced quantitative and qualitative growth of the productive forces of society. The concept of productive forces in the sense used here simply combines human capital (the Marxists would say 'subjective factor' – with its knowledge, skills and working habits) and tools of production (the so-called 'material factor' – machinery, physical and chemical ingredients). Additionally, the state is supposed to be an efficient crisis manager. Each political system tends to reproduce itself, and therefore its ruling élite should be very careful as to how they handle and channel the development of these forces. Productive forces that escape the engineering and control of the state-enforced relations of production are likely to be the undertakers of the legal and political system which sustained that state. If this happens, the character of the state itself becomes the subject of change and may lead to a radical redefinition of the relationship between state and society. This, according to Chai-Anan Samudavanija, involves three dimensions – security (S), development (D) and participation (P) (Samudavanija 1991:15–22). Such a conceptualisation presupposes that the consolidated and fully modernised Western state has established a reasonable level of harmony between the three dimensions. On the other hand, the non-consolidated modernising state in developing societies – societies that are still in flux – tends to give priority to one dimension, usually that of security of its ruling élite. The dominance of one dimension over others is due to four major variables: ideological domination, institutionalisation of structure, the capacity to control and utilise resources, and adaptive capacity (or the capacity to escape the surrounding societal forces). Using a non-Marxian terminology we came the other way round and back to the 'relations of production' which determine Samudavanija's variables. In his words, developing states, and I would say that the post-communist states of East Central Europe and the former Soviet Union belong to the same category (it seems, indeed, that the borderlines separating the Second World from the Third World have been blurred),

> encompass within themselves many apparently contradictory characteristics and structures, for example those of development and underdevelopment, democracy and authoritarianism, civilian and military rule, at the same time. [Such] ... political systems are the reflection of their economic and social structures and ... different modes of production that coexist within [such] ... societies. At the political level such structures and characteristics struggle against each other, but most of the time, they also come to terms with each other and continue to coexist in uneasy harmony. (Samudavanija 1991:19)

In the cases of communist-controlled political systems, which collapsed together with the decomposition of the Soviet, Yugoslav and Czecho-Slovak federations, such 'structures and characteristics' proved no longer able to coexist. Could the successor states that replaced the three defunct federations be more successful?

BREAK-UP OF MULTIETHNIC STATES, BALKANISATION, CAUCASIANISATION

The collapse of the Soviet Union and of Yugoslavia was more than the simple falling apart of two multi-ethnic political communities and the emergence, in their place, of a number of new ethnic states. It was at the same time the collapse of a whole social order that underwent a process of gradual delegitimation 'from below'. During this process, the communist-controlled communities of peoples lost their identities. The basic social consensus holding together these federations, which was maintained by a combination of consent and compliance, and coercion and manipulation, was, at one moment of no return, broken. A full-scale crisis erupted which had to be resolved in one way or another.

'Crises represent situations in which the society moves in a new direction. They are the major decisional points at which the society is redefined, and therefore relevant to sequential changes' (Verba 1971:306). Leonard Binder suggested a distinction between five different forms of crises of political development (Binder 1971:65), each one of them including a number of components of the 'modernization syndrome': (1) the crisis of legitimacy; (2) the crisis of identity, whose syndrome components are – the politicisation of identity, the failure of productive and administrative integration and thwarted individual adjustment; (3) the crisis of participation – essentially political shortcomings and an absence of democracy; (4) the crisis of distribution and redistribution – inequality of opportunities and benefits; (5) the crisis of penetration – failures to equalise obligations and duties, individualise citizenship, and mobilise the population. I simplified Binder's conceptualisation with the aim of showing that there are many overlapping dimensions of crises that resulted in the delegitimation of the Communist project of development.

The three federations were still in place when ethnic tensions erupted and when people started to affirm their separate ethno-national identities, which the party-state itself nurtured, but which until that moment were not obstacles to their co-habitation and intercourse. In fact, both in former Yugoslavia and in the Soviet Union the 'societies at large' consisted of a number of different ethno-national communities upheld by federal structures, which until recently seemed to cooperate under the watchful eye of the party-state. These ethnic communities shared the same habitat and were more or less mixed, but while they were included in one federation, internal boundaries were rather fluid and depended on the whims of the rulers. However, once fixed, these borders were not really challenged. The territorial units that were established in such a way – republics, regions, districts and towns – were administrative, but with different administrations providing different services: employment, housing, education and health facilities, transport and so forth, and that made all the difference. Of course, it was better for the individual to be located in more developed zones, where such services were of better quality, or in zones where the native language was an advantage. That is one of the reasons why spontaneous migrations from republic to republic tended to be ethnocentric, but local migrations were mostly directed towards the nearest regional pole of industrial development. The average citizen was little concerned with high politics which he or she couldn't influence in any way.

That was the reserved domain of the *nomenklatura* in which different factions, some of them with territorial power-bases (bureaucratic nationalism), eventually confronted each other over problems of redistribution of resources (authoritative allocation of material and immaterial values).

Then, suddenly, the fact that an individual identified himself or herself with one or another ethno-national community made the difference: he discovered that he may be better off if his ethno-national group prevailed, or that his situation in a particular surrounding or republic became untenable because he belonged to the 'wrong' ethnic group. By the same token his social status and role in what was still supposed to be the 'society at large' began to change for the better or worse. Those who refused to identify themselves with mutually opposed and exclusive ethno-nationalist projects soon found themselves in no man's land. The community to which one thought one belonged had disappeared, or was only surviving in one's memory. Those were the dilemmas of identity in which we were all caught up and which we had to resolve in one way or another.[5] The majority solved it by embracing ethno-national ideologies. Ethno-national ideologies were the main vehicles for the construction of a new sense of community and corresponding collective and individual identity. I am speaking of course of political ideologies that serve to explain, justify and motivate political action, and are presented as a more or less coherent system of concepts, assertions and beliefs that rationalise the 'nation', its continuity (history, historicism), political space (geopolitics) and 'national interests'.

TOWARDS SEGREGATED DEVELOPMENT?

Like the South African bantustans in the times of racial segregation, the ethnic states that emerged in the Balkans and Transcaucasia are based on the idea of separate homelands and segregated development (apartheid) of different ethno-national groups. In South Africa it was the racist state, controlled by the white Nationalist Party, that imposed such an arrangement on the black majority, but the bantustanisation of the country was also supported by tribal chiefs, their loyalists and followers. The Zulu Inkhata party of Chief Buthelezi, the most militant and massive black ethnic political organisation in the country, was the open political ally of the ruling Nationalist Party in its struggle against the African National Congress (ANC), and represents today, after the apartheid system has been rejected nation-wide and majority rule introduced, the most violent opposition to the central government of Nelson Mandela. The Inkhata is today the objective ally of the now isolated white racist groups, in their common struggle against the multicultural and multi-ethnic society that the Mandela government represents. Similarly, as paradoxical as it may seem at first sight, extreme ethno-chauvinists in the Yugoslav space and Transcaucasia, although situated on the opposite sides of the barricades, sustain each other through their confrontation and share objective common interests against the moderates in their own camps. While Yugoslavia was still in one piece, but ethnic homogenisation and polarisation processes reached breaking-point, both Milošević and Tuđman, personifying two mutually opposed ethno-national projects, perceived the central government of Prime-Minister Ante Marković and his programme of reforms as the 'main danger' that could eventually reshape the Yugoslav society and federation and therefore thwart their political ambitions of creating Greater Serbia and Greater Croatia. They indirectly cooperated in blocking these reforms, and Marković personally. They were joined by the Slovenes, and for their own obsolete reasons, by the 'party of generals' and the federal military establishment. Once Marković was incapacitated and finally eliminated politically, the ethnocrats could start their war games. In Bosnia and Herzegovina, the three ethno-national parties – Muslim, Serb and Croat – initially even formed a precarious coalition government whose only *raison d'être* was to block the path to Marković and other reformers of communist or liberal origin. Once these heterogeneous, non-ethnic interest groups were politically marginalised, the coalition fell apart and violence broke out. After the stalemate in Croatia, Milošević and Tuđman fought their war by proxy in Bosnia, both with the ambition of annexing as much territory as possible.

In former Soviet space, the members of the Commonwealth of Independent States (CIS) officially recognised each other as they existed under the union republics' boundaries. Those who did not join the CIS at that time were already embattled over their own territorial disputes. From the three Transcaucasian countries only Armenia joined the second founding meeting of the CIS in Alma Ata, because at that time Armenian territorial ambitions were supported by an important section of the Russian establishment. Georgia, already in civil war, was absent, and Azerbaijan joined the Commonwealth, but soon pulled out. A more complicated situation prevailed in decomposing Yugoslavia, where the Milošević offensive was already in full swing. Serbia refused to recognise the internal 'administrative borders' left over from the communist state and vowed to establish a Serbian state 'wherever there are Serbian people, wherever there are Serbian homes and fields' (Ćosić 1993:1). Strengthened by the support of what remained of the former Yugoslav army, such a project would amputate a substantial part of breakaway Croatia and annex the whole of Bosnia-Herzegovina and Macedonia.

Similarly, Armenian military successes in and around Nagorno Karabagh have amputated Azerbaijan, and today's Georgia has not yet succeeded in re-establishing its control over breakaway Abkhazia and Southern Ossetia.

THE ROLE OF ASYMMETRICAL CLIENT-STATES

Theories of interdependence as elaborated by Keohane and Nye (1989), even when they point to the unequal cost of inter-state transactions and elaborate the shifts of power in the international system of nation-states, are perhaps able to explain the complex relationships that are established between Western industrial liberal economies, but are hopelessly useless when they have to deal with peripheral or semi-peripheral countries whose national economies are not yet fully integrated into the global system. To put it differently, they may eventually explain the actual international position and the dominant role of the US and describe the nature of its relationship with major Western industrial partners and allies, but the voices become elusive and conspicuously silent the moment they have to define the new role of Second- and Third-World countries in the emerging international liberal order. They are written from the perspective of American hegemony and directly or indirectly justify this hegemony, ignoring the other side of the same international equation.

What is the position and role of countries such as the FR of Yugoslavia (Serbia/Montenegro), Croatia or Bosnia Herzegovina? Is the last an independent country or a mandated territory of the UN/NATO, and how much is the Milošević government really an independent international actor? All three of them are clearly dependent on the wills and whims of the 'international community' and, as we have seen in Dayton and later in Paris, they behaved, at least in this phase of the conflict resolution process, like classical client-states. Even Russia itself, which was given a decorative role in the international contact group for former Yugoslavia, has for the time being no alternative other than to acquiesce on what others have decided in the Balkans. At the same time, Russia acts as a major external power-broker in Transcaucasia, and although it has not yet succeeded in imposing a full capitulation on local belligerents, it is investing a great effort in transforming them into clients. Perhaps its most important achievement was to force Georgia and Azerbaijan to come under the CIS umbrella. However, state power in Russia itself is challenged, both in the centre by a consolidated communist opposition and extremist nationalist groupings, and at the non-Russian periphery of the federation by separatist ethno-nationalist movements, such as in the case of breakaway Chechnya. How does such an asymmetrical state as Russia fit into the increasingly 'interdependent' world? What about the cases of

Azerbaijan or Georgia, and what is the real meaning of their nominal 'independence'? What is the autonomous international manoeuvring space which is left at their disposal?

In trying to answer such questions, and faced with less than adequate concepts, I use here the old term of 'client-states', which is more precise than 'peripheral states'. This reintroduced term means that the international autonomy of Balkan and Transcaucasian state-entities is objectively reduced, and that they are forced to behave in the international arena, at least when it comes to options which have a wider geopolitical significance, as 'clients' of powerful 'patrons'. To describe such a relationship, the term of 'new medievalism has been suggested, although this new type of vassalage is no longer personalised, linked to a particular suzerain or a single foreign power. Exclusive *chasses gardées* belong to the colonial and mercantilist past, and although peripheral markets may be temporarily divided between industrial powers or cartels of companies, the ineluctable process of globalisation is opening them up to international capital and competition. Although the US in reality acts as a world hegemony, it is not as a 'supreme patron' but rather as 'multilateral manager'.

The emerging global system is rather impersonal, and it operates under a corporate leadership, which presently plays the role of collective 'supreme patron'. The personality of individual members of its presumed 'executive board' , and even their names, are irrelevant. The system works, regardless of whether Reagan, Bush or Clinton is the US President, or whether Japan has a Liberal Democrat or Socialist prime-minister, or whether or not Italy has a 'technocratic government'. From the point of view of the global system, all of them are individually replaceable, a reality which the 'fathers' of new/old nations in the Balkans and Transcaucasia, who have a concentration of so much personal power, have difficulty in understanding. These two types of power, one more or less personalised at the level of the ethnic state, and the other impersonal and corporate at the level of the global system, legitimised in different ways with a variety of formulas, complicate the analysis of contemporary international relations. However, the post-cold war system of states may be represented as a stepped pyramid in whose structure different states occupy different moving positions. The relative position of each state depends primarily on the level of development of its productive forces and of its place in the global division of labour. Military force, unrelated to industrial power, is of secondary importance. The top of the pyramid is occupied by industrial powers, that is by the G7 countries presided over by the United States. Smaller industrialised countries are located just below, while its base is crowded with weak and peripheral client-states, whose modernisation process has been retarded, but which aspire to improve their precarious position. They will be upgraded only when their productive forces have been rearranged in the manner that suits the requirements of the global liberal system. Only then may they be co-opted into the EU and NATO. But even then, non-economic criteria (geopolitical or ideological considerations) may prevail and postpone their co-option.

The concept of 'asymmetrical state'[6] was introduced here in order to underline that contemporary ethnocracies do not behave in accordance with standard norms. It may even appear that they have cut out for themselves an unprecedented autonomous space, both in the international arena and in internal politics. Yet their seemingly 'independent' moves, and their 'challenges' to the international community, were in fact monitored and channelled from the very beginning by more powerful external actors, and were fitting into regional 'grand scenarios' written by somebody else. Earlier, I described the role played by ethno-nationalist élites in the political fragmentation of what was formerly communist-controlled space. Milošević's move to carve out his Greater Serbia not only precipitated the collapse of Yugoslavia, but was also the introduction to a major rearrangement of the Balkan political space. This is still in progress and has to be included in one way or another into the future European 'architecture'. Hussein's invasion of Kuwait, and the Iraqi defeat in 'the Mother of Battles', opened up the process of regional political readjustment in the Middle East, now exclusively monitored by the United States. When Washington finally decided to do something about Bosnia as well, everybody involved in the conflict, belligerents and European powers alike, stood to attention and obediently lined up to sign the documents presented by Richard Holbrook. Milošević, previously nicknamed 'the Balkan Butcher', transformed himself overnight into 'peacemonger' and began to behave, at least for a while, as any other ordinary client. A similar show of diplomatic muscle could have prevented war tragedies long time ago, but clearly the Americans were not ready earlier and perhaps in Washington's views other circumstances were not ripe either.

Balkan and Transcaucasian ethnocracies are also 'asymmetrical' when it comes to the political economy of international relations. As we have seen, they were legitimised by major industrial powers who pressed for the opening of Eastern European and CIS markets. But they found themselves in a paradoxical situation which needs clarification. First, these state-entities, which were established in the name of ideals about national self-determination and political independence, are now not only forced to behave internationally as subservient client-states, but are also supposed to give up part of their newly acquired 'national sovereignty' as the price of their integration into global economic circuits. Second, nationalism, with which these ethnocrats legitimise their state-building projects, is supposed to include a dimension of 'economic independence', yet such an ethnocentric and, in principle, autarchic concept of development directly contradicts the imperative of open markets and permeable borders promoted by the neo-liberal model of the world economy. In short, exclusive nationalism and globalising markets are strange bed-fellows and their temporary alliance against state socialism has, in the meantime, lost its initial rationale.

THE COST OF MAINTAINING ETHNOCRACY

Ethno-nationalists will, ultimately, have to examine the rising cost of maintaining ethnocracy and their own privileges. They face, in fact, the same dilemma that had to be solved in the 1980s by the South African whites' ruling class. South Africa, in those days, was a typical Western asymmetrical client-state, playing a special regional role in the Cold War confrontation. Because the situation in which they found themselves is so strikingly similar, I will adapt for our purpose some of the arguments already used by Heribert Adam and Hermann Giliomee (1979), who analysed the options left open to Afrikaner rulers. For Balkan or Transcaucasian ethnocrats, the main concern will be how to assure the perpetuation of their new social status and economic interests. Formal political power, so decisive for the acquisition of status and wealth in the current transitional phase, may become of secondary importance once these two basic interests have been satisfied. There are three courses of action they may follow: (1) they may give in and sooner or later abdicate; (2) they may opt for further wars and internal repression, which can only increase the cost they will have to pay themselves; (3) they may attempt to manipulate the challenges by policy changes that would cut the costs.

In the short run, 'voluntary' departure from power may be envisaged only if the combination of external and internal pressures becomes unbearable, or if the regime is toppled by an internal coup or foreign military intervention, or defeated in an 'ethnic' war. All of the possible outcomes have to lead to a general 'national catharsis', which is the precondition for the downfall of authoritarian ethnocracy. However, the simple removal of the leader, similar to the overthrow of a Latin American caudillo does not necessarily mean the ending of ethnocratic rule. One caudillo may be replaced by another or by an impersonal directorate representing the military establishment. The ways in which Elchebey and Gamsakhurdia were replaced by Aliyev and Shevardnadze point to the feasibility of such a scenario. It is too early to say what would happen if the leader and/or his party are defeated in a regular electoral competition. As we know from past electoral exercises it is only a remote possibility, because bans imposed on parties and candidates, exclusions from electoral register and manipulation of public opinion and cheating, seem to be the rule. Armenian President Ter-Petrosyan did not hesitate to send tanks against demonstrators who protested against an obvious electoral fraud. Tuđman's regime arrogantly ignored the electoral results for the control of Zagreb Municipal Council which his party lost, and appointed an emergency city-governor of his own choice; Milošević's regime, which lost the municipal elections in all major Serbian cities, retroactively annulled their results. With such 'performances' in mind, it is doubtful whether a peaceful transfer of power, such as occurred in Czechoslovakia or Poland, is at all possible in the troubled areas discussed in this paper.

Nevertheless, it should be remembered that authoritarianism also operates under a double constraint: (1) there are limits imposed by foreign tutors that these ethnocrats may ignore for a certain time but not permanently; (2) more importantly perhaps, the need to maintain a basic consensus among different cliques that support the regime demands self-restraint. As Adam remarked for racist South Africa,

[R]adically extended repression would presuppose a one-party state and/ or military rule that would severely tax the cohesiveness of the white camp ... [in our case 'white' should be replaced with 'ethnic community' in whose name Balkan and Transcaucasian ethnocrats rule] ... with its wide tactical cleavages, interest constellations, and international dependency. It would invite costly repercussions of various kinds. Technocratically ruthless repression would defeat its purpose in an integrated, interdependent, industrialized economy ...' (Adam and Giliomee 1979:9–10)

But unlike the South African economy, Eastern European economies are not yet fully integrated into the global system.

There remains the politics of manipulation by co-optation which ultimately leads to compromise. The original sin of our ethnocrats was that they autistically refused any compromise with their rivals. Now that they are compelled to talk to each other, shake hands, sign different documents and seek solutions to common practical problems, perhaps they will start to realise what they have missed. As the South African experience has proved, compromises between élites across racial, tribal and linguistic boundaries are feasible and they may work for quite a time. In the previous apartheid system, which was in spite of its shortcomings and human rights abuses, remarkably stable and economically efficient, the Afrikaner regime bought the loyalty of a significant group of African élites, precisely with the creation of black 'homelands' (Bantustans). When the apartheid system became too costly and counter-productive, the same Afrikaner regime, with a slightly changed personnel and ideology, sought a compromise with the counter-élites represented by Nelson Mandela. It was done, not so much because of revolutionary pressures from the ANC, but out of economic necessity. Indeed, big mining and industrial corporations associated with transnational capital, which made their own cost calculations, provided strategic support to the deal.

A lesson relevant for European asymmetrical client-states may be drawn from the South African trajectory and its association with the global economic system. The country used to be a British protected market and colony. It is during this period that the process of modernisation was initiated. However, the growth of national productive forces required a new institutional framework and a new state-entity emerged, the racist South Africa with its apartheid system, on which international sanctions were imposed. Forced to rely on its own resources and pursuing essentially an autarchic concept of development, the country's productive forces were beefed up to the point that the RSA became the first industrial power of the continent. It may be said that the relative isolation of the country was an economic asset not a liability, until the moment the internal market became too limited for the output capacities of its industries. As in the case of the Soviet Union and Eastern Europe, its productive forces reached the threshold of a higher level of modernisation which necessitated the opening of the country to trans-border transactions. In short, autarchy became counter-productive for the country's economy itself. Although many other variables contributed, this fact alone is perhaps sufficient to explain why the collapse of state socialism and of the apartheid system was practically simultaneous.

In South Africa a new rearrangement of the 'national' legal-institutional framework became a must, and a new formula was found in the compromise with African counter-élites which seems already to have borne fruit in terms of economic growth. Most probably such a transition toward a 'multi-cultural and democratic' South Africa would not be possible without the effective push given by transnational capital already present in the country. The latter, as well as the fact that South Africa previously had a well-established market economy, makes the difference with the transition processes in the European East.

FRAGMENTATION AND THE AGENDA FOR INTEGRATION

The emergence of ethno-states in the Yugoslav and Transcaucasian spaces was a redefining response to internal and external economic pressures of modernisation. It also represents a response to the pressures of productive forces that beefed up under state-command economies. As the market principle eroded these economies, both from inside and outside, and the old system of state-redistribution was collapsing, generating new social differentiation and new conflicts of interest in the process, it became important to redefine the role of the state. The inability of the communist party-state to adapt itself to new realities naturally put on the agenda the formation of smaller state-units that would, on one side, allow the reorganisation of the society's productive forces and of the redistributive function of the state, and, on the other side, satisfy the power ambitions and material appetites of nationalist élites. Expansionist global markets speeded up the process of internal disintegration.

Global economic processes proceed gradually, sector by sector and country by country. Because their capacity of absorption is still relatively limited, they are predisposed to handle smaller and weaker productive units (state entities). Paradoxically, as it may seem, fragmentation on one side became the precondition for the globalisation of markets on the other side. It is quite symptomatic that the disintegration of the Soviet Union, Yugoslavia and Czechoslovakia occurred practically during the same time-sequence when Eastern Germany was being absorbed into the Bundesrepublik. Or, to put it simply, the fragmentation of the Soviet and East-Central European political space is only the other face of the uneven and convulsed process of (West) European integration. Or, to put it still differently, the 'resurgence' of ethno-national identities on one side is correlated with the construction of a European supra-national identity on the other side. It seems that today's Second and Third World states are reduced to flexible productive units which may be decomposed and recomposed according to the economic necessities of global markets. The idea is that these remodelled state-entities will fit better into the readjusted international division of labour, which is of course characterised by inequalities.

Globalising processes, which are more or less rational human projects, prefer to handle clusters of countries and not single, freelance state-units. The model of integration of the German Democratic Republic was unique and too costly even for the wealthy *Bundesrepublik* and it will not be repeated, although it was recently revealed that German Chancellor Khol and Czech President Havel 'discussed the need for integrating their economies, while retaining their cultural identities in the New Europe' (Khol 1997:5). Therefore, Eastern European countries have to be aggregated into clusters that have to be standardised in order that whole clusters may become candidates for integration into the global order. This is already promoted through international neo-liberal financial institutions and their 'structural adjustment programs', GATT rules and through regional economic-cooperation projects.

One such regional free-trade cluster in the politically fragmented Eastern European space is the Visegrad Group, which includes Poland, the Czech Republic, Slovakia, and Hungary. Slovenia has a type of associate membership status only. These countries form a *cordon sanitaire* bordering the

European Union, from which the first candidates for integration into the EU will be hand-picked. The three Baltic states, Lithuania, Latvia and Estonia, represent a similar cluster separating Russia from Scandinavian countries. Romania and Bulgaria, with their shaky crypto-communist regimes, constituted until recently a group apart. The Yugoslav successor states (with the exception of Slovenia) and Albania are, for the time being, not on even the official waiting list prepared by the European Commission, which means that these ethnocracies are, for now, excluded. A statement that was leaked in January 1997 from EU's headquarters in Brussels asserted that eventually only ten East European countries (the first three clusters) could qualify for membership, but only after lengthy negotiations and adjustments, not earlier than 2002, and that even this date is perhaps too optimistic and not for all the aspirants (European Union 1997:1 and 6). The European Commission was charged to prepare the assessments of the ten candidate countries that the EU leaders will use to select the first group of East European countries to enter membership talks in 1998.

On the other hand, Washington seems to promote an overlapping agenda but one not fully congruent with the European project of economic integration: the expansion of NATO eastwards is supposed to include in the Western military alliance former Eastern Bloc countries; however, the move, already announced with the Partnership for Peace formula, became a major stumbling bloc in US–Russian relations. By-passing the Organisation for Security and Cooperation in Europe (OSCE), in which the United States has one voice only, equal to any other member-state, and which could have been used as the umbrella for the construction of the post-cold war European security 'architecture', Clinton's administration argues that NATO, in which Washington has a decisive say, is the optimal framework for security. Poland, the Czech Republic and Hungary have already been sorted out as first candidates for membership. The Russians, both government and opposition, resist NATO's expansion, although Moscow was practically given a free hand in most of its 'Near Abroad' (but not in the Baltic states and not in the Ukraine). The French, who would like to build up a 'European pillar' of NATO, are also unconvinced, while the Germans, concerned with Yeltsin's precarious internal position, advise moderation. Those most interested in NATO's expansion are the candidates themselves, and the most vociferous supporters are the Polish reformed communists, who believe that their country's membership in NATO would be a guarantee against possible future Russian and/or German encroachment. However, besides geopolitical considerations, NATO's expansion is primarily a business operation: the inclusion of new members means that they will have to adopt NATO's standard armament, which will beef up the profits of Western gun manufacturers (again dominated by US corporations) and definitely close up these markets to Russian producers. It is perhaps a short-sighted policy, because Russia will be pushed to countries such as China and Iran, but this is a policy which nevertheless brings money. By the same token, the markets of Third World countries will be flooded with cheap weaponry of Russian origin discarded from the arsenals of NATO's new members, which will further reduce direct Russian outlets. No wonder that the Russians protest.

THE 'DOUBLE MOVEMENT'

In today's era of expanding markets, states are gradually transformed 'from being buffers between external economic forces and domestic economy into agencies for adapting domestic economies to the exigencies of the global economy' (Cox 1995:55). But this transformation process is a contradictory and dialectical one. In the European East, we are still living in this transitional time-sequence and we know how painful and hectic it is. It seems that we are reliving the experience of nineteenth-century English capitalism, which, according to Karl Polanyi, was characterised by a 'double movement': one element was the unprecedented expansion of commodity markets, and the other was a counter-bore attempting to protect society from the pernicious effects of a market-controlled economy (Polanyi 1957:76).

In my free interpretation, the 'first movement' in the European East was stimulated by a utopian vision of capitalism, assuming that the dismantling of state-command economies, privatisation and the introduction of a self-regulating market will automatically bring material abundance, welfare and, most important, the reaffirmation of 'national values'. The 'second movement' brings the state back into the picture, and re-establishes state control over the productive forces (not necessarily state ownership), thwarting, temporarily at least, the integration of post-communist economies into the global economy. Such a 'second movement' may be interpreted as a protective reaction by nationalist elites who face growing popular dissatisfaction over their performance and feel threatened.

As underlined earlier, another 'double movement' occurring at the same time takes shape in the rearranged relationship between the semi-periphery and core countries: while core countries pursue their process of integration (first movement) in spite of all their mutual contradictions, peripheral countries are politically fragmented (second movement) in order to be better swallowed and digested by the global economy. James Rosenau went further when he related supra-national globalisation to sub-national contractions, localisation and fragmentation.

Globalizing and centralizing processes are conceived to be any developments that facilitate the expansion of authority, activities and interests beyond the existing (usually national) territorial boundaries, whereas
localizing and decentralizing processes involve any developments in which
the scope of authority and action undergoes contraction and reverts to
concerns, issues, groups and/or institutions that are less encompassing
than the prevailing territorial or socially constructed boundaries. (Rosenau
1995:49)

Although apparently contradictory and moving in opposite directions,
the two processes are dialectically interrelated and both promote and
culminate in change. Rosenau even suggested the term of 'fragmegration'
and concluded that

[n]either set of dynamics is fully independent. In recent years ever more
numerous occasions have arisen when the dynamics have interacted
directly and, in effect, operated as causal sources to each other. From
a short-time perspective, moreover, this interaction appears to have
acquired a momentum of its own. And as the pace increases, as new
increments of globalization foster new increments of localization, and
vice versa, enormous social and political power is unleashed. (Rosenau
1995:51).

This energy, freed by the ending of the cold war, is destructive and constructive at the same time, although for the time being its negative side
is more visible. It provoked major disturbances both on the international
level (new world disorder) and at the level of individual societies (ethnic
conflict). The disorder of 'fragmegration' fostered major shifts in the
perceptions people had of themselves and of their environment, which in
turn provoked shifts in their loyalties, including their new identification
with ethno-nationally redefined communities.

According to Stephen Gill, global finance capital draws much of its
strength from such a division of the globe into competing state jurisdic-
tions which can be played one against the other. He directly related fragmentation and the weakening of the national welfare state to the gradual
globalisation of the neo-liberal model and universalisation of the neo-
liberal discourse, which demand changes in the prevailing forms of state
through the redefinition of its external sovereignty and internal practices
(Gill 1995:65–99). Furthermore,

[t]hese developments, then, helped to give rise to a more competitive,
social Darwinist struggle of a survival of the fittest, and a growth of
inequality within and between nations, [which in turn generated] simultaneous and interlinked processes of incorporation and/or marginalisation into/from the global political economy. (Gill 1995:77)

This describes fairly recent political conflicts and developments in the regional laboratories of the Balkans and Transcaucasia. For Samir Amin, there is no doubt that

> [m]anaging the world like a market implies a maximum fragmentation of political forces, or, in other words, a practical destruction of state forces (an objective anti-state ideology attempts to legitimize), the collapse of nations in favour of infra-national communities (ethnic, religious or other), and their weakening in favour of supra-national ideological solidarities. For this idea of global management, the ideal is that not one state (and especially not one independent military power) worthy of the name should survive – the United States having become the only global policeman – while other powers are restricted to the modest tasks of daily market management. The European project itself is conceived in these terms, as the communal management of the market and no more, while beyond its borders maximum fragmentation (as many Slovenias, Macedonias, Chechnyas as possible) is systematically sought. (Amin 1996:9)

But things are not as simple as Amin presents them, because nationalist projects usually have an economic dimension as well and therefore, as already underlined, they may resist any encroachment on their 'national sovereignty'.

GLOBALISING PROCESSES

From the point of view of political economy and contemporary international relations, the framework of the modern nation-state itself is as rational as a political construct can be. Its 'rationality' derives from the global system, not from the isolated state. From this point of view, it is irrelevant what and who fills the shelf of the state, as long as this state-unit is integrated into the global system and plays its role in the international division of labour. The size of the individual state-unit is also irrelevant. Luxembourg, Andorra and San Marino are performing reasonably well, not to mention South Korea or Hong Kong. In Hong Kong even political independence was not an indispensable precondition for economic growth and a respectable standard of living, as the latter was certainly much higher than in neighbouring communist China which Amin uses as a positive reference, neglecting to explain that China's spectacular economic boom was achieved not in confrontation to global capitalism but in cooperation with it. As we know from other examples, in many former colonies the standard of living for the masses has, in fact, deteriorated after they achieved political independence in spite of the revolutionary and anti-imperialist rhetoric of their nationalist elites. Indeed, from the point of view of an individual living in such an ex-colony or new state-unit or from the point of view of a larger community (minority or even majority) within the newly created nation-state, it may appear that the previous state-formation was 'better'. In our parts it was better for those who are presently persecuted, cleansed, excluded and raped, for the refugees and displaced persons, for those who lost their relatives, security, jobs and houses. From their point of view, former Yugoslavia and the Soviet Union were certainly 'better' than the actual wars, disorder and deprivation. That does not mean that they were more 'rational' from the point of view of the global economy. In fact, it may be argued that their respective state-command economies collapsed, and the two federations decomposed, precisely because they were not rational enough for the global system.

At this point it may be useful to offer a short explanation of the relationship that was established between the 'world capitalist system' and state-socialist economies. We know everything about their cold war ideological confrontation and mutual containment. However, the two types of economy not only 'coexisted' but did engage in trade. It was essentially a mercantilist relationship, although real socialist states were increasingly willing to import Western technology through direct joint venture projects and partnerships with foreign capital. The terms of trade were those of the global system, which means, using the terminology of the dependency school, that they were 'unequal', and that the capitalist core exploited the East European and Soviet semi-periphery through unequal exchange. Economically speaking, the 'world socialist system', as a self- or Soviet-centred alternative to the existing system of international economic relations, never took shape. The COMECON never became a counterweight to the EC. The most ambitious individual attempts to 'break up the bonds' with the world capitalist system, the Chinese Great Leap Forward and the Khmer Rouge social vivisection, ended up as colossal economic and human catastrophes. From its beginning, the so-called world socialist system, that is the addition of mutually non-integrated and essentially autarchic, national, state-command 'socialist' economies was, and remained until their collapse, an underdeveloped appendix of the global capitalist system.

The global system of course benefited from such an unequal relationship, yet the character of the now defunct real socialist economies was such that it did not permit the maximisation of profits similar to those achieved in the bold Chinese experiment with a market economy. The global system can accommodate itself to the existence of a public sector as such, or to bureaucratic state management, or even to the political monopoly of communist elites in individual peripheral countries. The examples of South Korea, with its huge public sector managed by military officers, and that of Communist China, demonstrate this conclusively. In fact, the Chinese 'experiment' with capitalism, which has already gone on for some twenty years, may prove that communists may be better local managers for the global market than outright nationalists.

It should not be forgotten that Marx himself was fascinated with capitalism, which he described as the most progressive historical formation of a class-divided society. And Marx, the theoretician, was personally financed by Engels, the industrialist. So why should such a relationship be an obstacle to globalising capitalist processes? The obstacle is not the communist ideology itself, which was always malleable, but the problem created by the absence of a free internal capital–commodities–manpower market and state-imposed regulations against cross-border economic transactions. Combating communism, the US-led Western alliance sought to eliminate these protectionist barriers. Once such an economic Iron Curtain was dismantled, it became of secondary importance who the local managers for the global market would be. Reformed communists, as long as they abide to global rules, may manage domestic affairs. In an unprecedented move, President Clinton even gave his advance blessing to the left-of-centre government coalition in Italy, dominated by former communists. For the global market, it is also of marginal importance if, in the course of political developments, some state-units disappear and some others appear.

The globalisation of the neo-liberal model is related to the development of productive forces both worldwide and in individual countries. It seems indeed that neo-liberal relations of production, articulated in different ways in core capitalist countries, in the semi-periphery and periphery, may provide for the time-being the most efficient framework for a new cycle of economic development. While the productive forces of core capitalist countries have already reached the level of technological maturity and their industries flood world markets with their commodities, in the Eastern European periphery 'national' productive forces had been frozen at a much lower level, not only because of communist mismanagement but also because of the legacy of backwardness, which is much older.[7] The autarchic and stationary state-socialist economy, which successfully upgraded the national productive forces to a certain level, proved to be a structural obstacle for their further qualitative growth.

The presently projected neo-liberalisation of Eastern European economies is supposed to break the barriers imposed by state socialism and to gradually absorb the reshaped countries into the global system. To do so, it must destroy the legacy of state socialism, which in turn means that at least a part of the inherited productive forces will have to be destroyed as well. I am speaking of whole productive sectors that cannot survive cheap imports and free market competition and I am speaking of the labour force that suddenly becomes a surplus. I am also speaking of massive disinvestment and of the corresponding disaccumulation of capital that inevitably leads to the destruction of a part of the economy. Localised and transitional economic retrogression thus becomes the precondition for further development of the rearranged and reorganised productive forces that are supposed to fit more adequately into the global system. This is in theory only. It remains to be demonstrated in practice that East European countries and Soviet successor states could escape, in the long run, the 'development of underdevelopment'.

It seems that the main instrument of the new global revolution is privatisation monitored by international monetary institutions, whose goal is the opening up of national markets to transnational capital. Only when the means of production are fully privatised will the East Europeans have their own entrepreneurial class, a true native bourgeoisie, ready to manage local markets. The process of privatisation may be gradual or experienced as a 'shock', but is equal in brutality to earlier communist confiscation and nationalisation. The actual distribution of coupons or shares, which is supposed to offer a kind of compensation to the citizenry and/or to the employed or even unemployed, is of little consolation to the average individual who has lost his or her security and has to struggle for basic physical survival in a social surrounding that has suddenly turned Malthusian. Their desperation compares to that of 'the enemies of the people' who were dispossessed by Soviet communist rulers and sent to Siberia or forced into exile.

Like communist nationalisation, the process of privatisation has to accomplish once again the 'primitive accumulation of capital', but in contrast to the monopolisation of capital by the communist party-state, now capital is being concentrated in the hands of tiny native cliques of private entrepreneurs or/and its ownership sold to foreign companies. Communist nationalisations were done in the name of the society: the process of privatisation is now done in the name of the individual. As Balkan, Caucasian or Russian individuals, these former communist citizens have no legal capital of their own. Money drawn from the informal economy, or even from Mafia activities, is invested into dirty 'financial engineering' operations through which social property is transferred into private hands. This process cannot work without the active role of the new state, which has to decide what should be privatised, at what pace and what percentage, what are the modalities for ownership over the privatised means of production. This choice is essentially ideological, which means that it is also discriminatory for at least two reasons: (1) because the natives have no capital of their own, which gives the advantage to foreigners; (2) because members of ethnic minorities have been excluded from the system (ethnic cleansing, voluntary emigration) and effectively dispossessed of their property.

The states that have emerged are authoritarian ethnocracies based on ethnic exclusion and discrimination, although the character of the regimes themselves is masked by formal political pluralism (clique politics) and electoral rituals. The international community, both political and academic, was conceptually unprepared for such a 'resurgence of the past', and in the name of the time-honoured principle of national self-determination promptly legitimised these new apartheid regimes and, indirectly, their discriminatory and non-democratic practices. The problem lies not in the recognition of new states as such. After all, states have always been political artefacts. The problem lies in the recognition of specific state-entities that are built on crime, ethnic discrimination and exclusion.

The same phenomenon may be viewed from another perspective. As already underlined, perhaps such a 'bantustanisation of the European periphery is an integral part of the dialectical process of global integration–fragmentation, or, that the fragmentation of the European East is the other face of the process of Western European integration. If that is the case, then even the apparently irrational destruction of the economic infrastructure and human capital all over the European East, as well as the multiplication of nation-states, has a kind of external rationale. Smaller and weaker post-communist state-units, all of them on the waiting list for integration into the EU, WEU and NATO, are likely to be swallowed and digested more easily. If that is so, then the ethno-national exclusiveness (economic nationalism) and the petty-commodity mentality of the local ethnocrats (all of them recruited from the bureaucratic petite bourgeoisie or the former *nomenklatura*) may prove to be major obstacles for the integration of these new peripheral countries into the global mass industrial society of the twenty-first century. The logic of segregated ethnic development directly contradicts globalisation processes. Because of that, the established ethnocracies are likely to be unstable political constructs and transitional types of regimes. They are historically condemned to evolve or they will be toppled by their own disillusioned subjects, the same ones who had previously enthusiastically supported the establishing of ethnocracy. If my reading of the mass protests that shook Serbia early in 1997 is correct, then it may be asserted that the process of delegitimation of ethnocracy 'from below' has already started. And it may spill over, because all the ethnocracies in question contained within themselves, from the very beginning, the seeds of their own destruction.

PAX AMERICANA, OR THE MOVING DISEQUILIBRIUM

Western democracies and globalising forces, the very ones which had fa-
cilitated the emergence of ethnocracy, will support this new evolution
because of their own interests. Nevertheless, the 'world capitalist system'
is not such a monolith as its ideological adversaries like to believe. Nor
is it the *deus ex machina* that the Western apologists of free trade and
democracy claim. The global system of trade liberalisation, stable currencies and expanding interdependence based on the Bretton Woods
agreements has, in fact, been in deep trouble since the mid-1970s. The
serial collapse of autarchic and state-commanding economies was not such
a blessing for the system after all, because too many countries opened
themselves to transnational capital. The last five years have already demonstrated that the morsel was too big to swallow whole. It is beyond the
scope of this chapter to discuss dependency theories and their academic
elaboration, but if we wish to explain actual challenges to the nation-
state, to its 'sovereignty' and 'independence',[8] we have to analyse the
relationship between the state, the market and the global system. From
the very beginning we should recognise that there is a tension between
the global economy based on market principles and domestic economies
based on state interventionism. In the following sketch of the global system and its actual problems, which is a theme of crucial importance for
all post-communist nation-states, I will rely more on pragmatic interpretations of the contemporary international political economy as elaborated
by Robert Gilpin (1987).

In short, the international economy that emerged after the Second World
War was a liberal economy based on American economic and military
hegemony in an hierarchical system of nation-states. This unchallenged
American pre-eminence was due essentially to the wartime destruction
of other industrial economies.

> The political and security ties between the United States and its prin-
> cipal West European and Japanese allies provided the political frame-
> work within which the liberal world market economy could operate
> with relative ease ... American leadership and the alliance framework
> provided a secure and stable basis for the development of global econ-
> omic relations. For the first time ever, all capitalist economies were
> political allies. American initiatives in the area of trade led to succes-
> sive rounds of tariff liberalisation. The dollar served as the basis of the
> international monetary system ... The United States assumed the de-
> fense burden of the industrial democracies, thus enabling the West
> Europeans and especially the Japanese to concentrate their energies
> and resources on economic development. American hegemony provided

the favorable environment within which supply and demand forces created an era of unprecedented growth and an increasingly open international economy. (Gilpin 1987:343–4)

Signs of the decline in American power began to appear during the Vietnam War and became evident with the breakdown of the Bretton Woods world monetary system and with the energy crisis in the 1970s. The US share in gross world product rapidly declined, its productivity became eroded and its self-sufficiency in raw materials decreased. However, the US continued to be the dominant economic and military power, financed by an increasing budget deficit of $200 billion or more annually. With tax cuts, the Reagan administration managed to launch a temporary economic recovery, but the side-effect was a huge accumulation of private, public and foreign debts which between 1980 and 1985 nearly doubled, passing from $ 4.3 to $ 8.2 trillion (Gilpin 1987:346), resulting in the fact that the United States is today the most indebted country in the world and, therefore, potentially vulnerable. In fact, the US was financing its massive military build-up and the maintenance of its grip on world hegemony mainly through foreign borrowing, especially with the financial assistance of the Japanese, Germans and certain Arab oil exporters. To repay the foreign debt, the US will need a trade surplus of approximately $100 billion annually, stretching well into the next century. It seems that the Bush–Baker team had succeeded in initiating a new although slow cycle of domestic growth, but its benefits were reaped by the Clinton administration.

Nevertheless, 'the relative decline of American hegemony has seriously undermined the stable political framework that sustained the expansion of a liberal world economy in the post-war era, and increasing protectionism, monetary instability, and economic crisis have developed' (Gilpin 1987:345). At the same time, US exploitation of its dominant economic position is increasingly resented by its economic partners, namely, the Europeans and Japanese, who are themselves unable or unwilling to assume a greater share of the responsibilities for the managing the system and are pursuing their own narrowly defined goals. The parochial interests of different European countries, emphasised by internal political competition and a protracted economic recession, pushed the process of Western European integration well into the next century. Challenged internally and disunited, European decision-makers had to accept American demands for the liberalisation of their agricultural policies and to remove certain of the artificial protectionist trade-barriers they had erected. The very authority of the state was undermined, not only as a result of the process of internationalisation of markets, but also by a series of internal corruption scandals that hit a number of key European countries such as Italy, Spain and France. It led to the undignified retirement of the whole old guard of Italian politicians and in France to the destitution of the ageing Socialist Party, without solving any of the crucial problems in the two countries. In Britain, the Conservatives, the most faithful US allies in Europe, have been voted out from power. It is no wonder then that such weakened political élites so easily subscribe to US leadership. Japan is, on the other hand, shaken by is own internal political crisis, but still resists America's extravagant demands for trade capitulation. Not the shaky state, which more or less graciously accepted Mikey Cantor's demands, but Japanese civil society, which is not rushing to 'buy American'. If my reading of the last devaluation of the US dollar is correct, then its intention was not just to enhance, temporarily, American exports, but to simultaneously compel the expanding Japanese and German export-oriented economies into obedience. This 'weakness' of the dollar was, clearly, not a liability, but a proof of the recovered vigour of the US economy, which depends only partly on exports. Indeed, it seems that the Americans once again produce 'bigger, better and cheaper' than their economic rivals. A 'cheap' dollar was buying off the American debt and once again muzzling the mark and the yen.

American partners often resent such an 'interdependence'. We may speak of an increased asymmetry in the distribution of power within the global economy between the US and their major industrial allies. The only exceptions are, perhaps, Germany and Japan. German self-esteem has been enhanced by the annexation of the former GDR, but because of that the Bundesrepublik still suffers from economic indigestion. The latter proves that expanded territories and population are key assets no more, and that an excess population may even become a fetter to the attainment of a higher level of economic growth. Anyway, German business, associated with American capital, understood very well the foremost importance of open markets and is strategically interested to maintain the state-to-state partnership with the US. The largely virgin markets in Eastern Europe, the CIS and China offer so many business opportunities that nobody in the West is, for the time being, interested in solo roles. This potential cannot be exhausted in a short time, and will take at least another half a century or more. Furthermore, because they are so huge and offer so many opportunities, they will probably round up the angles of competition between core industrial countries. This is the main reason why the German political class is satisfied with its status as junior partner to the US and is not likely to shake the global boat as long as the boat has enough steam. Paradoxically, perhaps, its relationship with the rest of Europe is more ambiguous, a dilemma that may be summarised as: 'whether Europe will Europeanise Germany, or Germany will Germanise Europe'. Because both Germany and their main European partners have lasting interests in continuing the process of European integration, it is unlikely that they will clash over the distribution of Eastern European spoils.

Of course, it is possible that, during this process of economic globalisation, the increased interdependence of core industrial economies will lead to competition and conflict. The 'mad cows' inter-European war, although the disease was known about for quite some time, shows how fierce is the competition. The elimination of British and Irish cows was an omen for German and French cattle-breeders. And I suspect that today, a number of specialised laboratories all over Europe, sponsored by whole domestic production sectors, large corporations and even state-agencies, try to discover defects and imperfections in other countries' products.

As Robert Keohane and Joseph Nye have warned,

[R]apidly rising economic interdependence can create fear and insecurity among politically important groups . . . Thus protectionism may increase as economic interdependence becomes more extensive. Protectionism has always been with us. But as the technology of communication and large-scale corporate organisation has reduced the natural buffers between markets, many domestic groups have turned to government demanding the establishing of political buffers. Even when a country is not threatened by increased vulnerability, the sensitivity of its interest groups can stimulate it to adopt policies that restrict international transaction. (Keohane and Nye 1989:41)

They also explained how hegemonial systems and their corresponding economic regimes are eroded by economic and technological change and are from time to time replaced by new networks of rules, norms, and procedures that regularise the behaviour of international actors. Regimes, such as for example the international monetary agreements developed at Bretton Woods in 1944, are defined as 'sets of governing arrangements that affect relations of interdependence' (Keohane and Nye 1989:19). The abandonment of the convertibility of the dollar into gold in 1971 marked a radical change in the Bretton Woods monetary regime, but did not undermine US hegemony. However, this hegemony is presently being challenged by a more nationalistic perspective in the US itself (Republican right-wing parochialism which may lead to isolationism) and abroad (protectionist reactions of weaker economies). As a consequence it may happen that in the more or less distant future the rule-making and rule-enforcing powers of the US could be eroded, creating a new manoeuvring space for secondary states which are now accepting American supremacy.

Now to return to developing and post-communist countries and to their inclusion into the global system. Their problem is not that they would not like to be integrated, because each one of them may be, ultimately, compelled in that direction, but that the fluctuating global system is unable to absorb all of them at once. As we have seen, 'Eurocrats' are devising waiting and time lists for the future gradual integration of individual nation-states into the EU, but the global economy itself, especially transnational capital, is proceeding sectorially. In the whole of Eurasia a fierce competition is underway for the best positions in the most lucrative and strategically important economic sectors. In Eastern Europe and in the successor states of the USSR, the focus is for the time being on banking and finance, where immediate returns are expected, and on oil and gas, strategically indispensable for the running of core countries' industrial machines. Eventually, at a later stage, similar to the competition over the Chinese market, the dislocation of certain industries will move towards this periphery. In this scramble, local ruling élites will be courted, pressed, bribed, bought or eliminated. But more importantly, different companies from core states will seek the support and protection of their own governments, and/or will enter into cartel alliances with other corporations, dividing the markets among themselves and eliminating competitors. This is what is called 'liberal protectionism' (Aggarval 1985). Its general importance within the global system is likely to increase, reducing further the independent manoeuvring space and economic sovereignty of weaker and less developed state-units. On the other hand, there is a parallel tendency toward regionalisation in the world economy around the three most important poles of economic development, that is, North America, Western Europe and the Japan–Pacific region. If this tendency prevails, the rest of the world will be subdivided into market reserves of these three poles. In the long run, the first trend may lead to trade wars between states and the second to war between economic clusters.

The new rhetoric associated with transnational capital and US hegemony tries to convince us that we are living in a 'global village' in which national boundaries are rapidly diluted by the accelerated cross-border circulation of knowledge, capital and commodities, and intensified social communications. It claims that such a growing interdependence will ultimately be beneficial to everybody and will eliminate international conflict. Evidence, on the other hand, tends to demonstrate that after the collapse of the Cold War order a disorder has emerged and that new hotbed of international conflict have proliferated, validating more traditional 'realist' theories which have the famous 'national interest' as their focus and are obsessed with concerns about 'national security'. For the ethnocrats who rule new Balkan and Transcaucasian states, 'national sovereignty' within secured borders has become a question of life or death. It seems, indeed, that these ethnocrats are unconsciously guided by realist theories that assume that force, and only force, is a usable and effective instrument of both international and internal politics. In Samudavanija's

(1991) three-dimensional conceptualisation of the state, these ethnocrats give absolute priority to their own security (S) and accumulation of wealth masked under the slogan of 'national interest', and only then may they eventually think about long-term strategies of economic development (D). Although they may believe that they are God-chosen, all their policies are in fact reduced to a day-to-day struggle for survival. Popular participation (P) and pseudo-democratic rituals serve only to camouflage the ugly reality of their rule.

It seems that we are living in a transitional phase of economic disequilibrium, in which the actual dominant position of the US is challenged both by its own internal developments and by external factors, but no alternative to its hegemony is on the horizon. We may of course speculate about a 'trilateral' or 'multi-polar' world of tomorrow or about a post-hegemonic era. However, altogether, this is not going to help our weak new ethnic states. For the time-being, they still represent marginal lands, not yet fully integrated into any system or cluster, where the hunting season has just been opened.

Notes

1. In a previous paper, 'State, Development and the Political Economy of International Relations: the Asymmetrical Client-State in the Balkans and Transcaucasia', presented at the Europe & The Balkans Conference at Bertinoro, Italy, 16–18 February 1996, the topic was expanded with an elaboration of theories of development. Both papers are parts of a larger research project, 'Social Change, Politics and Ethnic Conflict in Yugoslavia and Transcaucasia'.
2. The phrase was coined by Skocpol (1985).
3. For the critique of the erroneous interpretation of Weber, see Cohen *et al.* (1975).
4. For an accurate interpretation of List's views see Szporluk (1988).
5. I elaborated the topic in a paper, *'Identity: Usual Bias, Political Manipulations and Historical Forgeries. The Yugoslav Drama'*, presented at the Europe & The Balkans Network Conference, Bologna/Forli, Italy, 5–7 December 1996.
6. I borrowed the term from Cohen *et al.* (1975).
7. The legacy of backwardness in Eastern Europe was described in a volume edited by Chirot (1989).
8. See for example Camilleri and Falk (1992).

4 The 'Abnormal' Economy of Bosnia-Herzegovina
Vesna Bojičić and Mary Kaldor

Attempts by the international community to implement the Dayton Agreement are floundering. Despite the expenditure of billions of dollars, reconstruction has been painfully slow, the return of refugees has been minimal, there continues to be sporadic violence, with widespread human rights violations and evictions of 'minorities', especially in Serb- and Croat-controlled areas, and the majority of people are still without jobs and dependent on humanitarian assistance.

Part of the problem is cognitive – the difficulty of comprehending the character of the war that has taken place and its effects on the underlying functioning of society has resulted in an inadequate response. Terms like 'reconstruction' and 'transition' are drawn from experiences in other places and other times and are not applicable in the current Balkan context. The term 'reconstruction' for example, which conjures up the post Second-World-War experience, typically presupposes a war fought for rational political ends, a war which has a beginning and an end, a political outcome which provides for the basis for the restoration of 'normal' political institutions capable of implementing a programme of reconstruction. Yet the war in Bosnia-Herzegovina was quite a different type of conflict. It was a war about ethnic nationalism, a deeply immoral and irrational phenomenon that feeds on violence and criminality and cannot survive in a 'normal' context. The Dayton Agreement was not a solution; it was an uneasy temporary truce, a set of contradictory compromises in a situation in which the only possible compromise was one that rewarded the ethnic nationalists.

The term 'transition' generally refers to a set of policy recommendations intended to guide the transition from a command economy to a market economy; these include macro-economic stabilisation mainly through cuts in public expenditure, liberalisation of domestic prices and foreign trade, and privatisation. It is true that despite the rhetoric about self-management and the 'soft' character of Yugoslav totalitarianism,[1] Yugoslavia was a typical command economy characterised by shortage of resources. At the same time, however, it is also the case that Yugoslavia experienced the pains of transition to the market some ten years earlier than other East European countries. Cuts in public spending and opening up to the world economy led to high levels of unemployment and the growth of a large, semi-legal parallel economy. Levels of unemployment were highest in Bosnia-Herzegovina. Nationalism can, in part, be explained by these characteristics of the Yugoslav economy. On the one hand, it was the consequence of the shortage economy. Competition existed but it was not market competition; rather, it was bureaucratic competition for resources. Because of the decentralised nature of the Yugoslav political system and because of the absence of democracy, republican elites used nationalism to bid for resources and power. On the other hand, nationalism became an umbrella under which former communist aparatchiks seeking to sustain power and new 'entrepreneurs' could shelter and seek legitimacy in the brave new post-communist world.[2]

These tendencies were accelerated by the war. Our basic argument is that the war was a form of compressed transition which destroyed the normal functioning of institutions – something similar is happening in Albania, even without a war. The role of the state was reduced to the point that it literally disintegrated. Traditional heavy industry was destroyed. The economy was completely opened up to the outside world; indeed there was full convertibility, because the Deutschmark circulated throughout the region as currency. What came into being is what we call an 'abnormal' economy. Without comprehending the nature of an 'abnormal' economy and creating the conditions for the restoration of normality, reconstruction cannot succeed. In what follows, we describe the economic impact of the war. This is illustrated by two case-studies of Mostar and Tuzla, which exhibit varying degrees of 'abnormality'. In the last section, we briefly summarise the experience of reconstruction so far.

THE IMPACT OF THE WAR

The 'abnormality' of the situation is reflected, first of all, in devastating economic statistics.[3] Human losses in Bosnia-Herzegovina are estimated at 200 000 civilians[4] and around 60 000 military casualties. These figures are less than the comparable casualty figures in the Second World War, although the ratio of civilian to military casualties is dramatically higher. Even more striking have been the demographic changes. The goal of this war was ethnic cleansing – the expulsion of particular ethnic groups from particular territories. The population of Bosnia-Herzegovina, according to the latest official estimates, is down to 3 437 708, or roughly one million less than before the war. Around two and a half million citizens of Bosnia-Herzegovina are displaced, of which 509 714 live in the EU countries, and 750 000[5] in all of Europe. A significant proportion of these are qualified people, producing a 'brain drain' effect on the economy and society of Bosnia-Herzegovina and its post-war development perspectives. The exodus of people continues even now, despite the pressures to return, and represents one of the most critical aspects of the present situation as well as of any future arrangements in the region.

Official estimates on the Bosnian government side suggested that some 250 000 people were engaged in defence on the Bosnian side. Figures are not available for the Serb-controlled and Croat-controlled parts, but since the Bosnians had much greater military manpower(though much less equipment) than the Serbs and the Croats, it is reasonable to assume that the numbers were lower in these parts. Thus, compared with the Second World War, participation in the war was relatively low. Around 85 000 people (Bačković 1995) are estimated to be working in a civil sector, or only 6.5 per cent of the republic's pre-war active population. This represents a sharp contrast to the Second World War, which involved a total mobilisation. Unemployment throughout the republic at the end of the war was estimated at 90 per cent.

Physical damage has been extensive, much greater than during the Second World War. The greatest damage was inflicted on the infrastructure, especially railways, roads, the energy system (gas and electricity), and telecommunications – the basic foundations of modern existence. Around 45 per cent of all industrial plants were destroyed[6] and a significantly higher percentage robbed of machinery and equipment. During the war, it is estimated that industry operated at five to six per cent of its pre-war capacity (Bačković 1995). Coal-mining, for example, continued throughout the war, although its output fell from over 18 million tons in 1990 to around 1 million in 1994. Also, all operable sectors of military industry continued production, albeit only marginally compared with the scale and range of production before the war. Agricultural production, which accounted for 9 per cent of the GDP of Bosnia-Herzegovina and employed over 23 per cent of the population, has also fallen to a minimum. (Imports of food have always been necessary, even in peacetime.)[7]

Health-care facilities, schools and housing stock also suffered extensive damage. Seventy per cent of the total housing stock is either destroyed or damaged. The cost of rebuilding or repairing buildings has been estimated at about $10.8 billion (Bačković 1995). Alongside the physical destruction is disruption of most of the functions of urban living, which in itself adds to the 'abnormality' of the situation. The destruction of the economic base is augmented by the extensive damage to historic and cultural sites.[8]

Given the low level of production, the high level of unemployment and the extensive physical damage, the economy was dependent on the outside for food and military supplies. All in all, in the three years of

Economic Flows: Bosnia-Herzogovia 1992-4

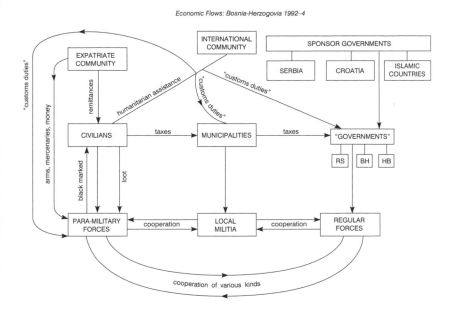

Figure 4.1   Economic flows: Bosnia-Herzogovina 1992–4

war, GDP per capita of Bosnia-Herzegovina fell from $2 719 to just $250.

To understand what lies behind the statistics, it is necessary to understand the character of the war economy and how military activities and subsistence were financed. (See Figure 4.1.)

On the Serb and Croat side, there were two types of military forces. There were regular forces based on the remnants of the Yugoslav National Army (JNA) and the republic-based Territorial Defence forces (TDs) created after the Soviet invasion of Czechoslovakia in 1968. The remnants of the JNA were almost entirely on the Serb side, but the Croat regular army was based on the Croat TD. And there were paramilitary groups composed of criminals and extreme nationalists, especially on the Serb side; thus Scselj was the leader of the most extreme Serb nationalist party and his 'Chetniks' were the military arm of his party, while Arkan was a notorious figure in the Belgrade underworld and his 'Tigers' were recruited from the fan club of the main Belgrade football team which he owned. The regular forces seem to have been largely supported from outside by the Serbian and Croatian governments respectively, perhaps indirectly through support for the ethnic statelets that were created – Herceg-Bosna and Republika Srpska. The paramilitary groups were financed by 'taxation' of humanitarian assistance from abroad, by black market activities of various kinds, and through loot from the displaced population. The war provided an enormous opportunity for organised criminal groups to augment their sources of revenue.

On the Bosnian side, there was no regular army for the first two years of the war. Defence against Serb and Croat forces varied from place to place. Thus Sarajevo was initially defended by two notorious criminals, Caco and Ćelo. In other places, local militia were created out of local police forces and volunteers known as 'Patriotic Leagues'. This was the case in Tuzla or Bihac, where the workers from the big enterprises Soda So and Agrokomerc were mobilised. Local militia were financed by local municipalities, which 'taxed' humanitarian assistance and levied local taxes of various kinds. At the height of the war, there was almost no money in circulation, so soldiers and workers were paid in kind, in food parcels and in basic services.

There were also foreign mercenaries, directly financed from abroad on all sides – mainly Russians on the Serb side, Italians and diaspora volunteers on the Croat side (the so-called Garibaldi Brigade), and the Mujahadeen, Afghan veterans, on the Bosnian side.

Except in a few places, for example, Brčko and Mostar, there was very little fighting between opposing sides. Rather, the war was directed against *civilians*. Hence most of the violence consisted of attacks on besieged towns and atrocities committed against civilians once towns or villages were captured. It was the paramilitary groups who were responsible for the worst atrocities; indeed, it seems clear that, on the Serb side, this was deliberate strategy. The regular forces would start shelling a village or town, wearing down the inhabitants. Once they had entered the area, the paramilitary groups would be given free rein to go on the rampage. Arkan is said to have had lists of rich Muslims who were killed, while other men were taken to detention camps, women were systematically raped so that the memory of shame would prevent them from ever wanting to return. The 'right to be the first to loot' was regarded as a form of payment.[9] It was the Mujahadeen (reportedly mobilised from the Palma video shop in Travnik) who were responsible for most atrocities committed on the Bosnian side.

Thus, for most of the war, there was no single front line. Rather, Bosnia-Herzegovina became a patchwork of enclaves surrounded by front lines and checkpoints. Among the paramilitary groups and regular forces, there was cooperation across the front-lines both for military purposes, for example, the Muslims of Mostar 'purchased' Serb artillery fire, and, more importantly, for commercial purposes. Certain places, such as Croat-held towns in Central Bosnia, for example, Kiseljak or Vareš, became centres for black market activities. The delivery of humanitarian aid, which was based on negotiation among the various groups, was carefully controlled.

If too little was allowed through, the paramilitary groups would lose their sources of 'taxation'. If too much was allowed through, black market prices would fall.

Towards the end of the war, particularly after the Croat–Muslim ceasefire, there were attempts to regularise the armed forces and to centralise finance. The local militia became local brigades of the regular armies and the para-military groups became 'special units'. Thus the capture of Srebrenica was undertaken entirely by the regular Serb army, but the Special Units were sent in on the third day to 'mop up' resistance in the traditional fashion – indeed, to judge by the huge number of disappearances, they were probably even more brutal than formerly.

Attempts to centralise finances and thus mobilise a centralised war effort were continually thwarted. Some success was achieved by Haris Silajdžić when he became prime minister of the republic of Bosnia-Herzegovina in October 1993. He succeeded in getting rid of Celo and Caco and es-tablishing a regular army, Armija, which integrated the local militia. Es-pecially after the Croat–Muslim ceasefire, he was able to create something approximating a single Bosnian economic space; nevertheless, there were huge obstacles to restarting the formal economy, and he remained de-pendent on outside support, mainly Islamic governments and, indirectly, the United States, to finance government activities including the Army. Parallel efforts on the Serb side seem to have been even less successful. After Miloševic reportedly closed the border with Republika Srpska in the summer of 1994, the Serbian forces found themselves in consider-able difficulty. In the spring of 1995, Mladić told the Serb parliament that they must choose between a negotiated peace and a mobilisation economy. The 'parliament' rejected total mobilisation because so many criminal elements who profited from informality were members of the parliament.[10]

Typically, a war economy is similar to a command economy. The war economies of the Second World War were closed economies in which there was a total mobilisation for the war effort and in which the economy was centrally administered. All those not conscripted for the war effort, including women, were employed in production. Although lendlease was significant for Britain and the Soviet Union, these were largely self-sufficient economies.

This war was quite the opposite. There was some limited production, but the war economy was totally dependent on outside supplies for food, fuel, spare parts and weapons (despite the arms embargo). Outside sup-port took the form of humanitarian assistance, remittances, support from sympathetic governments (Serb, Croat and Islamic) and black market trad-ing. Physical damage was much greater and at the same time participa-tion in the war was relatively low compared with the Second World War, even though all sides experienced shortages of military manpower and unemployment remained high. The shortages can be explained by the lack of legitimacy of the warring parties and the lack of regular means of payment. Thus, in contrast to the Second World War, the war economy is characterised by high levels of unemployment, high levels of imports and weak, fragmented and decentralised economic administration. In effect, to survive, individuals faced the choice of leaving, joining the army and/or becoming a criminal.

It could be said the war economy represents a new type of dual economy, typical of peripheral regions exposed to globalisation. On the one hand, the public sector is destroyed and replaced by a humanitarian economy, supported entirely from abroad, based on handouts, in which nobody is paid and no-one works, and in which beneficiaries experience repeated humiliation. On the other hand, the new market economy is largely criminalised; it consists of a 'gangster economy', made up of loot and pillage, black marketeering, arms trade, drug trade, etc. These two types of economy feed on each other,[11] perpetuating a material basis for ethnic nationalism. Both types of economy radiate outwards. The humanitarian economy radiates outwards through refugee networks, and the gangster economy through various Mafia rings and other transnational criminal networks.

TUZLA AND MOSTAR

The nature of this 'abnormal' economy can be best illustrated on the basis of a study of local economies. During the worst phase of the war, there were no institutions functioning at the level of the state in Bosnia-Herzegovina. Essentially, administrative structures disintegrated and the war was organised locally. How local administrative units functioned determined to a large extent conduct in the war and the nature of the local economies. These different experiences are also reflected in the post-war period and the progress in reconstruction of various communities.

The cases of Tuzla and Mostar are two illustrative contrasting examples of how this abnormal economy works. Before the war, these two towns were rather similar. Historically, both towns were significant economic centres during the Ottoman empire; Mostar was an important merchant town and Tuzla was a centre for salt-mining. Both have a rich Turkish and Austro-Hungarian heritage; in particular, the old Turkish parts of Mostar were a famous historic site. After the Second World War, both towns were heavily industrialised, and turned into economic, administrative and cultural centres of their respective regions. When the wars began, they enjoyed relatively high wage levels compared with the Yugoslav average. Nearly half of employment was accounted for by industry and mining.

These were medium-sized towns with populations of 130 000 and 80 000 respectively. Both towns had very mixed populations, with a high number of people declaring themselves as Yugoslavs (24 per cent and 18 per cent respectively, although the figure for Mostar is much higher if outlying rural districts are excluded).[12] They are both situated on rivers surrounded by rich agricultural lands. Both towns were successful exporters and appeared to benefit from the Marković reforms which preceded the break-up of Yugoslavia. Tuzla had ecological problems before the war; it suffered both from polluting chemical factories and from the danger of subsidence arising from centuries of salt-mining.

In the first democratic elections in 1990, Mostar elected a coalition of nationalist parties (SDA, the Muslim nationalist party, HDZ, the Croat nationalist party, and SDS, the Serb nationalist party) to run the municipal administration. This coalition broke down shortly after Bosnian Serb forces around Mostar were defeated; from then on, two separate single-party-based administrations took over. Tuzla elected a coalition of non-nationalist parties (Social Democrats, Reformists, and Liberals), which continued to govern the town throughout the war.

When the war broke out in April 1992, the local Tuzla militia succeeded in expelling, relatively peacefully, a division of the JNA, unlike in Mostar where the JNA launched an attack on the town while withdrawing. Subsequently, there was no fighting in Tuzla, although the Serbs continued to shell the town almost until the very end of the war. During the fighting between Muslims and Croats, Tuzla was, however, completely blockaded because all the main routes into Tuzla were cut off by fighting. In the case of Mostar, the war with the Serbs lasted from April 1992 to July 1992. This was followed by war between Croats and Muslims which lasted from April 1993 to March 1994, with frequent shelling from the Bosnian Serb positions at the eastern edge of the town.

The Tuzla municipality is still in charge in Tuzla. After the establishment of the Croat–Muslim federation, on the basis of the Washington Agreement signed in March 1994, a cantonal government was also established in Tuzla, controlled by the SDA, although effective power, for the time being, still rests with the municipality. In Mostar, the administration is effectively divided between an SDA-controlled administration on the East side of the River Neretva and an HDZ administration on the West, although the joint city administration was formally established following the July 1996 local elections. The functioning of the cantonal government (Herzegovina-Neretva canton is a mixed one and thus presupposes power sharing between the two peoples) is blocked by obstructions mainly from the Bosnian Croat side.

In addition to the local administration, during the war there were two governments in the federation: Herceg-Bosna and the Republic of Bosnia-Herzegovina. Those taxes levied at a local level which were passed on, mainly towards the end of the war, went to the respective governments and were used primarily for the armies – the HVO and the army of Bosnia-Herzegovina. The federation was largely a paper organisation. The implementation of the Dayton Agreement is supposed to bring an end to the existence of para-state of Herceg-Bosna and the transfer of taxation powers from the Republic to the federation.

Under the Washington agreement, an EU administration was established for the whole of Mostar with a mandate to integrate the city. Through the process of reconstruction and political and social reunification, this was meant to be a model for strengthening peace and reconciliation within the federation (Reichel 1996). This has not happened. The EU administration adopted a 'top-down' diplomatic approach and opted for negotiations with the local political and military structures that were established and reinforced in the course of the conflict rather than direct administration. Members of the administration continually stressed that they had not established a colonial-type protectorate. The pre-war city council, the *de facto* and only legitimate governing body, was simply sidelined, and the entire project became dependent on the good will and cooperation of the parties on the ground, including those who saw no interest whatsoever in the reconstruction proposed by the EU administration. Given that the EU administration was not provided with real executive powers, the whole endeavour stood on very fragile legs from the start.

Demilitarisation of Mostar as a precondition for the start of the EU administration operation meant that soldiers on both sides were transformed into large separate police forces. Although the EU brought in a WEU police force with a mandate to create a unified police force, freedom of movement and security, this did not happen during the term of the EU administration, mainly because the EU did not have the power to overrule the local authorities.[13] Movement between the two sides was initially extremely limited; 250 people a day were allowed to cross from East to West, but only women and children. Even now, well into implementation of Dayton Agreement, security is still very poor and, on the West side, murders and evictions of non-Croats still continue.[14] Well-organised gangs of criminals also make life difficult for the Croat population on the West side.

The main area where the EU administration has made progress is in reconstruction. However, this has largely consisted of two reconstruction programmes, one for the East and one for the West, and may thus have contributed to a legitimisation of separate development.

Different experiences of the workings of the local economies in these two towns were greatly influenced by the demographic changes that took place as a result of war. In both towns the populations have changed dramatically, although the changes have been much greater in Mostar than in Tuzla. Many people have died and many people have left either for reasons of safety or for economic reasons. In Mostar, the population has declined to around 62 000, of which some 26 000 are displaced persons; thus only some 36 000 of the original resident population remain in their homes and a further 6000 remain in Mostar as displaced persons.[15] In Tuzla, the local population has declined to 110 500 and, according to figures from the cantonal government, there has been an influx of 53 700 refugees of which some 20 per cent are settled in permanent living places. (This figure does not include the influx of some 20 000 refugees from Srebrenica, some of whom were subsequently resettled across Bosnia-Herzegovina.) Displaced people represent 27.3 per cent of the current population of Tuzla, while the remaining 72.7 per cent[16] consists of the indigenous population. The fact that most of Tuzla's population stayed throughout the war was an important factor in shaping the atmosphere conducive to reconstruction and maintaining the peace.

In Mostar, the population decline has been much greater on the East side than on the West side. On the East side, the population has declined to 19 300, of which 13 000 are displaced persons. In other words, only around 6000 people who lived there originally remain. Of the displaced persons, roughly a quarter come from the West side, a third come from Serb-occupied territories, and 17 per cent from Croat–occupied territories outside Mostar. On the West side, the population has declined to 33 700, of which 12 000 are displaced persons; in other words, some 13 000 original residents remain on the west side.[17] The category 'displaced persons' includes both people who have been expelled from their homes and those who have moved into the empty houses as a result of ethnic cleansing. The difference between the category of displaced persons on the West side and the East side is evidenced by the proportion of people on each side who want to go home. Nearly 90 per cent of the displaced persons on the East side want to go home, according to an EU survey, but only around half of displaced persons want to go home on the West side, and an even smaller percentage of those originally from central and northern Bosnia-Herzegovina wish to do so.

Physical damage has been extensive in Mostar, especially on the East side. Some 80 per cent of all buildings have been damaged. About 10 per cent, all on the East side, were so badly damaged as to be irreparable and a further 30 per cent suffered serious damage to supporting structures, again mainly on the East side. Nearly 60 per cent of all buildings were without roof structures when the fighting between Muslims and Croats ended. The EU administration estimated the cost of reconstruction of buildings at DM 300 million. The major part of the destruction has affected residential buildings. However, the damage also affected industry, infrastructure, public buildings including schools and kindergartens, and historic and religious buildings, especially mosques and the main orthodox church. All nine bridges over the Neretva have been destroyed, including two railway bridges and the historic Stari Most, described by Rebecca West in her book about travelling through Yugoslavia before the Second World War as one of 'the most beautiful bridges in the world' (West 1993[1944]:288).[18]

For twenty-two months, the East side had no water or electricity, because water and power utilities were situated on the West side. Discrepancies in living conditions between East and West side were enormous, and continue to be so. During the conflict, and shortly after, there was hardly any economic activity on the East side, while trade and catering were predominant activities on the West side. The war destroyed 40 per cent of Mostar's industrial infrastructure, including the railway and airport. Most industry is still halted either because of physical destruction or owing to lack of spare parts and working capital, as well as the loss of specialists, but also uncertainty surrounding the future of the town. Before the war, Mostar was producing helicopters, industrial freezers, cars, aluminium, electronics, beverages and textiles, mainly on the east side. It also had wood-processing production and the production of compressors for electrical appliances and industrial machines. The only enterprise which functioned during the conflict on the east side was Hepok, producing wine, juice, and spirits. With the reconstruction effort launched by the international community as a part of the peace agreement, some industries on both sides are twitching back to life, although at a fraction of their capacity.

The health system collapsed at the beginning of the war, and with most health facilities located on the West side, the level of health service on the East side was almost non-existent. The education system, apart from the physical damage and loss of staff, also suffered from the partition brought about by war, in particular secondary schools and the university. The 'Džemal Bijedić' university has split into two under-staffed and under-funded independent units, with many fewer students than pre-war – one on each side of the town. The survival of the university on the West side has been enabled by the financial and staff support from Croatia, while the university on the East side equally depends on Sarajevo. Indeed, the two university 'centres', as they are called, seem to have become little more than political symbols and hardly function as centres of education. They cannot survive in their present form. According to the new constitutional arrangements, higher education is to be financed at the cantonal level. Far from anything else, it is clear that the economy of the

Herzegovina-Neretva canton cannot support two university centres on its territory.

In Tuzla, physical damage was much less. However, the economy was hit by the disintegration of Yugoslavia, which meant an important loss of markets, by the blockade, which meant both a loss of markets and enormous difficulty in getting spare parts, equipment and raw materials, and by the loss of specialists – some 50 per cent of people with the equivalent of a BA degree have left Tuzla. During the war about 30 per cent of those employed in industry before the war continued to work although not all the time; most of them were also in the army of Bosnia and Herzegovina.

Before the war, the main sources of employment were mining (coal, bauxite, lead, zinc, quartz, sandstone and various types of salt), the power utilities and the chemical industry. With tremendous ingenuity, one power plant was kept operating throughout the conflict; a new power plant had been built before the war to export electricity to Croatia and Slovenia. The coalmines also continued to function, employing some 5000 people compared with 12 000 before the war. The salt factory operated throughout the conflict at a much lower level than before; it had to go on producing because of the dangers of subsidence. It even managed to export some salt to Croatia. One chemical enterprise, DITA, also continued to produce detergents when it was able to get raw materials. The other chemical enterprises were more or less closed.

Small-scale production to meet local need continued and even in some cases has expanded during the conflict. This includes the manufacture of building materials, including gas-concrete and construction sand, the manufacture of food products (milk products, meat products, yeast, spirits) and the manufacture of textiles and shoes. The latter were purchased by non-governmental humanitarian agencies for refugees and by the Bosnia and Herzegovina government for the army.

In both Mostar and Tuzla, but especially in the former, there has been a growth of small enterprises since the war began, almost exclusively in services – shops, restaurants and coffee bars, which was at least to some extent linked to black marketeering. The mushrooming of shops and coffee bars on the East side as soon as the ceasefire came into effect has been striking. In Mostar, the EU administration begun an innovative small business programme, which ended as two separate programmes – one for the West side and one for the East. Most of the total (DM 8 million) provided in loans and grants was at the end channelled to some 70 medium-sized companies and 400 small businesses, mostly in services. The EU administration also initiated an 'Investment Support Programme' for large public companies in the textile, concrete, construction equipment and soft beverages industries (Reichel 1996:20), but the effects have been disappointing.

On the other hand, Tuzla, which during the war and even after received a fraction of the money poured into Mostar, has been the most successful example of local development initiative programmes and micro-credit finance schemes, and is becoming, economically, the most powerful region in Bosnia-Herzegovina. A pilot project of micro-credit financed by the World Bank during 1996 has become the model for the whole country.

The disintegration of the Bosnian state, and different coping strategies, can be traced through the use of money. During the worst of the fighting, up to March 1994, there was no money in Bosnian-controlled parts except in the black market, where the Deutschmark circulated. Those in work were paid in food parcels or in meals at public kitchens, based largely on humanitarian assistance. In Tuzla, where there was some production, a barter system operated; for example, the cheese factory exchanged cheese for detergents and workers in the detergents factory got cheese in their food parcels. All humanitarian assistance coming into Tuzla was taxed by the municipality in goods, which were then used to control prices on the black market. Likewise, UNPROFOR paid for its facilities in fuel and not money. In the Croat-controlled parts that were not blockaded, the Croatian kuna circulated as currency along with the Deutschmark, and workers received income in kunas.

The monetary division of the federation as a whole, and Mostar in particular, persists. The kuna is still the main currency in Croat-controlled parts and has actually appreciated in relation to the Deutschmark. The Bosnia-Herzegovina government issues its own currency, the dinar, but it is fixed in relation to the Deutschmark and is mainly used for small change, that is, as a way of increasing liquidity. There is no inflation in either part of the federation and prices are comparable.

Given the low level of production, both of these economies were dependent on outside assistance. This assistance took the following forms: humanitarian assistance, rent and expenditure from UNPROFOR forces, and remittances from families living abroad. Figures on the scale of outside assistance to each local economy are not available. However, it is clear that outside assistance to Mostar has been much greater than to Tuzla. Total EU expenditure in Mostar was about 144 MECU in two and a half years of the administration's term. The main official outside donor to Tuzla was the British ODA; its expenditure over the comparable period was £5 million (around 6.5 MECU).[19] This discrepancy, although on a smaller scale, has been maintained in the reconstruction programme financed by the international community. At the end of 1996, projects worth US$55 million were being implemented in the Tuzla-Podrinje canton, compared with $60 million in Mostar and Konjić – a part of Herzegovina-Neretva canton.[20] Tuzla pursued a deliberate strategy of mobilising support from NGOs and European municipalities. It is twinned with Bologna in Italy, and during the war received humanitarian assistance from German and Dutch towns. Subsequently, it has received reconstruction assistance from a group of Dutch cities amounting to some 5 million guilder (approximately $2.5 million) per year.

Some indication of the structure of the two economies can be gleaned from municipal finance during and immediately after the conflict. In Tuzla, taxes were raised by the Tuzla municipality in the whole Tuzla canton; some 60 per cent were raised in the municipality itself. Taxes consisted mainly of customs duties on all goods entering the canton and taxes per head on all Tuzla citizens including families living abroad. During the blockade, all taxes were spent locally. Following the end of fighting, the municipality kept 40 per cent and 60 per cent was transferred to the Bosnia and Herzegovina government. The capacity for self-sufficiency in Tuzla both as a result of the functioning of the local economy and due to the effectiveness of the administration is suggested by the fact that 60 to 65 per cent of BiH tax revenue in 1995 consisted of taxes raised in Tuzla.[21]

The situation in Mostar was very different. The East Mostar authorities were reliant, and still are to a great extent, on transfers from the Bosnia and Herzegovina government. The major part of municipal finance in West Mostar came from the government of Herceg-Bosna, which raised revenue mainly through customs duties on cross-border trade but also through income tax, profits tax and surplus income from state and municipal-owned enterprises; the Croatian government is also thought to supply additional assistance.[22] The municipality also raises local taxes from car licence fees, sales tax and advertising taxes but these yield very little. Despite the relatively heavy customs duties (or perhaps because of it), tax-gathering is said to be rather inefficient and this is reflected in the scale of the black market.

The different war experiences of Tuzla and Mostar during the war has greatly influenced the way the two towns and their inhabitants have been able to respond to the post-war reconstruction challenge. In Tuzla, where social, economic and administrative structures were preserved throughout the war, the task has been one of maintaining the peace through reconstruction. Governed by non-nationalist authorities, relying on locally defined priorities and insisting on inclusion of all the existing human and economic potentials and local coordination of the reconstruction effort, with far less resources, Tuzla has become an example of a relatively successful transition from war to peace. Numerous local initiatives such as the second international trade fair in April 1997, which attracted around 50 000 participants and visitors, a new holiday resort built on a local lake, since access to the coast is now so difficult, a joint project of the local clinical centre with one of the leading US institutions in the field of open-heart surgery, and various academic and educational activities, illustrate the huge leap forward Tuzla has taken as a result of its survival strategy during the war. Although the economy is still waiting for the major kick-start, the scale of new private investment in the town is an indication of trust in its political stability and economic prosperity of this region, as is the building boom, which is based largely on local finance and local companies. This is an even more important indicator of Tuzla's local capacity and the energies of its inhabitants, given that the external constraints to faster economic recovery of the Tuzla region still persist. The rail transport vital for Tuzla's industry is still halted, the bridge over the Sava at Orasje, one of the main transport routes, is not yet rebuilt, and the airport is closed.

In contrast, the EU administration in Mostar has been successful in restoring most of the basic facilities in the town, and some of the key infrastructure projects were completed, ending the physical isolation of the East side. A large portion of the housing stock has been repaired as well as all primary schools, several primary care medical facilities, two libraries, two hotels, several administrative buildings, etc. (Reichel 1996:18). Efforts at rehabilitation of education, culture and sport activities have also brought significant improvement in the life of Mostar citizens. However, the town remains divided, controlled by the nationalist parties, and constantly on the brink of renewed conflict. East Mostar is still a ghetto, with limited freedom of movement across the separation line, and has little resemblance with urban life elsewhere in Europe. West Mostar is a place of uneasy living, where numerous refugees and strong criminal elements create an atmosphere of apprehension and mistrust.

Economic recovery is lacking to any significant degree, although the booming trade and services on the West side conceal the low level of minimal industrial and other production. The fact that most new investment on the Croat side is not in Mostar but in Western Herzegovina indicates the lack of trust in the stability of peace in this part of Bosnia-Herzegovina, pending the final political settlement. Economic recovery and local initiative are strangled by the political manoeuvring of the nationalist parties, so much so that many of the industrial capacities rehabilitated by the EU-administration-led investment programme are lying idle. On the other hand, many vested interests, including those of the present governing structure, act as another strong impediment to genuine change in the present economic situation. On both sides, particularly among the businesspeople, there is a palpable lack of a sense of economic direction. The ending of a generous financial inflow, which accompanied the EU administration term in Mostar, has already been felt and prospects for the revival of the local economy are not very good.

The contrast between Mostar and Tuzla is also clearly evident in social and cultural life. There are no independent media in Mostar; the media are controlled by SDA on the East side and HDZ on the West side. Radio Mostar, on the East side, claims to be independent but 'very close to the government'.[23] In Tuzla there are SDA- and HDZ-controlled newspapers and radio stations, as well as Serb-controlled radio and television which broadcast from the hills north of Tuzla, and all are very shrill in their criticisms of the municipality and the Tuzla model. (The newspaper *Dragon of Bosnia* is particularly notorious.) Radio Tuzla and TV Tuzla are state-controlled. There is also an independent radio station, Radio Cameleon, which is widely listened to, and an independent newspaper, *Front Slobode*, which used to be controlled by the communist party and has a circulation of 3000. Cultural activity is extremely lively in Tuzla, more so than before the war, especially theatre and youth culture. Tuzla was also rather successful in attracting outside funding for the independent media and for cultural activities. Nevertheless, the independent media are still weak compared with government-controlled ones. Given Tuzla's relative isolation, this does call into question the capacity of the Tuzla model to survive.

The main differences between Tuzla and Mostar can be summarised as follows:

- The administration is divided in Mostar, and social, cultural and economic life on each side is controlled by nationalist parties; the degree of control is probably greater on the West side. Tuzla is unified under a non-nationalist administration with a relatively pluralist and tolerant culture.
- Mostar suffered much more than Tuzla from the war, both in terms of population displacement and physical damage. Tuzla suffered from physical isolation and the burden of large numbers of refugees.
- Both economies have very little local production and are dependent on external assistance. Mostar is much more dependent than Tuzla; the latter has more local production, less outside assistance and has been more effective in generating municipal revenue.
- Both internal and external security is better in Tuzla than in Mostar. The town of Tuzla has been successfully defended and crime rates are much lower than in Mostar. In Mostar, the black market is much more extensive (with cooperation between East and West) and evictions (ethnic cleansing) continue[24] on the West side.
- A final difference concerns the nature of outside assistance. Mostar is characterised by a top-down approach, which has resulted in investment being on a much larger scale but which may be less effective in establishing long-term self-sufficiency. Because it is top down, all

programmes have to be agreed by the local authorities and political criteria often override economic or social criteria, including the goal of integration. Tuzla has attempted a more decentralised and diversified approach seeking cooperation between other European municipalities and NGOs as well as governments.

RECONSTRUCTION EXPERIENCE

Following the signing of the Dayton Agreement, the international community initiated an 'emergency' programme for the revival of Bosnia-Herzegovina's economy. It was estimated that a minimum of $5.1bn would be needed over the four-year period to create the basic preconditions for the economic and social rehabilitation of the country.

The reconstruction programme, which has been supervised and financed by the international community, involves various activities. These range from the initial restoration of basic infrastructure and the rehabilitation of at least some productive activity to the establishment of an elementary institutional framework necessary for the process of economic and social development. The aim has been to provide a springboard for the creation of necessary structures, and the implementation of policies that will eventually enable sustained growth of the economy of Bosnia-Herzegovina on the basis of its own resources. The understanding was that the sooner the economic recovery filtered through to the population at large, the more likely would a final political arrangement leading to a stable peace be reached. Furthermore, the political conditionality attached to the aid for reconstruction was to function as the strongest lever in securing progress in the implementation of the overall aims of the Dayton Agreement and promoting reconciliation among people and communities.

The first donors conference, sponsored by the World Bank and European Commission to raise finance for the reconstruction of Bosnia and Herzegovina, took place shortly after the signing of the peace agreement in Paris, thus underlining the importance attached to the civilian aspect of the Dayton Agreement for a peace-building process in Bosnia and Herzegovina. It was followed by a second donors conference four months later, which together secured $1.8 billion in pledges for the first year of the reconstruction programme, from over 50 countries and 10 institutions. The World Bank has been designated the lead agency for the overall reconstruction program, despite the fact that the European Union has been the largest donor so far.

The main emphasis in donors' activities in the initial months was on humanitarian and other 'quick fix' rehabilitation (World Bank 1996a).

Both because of the lengthy procedures for releasing the money and owing to the complex situation on the ground, the first genuine reconstruction projects began only in the second half of 1996. Substantial funding, provided by the EU and the World Bank, started arriving only in mid and late March 1996.

From the outset it was made clear that the international effort at reconstruction in Bosnia-Herzegovina would focus primarily on physical and social infrastructure, although the task at hand implied not only reconstructing a war destroyed economy, but also building a different kind of economy from that which existed before the war. Most of the $1.719 million designated for reconstruction activities in 1996 fitted within the framework of the Priority Reconstruction Programme, while the remaining $132[25] million was earmarked for the peace implementation activities such as support for elections, the media and the local police force. At the end of 1996, some $720 million out of a total of $1.8 billion in aid pledged at the two donor conferences was actually implemented, with wide discrepancies across sectors between the respective amounts required, committed and implemented, as well as discrepancies in the regional allocation of funds. Multilaterally administered programmes and projects accounted for 61 per cent of reconstruction aid, while bilaterally administered programmes and projects (through national aid agencies, NGOs or others) represented 39 per cent of the total. Grant money accounted for 75 per cent of the total, while the remaining 25 per cent came in the form of credit.[26]

Of amounts tendered, contracted and disbursed, projects focusing on the repair of transportation and electric power networks, the rebuilding of housing and support to government institutions accounted for 77 per cent. Although the overall funds were sufficient, the implementation of projects in some major sectors, such as telecommunications, transport, electric power and gas, lagged behind because of the lack of cooperation between entities and even within entities. Obstruction from the local authorities continued in some cases even after important and costly projects had been completed, indicating the overwhelming influence of politics over genuine economic interests.[27] This has been particularly the case with projects that cross the lines of separation between the two entities, or indeed the municipalities controlled by different nationalist authorities.

The complexity of aid coordination, in a situation where basic institutions at the local level were either missing or incapable of handling the reconstruction-related activities, was another impediment in the implementation of the reconstruction programme. At the time the reconstruction programme was launched, there were three separate administrative entities with hardly any functioning joint institutions even within the Moslem–Croat federation. The capacity of most local authorities to engage in reconstruction was limited, especially because of a lack of skilled workers and professionals.

There was also a problem of poorly defined responsibilities among the different international actors involved, in particular, between the World Bank and the European Union, reflecting the roles the United States and European countries had in ending the conflict. It is clearly in the interest of Europe to see the economic recovery and political stabilisation of Bosnia and Herzegovina as soon as possible, if for nothing else than purely geo-strategic reasons. At the same time, the engagement of the US, because of its role in the key international financial institutions, and its leverage in the way individual countries respond, is absolutely essential. This creates a complicated framework for the implementation of the reconstruction programme in which the World Bank, under the powerful influence of the US, has the leading role, while the European Union, through the Office of the High Representative, is in charge of the civilian aspect of the Dayton Agreement, the pillar of which is economic reconstruction.

Furthermore, although the entire effort to end the war and help reconstruct the economy and society of Bosnia-Herzegovina is predominantly shaped by political considerations and motives, the involvement of donors also accounts for certain commercial interests, which affects the way and the speed with which the projects are implemented. Most of the biggest donors have their own structures for project implementation, thus bypassing local agents.

In spite of numerous problems, the first results of the international community's efforts at economic reconstruction of Bosnia-Herzegovina were already reflected in basic economic indicators for 1996.[28]

- the economy grew by 40 per cent;
- industrial output recovered to some 15 per cent of the 1991 level;
- real wages grew to an average of 270 Deutschmarks,[29] and the average pension reached 150 Deutschmarks;
- the unemployment rate fell to some 60 per cent of the labour force;
- foreign trade turnover increased several-fold; and
- the proportion of the population dependent on humanitarian aid was reduced to 60 per cent.

This improvement in the economic situation can be attributed almost entirely to the reconstruction effort. There are, however, vast discrepancies between and within the entities. While the Federation is in general doing better than Republika Srpska, the Federation's areas under the control of the Bosnian Croats have had better results than the rest of the Federation. For example, it is estimated that on the territory controlled by the Bosnian Croats, industrial output has recovered to 85 per cent of its pre-war level, and that average wage is over 350 German marks.[30] In the Bosnian Serb entity in 1996, the economy operated at 20 per cent of its pre-war capacity; the average wage was 40 German marks, unemployment stood at over 90 per cent, and a much higher percentage of the population was dependent on humanitarian aid.[31] The scale of the grey economy in the Bosnian Serb territory has reached alarming proportions, costing the government most of the tax.[32] It is a public secret that most of the grey economy flows are directly or indirectly supervised by the Bosnian Serb political figures, including some at the highest level of the state and party leadership. The observed differences are partly explained by the fact that most of the reconstruction effort has been concentrated on the federation, whereas different starting positions in the process of reconstruction, as well as a close economic cooperation of the Bosnian Croat-controlled territories with Croatia, for most part account for the differences within the federation.

Notwithstanding the observed encouraging tendencies, the recovery of Bosnia-Herzegovina's economy and normalisation of life for its citizens has nevertheless hardly begun. A year since the peace agreement was signed there are still places across the country lacking regular supplies of water and electricity, with the basic infrastructure largely destroyed. Health care and education are often of poor quality. For many people lacking the opportunity to work, life is extremely difficult because the humanitarian aid is slowly being phased out. In many cases, those who are employed do not receive their salaries regularly, sometimes for months. Around 90 per cent of the housing stock damaged and destroyed during the war had not been repaired by the beginning of 1997 This makes the prospect of providing accommodation for 360 000 internally displaced and homeless people, and 1.3 million[33] refugees still abroad, extremely bleak. In the federation alone, some 650 000 people are seeking work, at least a third of them being demobilised soldiers and war invalids.[34] The economy of the Bosnian Serbs entity is close to collapse. Bosnia-Herzegovina's GDP is, even after last year's strong growth, only a third of its pre-war level.[35] Most of the country's economy, particularly its large enterprises – once the main employers and earners of foreign exchange – is dormant.

The issue of job creation, which is of critical importance, not only for economic reasons but also in relation to social and political stability, is only implicitly addressed in the programme, which envisages some help for restarting activity in small and medium-scale enterprises. There have been several successful examples of lines of micro-credit across the country, and support of local development initiatives, but the effects on job creation have been minimal given the scale of the problem. Around $135 million in annual terms, earmarked for the support of industry, formerly the backbone of Bosnia and Herzegovina's pre-war economy, also cannot create sufficient new jobs. The World Bank conditions the revitalisation of large enterprises upon privatisation, which implies that its restructuring should eventually be carried out by foreign involvement and private foreign capital – a process which seems a remote possibility, given the political uncertainties surrounding the future of Bosnia-Herzegovina and slow progress in achieving economic recovery, not to mention the fact that locals who have the money to engage in buying stakes of state enterprises are often war profiteers and criminals. Thus, the mass of unemployed people, and the heavy social burden, represent a time-bomb in the Bosnia and Herzegovina's peace process.

In parallel, the problem of a lack of educated people who could successfully engage in the implementation of the reconstruction projects is becoming increasingly acute. The presence of so many foreign agencies means that many in the existing small pool of remaining professionals are attracted by high salaries to do jobs outside their profession, for example, interpreters, administrative workers, drivers, etc., thus undermining local capacity building in the long run. Apart from the loss of their professional expertise for the local reconstruction effort, these people generally have little involvement in issues facing those whose immediate livelihood and long-term future depend on the recovery of the local economy. In that sense, their social energy, which is of crucial importance for the post-war societal rehabilitation, is, to a great extent, diverted.

Slow progress in the implementation of the reconstruction programme is, to a great extent, linked to the issues of conditionality of economic aid; the local parties are expected to comply with the terms of the Dayton Agreement on, for example, the release of war prisoners, freedom of movement, return of refugees, cooperation with the war crimes tribunal, etc. Despite tremendous pressure from the international community, only a minimum of cooperation from the representatives of the nationalist parties has been secured. Freedom of movement is still restricted, particularly across the inter-entity line, and a telephone link between the entities has still not been restored. The return of refugees in areas where they would be a minority has been almost negligible, and there has been limited, or in the case of Bosnian Serbs, non-existent cooperation regarding the arrest of war criminals. The nationalist parties continue to keep a firm grip over the media, with some exceptions in the territories controlled by the Bosnian Moslems, and in Republika Srpska where one independent magazine is published. Gross human-rights violations have persisted throughout the country. In many areas, basic security is still not guaranteed, as the firm link between the nationalist authorities and mafia elements remains steadily in place. Terror and the rule of fear, aimed particularly at ethnic minorities, continue to be employed in the absence of genuine progress in the establishment of the rule of law and the functioning of local authorities. This opens up the key dilemma as to what extent the concept of reconstruction aid, reduced to economic reconstruction and primarily based on engaging official governing structures, can be effective in the present context.

This dilemma is reaffirmed when looking at the experience of new joint institutions. The creation and functioning of these, both at the level of the republic and at that of the federation, following the September 1996 elections, has faced severe obstructions, particularly on the part of the Bosnian Serbs and the Bosnian Croats. The elections reinstated the nationalist rulers, while the opposition failed to make any significant progress. The attitudes of Bosnian Croats and Bosnian Serbs towards ethnic demarcation, and, in the case of the latter, their explicit aim of separation, have not changed.[36] In most aspects, the two entities, for example, the Federation and Republika Srpska, operate as two independent states, and the effects of the international reconstruction aid in bringing the two entities closer together are at best modest. For the majority of nationalist leaders their power base remains outside the realms of formal local economies, thus making them resilient to the acts of aid denial by the international community, particularly in the short term. So the existing state structures become nothing more than an empty shell, as the key actors in the character of ethnic nationalists and nationalist parties remain the same.

According to the institutional arrangements instilled by the Dayton Agreement, most of the powers relating to economic policy-making have been vested in the entities, which makes macroeconomic cooperation extremely complicated. As it is, Bosnia-Herzegovina at the moment does not even have a clearly defined territory over which macroeconomic policies could be implemented. It also lacks a country-wide institutional framework that such policies imply.

The progress on the part of the international community to get the basic economic institutions in place and working has been painstakingly slow, and based on compromises that make the survival of Bosnia-Herzegovina very uncertain.[37] The refusal of the parties to agree on the central bank and the common currency[38] until mid-April 1997 resulted in the third donors conference being postponed. This conference is of crucial importance to the implementation of the peace agreement. It is supposed to enable a shift in the reconstruction effort from emergency towards more sustained recovery, focusing on infrastructure, job creation, financial institutions and the resettlement of refugees. In just over a year, Bosnia-Herzegovina, a country and society grossly disabled by the destruction of four years of war, is supposed to have passed from the humanitarian through to the reconstruction phase and entered a phase of economic reform, according to the scenario devised by the international community.

This scenario is, however, highly questionable. A year after the peace agreement was signed, economic recovery in Bosnia-Herzegovina is very fragile, and the forces of disintegration led by the extreme nationalists are stronger than the forces of ethnic cooperation and integration. Whatever has been achieved has been the result intensive international pressure – in another words, imposed from outside. The basic framework of relations in all spheres of life, reworked through the conflict on principles of ethnic exclusiveness and ethnic homogenisation, has remained intact, thus paralysing any dynamic processes that would lead to progress in the economy and the society of Bosnia-Herzegovina. It is no surprise then that the country is presently in some kind of limbo, as further economic assistance is halted because of a dispute at the political level.

CONCLUSION

Neither 'reconstruction', in a traditional sense, nor 'transition' have much resonance in today's Bosnia-Herzegovina. Visions of privatisation, macroeconomic stabilisation and the removal of trade barriers seem almost irrelevant to the realities on the ground.[39] Those who provide economic assistance face an unpalatable dilemma. Either they withhold economic assistance for political reasons, tolerating the continued suffering of ordinary people, and increasing their dependence on the 'abnormal economy', or they provide economic assistance within the framework of relationships that characterise the 'abnormal economy', thus legitimising the separate development of different ethnically controlled parts and allowing the forces of ethnic separation to control whatever institutions that are in existence.

There are of course certain ways out of this dilemma. International pressure can be exerted in support of integration, concerning common infrastructure projects for example. Pockets of normality, such as Tuzla, can also be supported so as to offer forward-looking examples. But progress is bound to be slow and easily reversible without effective executive power. Effective executive power means the power to impose security, to undertake effective policing and to arrest war criminals, and to prevent evictions and other human rights violations. It means the power to put pressure on outside governments on whom ethnic warlords depend, especially the Croat and Serb governments. And, it means, above all, the re-establishment of legitimacy. By consorting with the nationalist leaders, the international community has gradually become just another player implicated and infected by the abnormalities of the situation.

The restoration of 'normality' has to become a political project, a crusade and not just a technical procedure. This is so because the problems of Bosnia-Herzegovina are as much the direct consequences of the war as they are a product of its underdevelopment and the long process of peripherilisation of its economy and society. Thus, there is a need to search for a structured approach that would eradicate the basic causes of the conflict instead of trying to ameliorate the effects.

Notes

1. See Ivan Vejvoda, 'Yugoslavia 1945–91: From Decentralization Without Democracy to Dissolution', in Vejvoda and Dyker (1996).
2. For a fuller description of the economic causes of the war, see Vesna Bojičić and Mary Kaldor, 'The Political Economy of the War in Bosnia-Herzegovina', in Kaldor and Vashee (1997).
3. Of course, economic statistics, quite apart from the issue of reliability in the current circumstances, provide insufficient insight into the nature and magnitude of the problem; nevertheless, they are relevant for no other reason than as a perception of the likely economic base from which the reconstruction effort is to begin.
4. *UNHCR Information Notes*, monthly.
5. *UNHCR Information Notes*, monthly.
6. In oil refining and the derivatives sector the percentage of destroyed plants is as high as 75 per cent.
7. Source: *Statistical Yearbook of SFR Yugoslavia* (1991).
8. See the information reports on war damage to the cultural heritage in Croatia and Bosnia-Herzegovina, Documents 6756, 6869, 6999, 6989, 7308, and Addendum 7070 and 7133, Parliamentary Assembly, Council of Europe, Strasbourg.
9. See the evidence collected by the UN Commission of Experts on War Crimes in the former Yugoslavia *Final Report of the Commission of Experts Pursuant to Security Council Resolution* 780 (1992) S/1994/674, 27 May 1994, Volume I, Annex IV.
10. See Bougarel (1996). Bougarel describes the 'abnormal' economy as *l'économie predatoire* (the predatory economy).
11. One report in the Sarajevo daily *Oslobodjenje* during the war claimed that over one thousand different humanitarian organisations were registered in Sarajevo, and yet the rationing of the humanitarian aid was insufficient. At the same, time the supply on the local market was abundant. This can partly be explained by a peculiar phenomen of individual grocers (small shop owners generally engaged in black marketeering) who registered as humanitarian organisations; this provided them with the freedom to move in and out the city and engage in murky deals, misusing humanitarian assistance. These people were put in advantageous position compared to the rest of population, who had no access to the outside world and were living in a social atmosphere to a great extent shaped by the attitudes of this category of people. Understandably, this caused animosities, often in ethnic form.
12. Figures from the 1991 census.
13. Agreement on joint police force in Mostar was finally reached in April 1997.

14. Evictions continued throughout 1996, and culminated in more than 40 fam-
    ilies evicted in two days in February 1997, following an incident in which the
    Bosnian Croat police killed two Muslims and wounded 20 during their visit
    to the cemetery on the West side.
15. Figures from EU Administration. Figures provided by the local authorities,
    on both sides, are much higher.
16. Source: *TALDI*, Tuzla, April 1997.
17. Data as of March 1995. The latest available data from the UNHCR for January
    1996 estimates the total population of the municipality of Mostar at 104 150
    persons with the following breakdown: West Mostar: total population 54,000
    with 12 000 displaced persons (approx. 800 Serbs, 3 000 Muslims); East Mostar:
    total population: 50 000 with 20 000 displaced persons (approx. 400 Serbs,
    2000 Croats) Data should be taken as an approximation, as there are vast
    discrepancies in figures from different sources.
18. A slender arch lies between two round towers, its parapet bent in a shal-
    low angle in the centre. To look at it is good; to stand on it is good. Over
    the grey-green river swoop hundreds of swallows and on the banks mosques
    and white houses stand among the glades and bushes . . . They build beau-
    tiful towns and villages. I know of no country, not even Italy or Spain,
    where each house in a group will be placed with such invariable taste and
    such pleasing results for those who look at it and out of it alike.
19. This covered: assistance to the power station and coalmines; more than 100
    public utilities, repairs and other infrastructure projects; support for NGOs,
    including £400 000 for Oxfam; helping Scottish European Aid with £200,000
    for water repairs and local roof tile manufacture (source: ODA).
20. Source: World Bank.
21. Tax revenues in March–April 1995 in the Tuzla canton were 50–60 million
    German marks.
22. The republic of Herceg-Bosna imposes 25–30 per cent customs duties on all
    goods passing through the republic including goods destined for Bosnia and
    Herzegovina. According to IMG, the authorities insist that any agency trans-
    porting goods through their territory must be registered in Herceg-Bosna
    and must have projects in Herceg-Bosna. They will not allow any equipment
    that they consider could be used in the production of weapons, e.g. pipes.
23. Interview with Alija Behram, head of Radio Mostar. He explains this by the
    fact that 'the SDA is not hard like in Tuzla and the HDZ is much more of
    an enemy.'
24. At the time of writing this chapter, April 1997, evictions are far fewer than
    before on the West side; however, tacit discrimination against non-Croat in-
    habitants continues by way of restricted access to employment, enforcement
    of payments for household electricity consumption and other bills, denial of
    travel documents, etc.
25. Source: OHR Brief.
26. Source: interview with Hasan Muratović, *Ekonomist*, no. 21, January 1997,
    Sarajevo, p. 1.
27. The case in point is the railway link between Sarajevo and the Croatian port
    of Ploce, which was ready for commercial traffic in the summer of 1996, but
    has been out of operation due to the political dispute between the Bosnian
    Moslem and Bosnian Croat authorities.
28. World Bank, *Ekonomist*, Sarajevo; various issues.
29. Source: *Ekonomist*, no. 17, December 1996, Sarajevo, p. 4.

30. *Ekonomist*, December 1996, p. 4
31. Source: World Bank.
32. An interview with B. Plavšić, the president of the Republika Srpska, quoted in *New York Times*, April 1997.
33. *Ekonomist*, no. 21, January 1997, Sarajevo, p. 1. Only 6 per cent of refugees abroad have returned to Bosnia-Herzegovina so far.
34. *Ekonomist*, no. 27, February 1997, Sarajevo, p. 13.
35. GDP per capita was estimated at $500 at the end of 1996, compared with $1 900 in 1991. Source: World Bank.
36. Bosnian Croats obstructed the work of the federal government and the Sarajevo city assembly until their request for the creation of new municipalities was finally accepted. Bosnian Serbs signed an agreement on special relations with Serbia and Montenegro.
37. An example of such a compromise is a recent decision by Carl Bildt, the EU High Representative, to accept such an interpretation of the Dayton agreement, giving the entities, rather than the state, the power to collect customs duties.
38. Even this agreement is a compromise; there is to be a transitional currency 'the Convertible Mark' – a coupon which will, in appearance, be different in the federation and Republika Srpska territory. So far, there have been four currencies in circulation in the territory of Bosnia-Herzegovina, that is, Bosnian dinar, Croatian kuna, Serbian dinar and German mark.
39. According to the World Bank, the people of Bosnia share a 'common vision' of a 'modern market economy, underpinned by a flourishing private sector and complemented by a small but effective government ... of private ownership and private initiatives for trade, production and finance ... with minimal barriers on trade, finance and labour mobility ... (in which) public expenditure is substantially reduced and is very targeted in scope ...'. World bank (1996a).

5 Lunching with Killers: Aid, Security and the Balkan Crisis

Mark Duffield

RECONSTITUTING THE PROBLEM

The breakup of Yugoslavia has played an important role in the emergence of a new international aid security paradigm. While aspects of this framework had been developing during the previous decade, the depth of the crisis and its proximity to Western Europe served to accelerate its elaboration. Refined during the course of the Balkan war and its aftermath, the new aid paradigm has a wide historic and global significance. In an increasingly divided world, it is adapted to manage the effects of economic polarisation and political fragmentation.

The 1970s marked the end of an unprecedented period of Western economic growth and social cohesion. Since then, the world-system has entered a period of profound systemic change (Hopkins and Wallerstein 1996). In place of the old certainties, the relationship between core and periphery has been reproblematised. One can no longer automatically assume, for example, that a process of modernisation will eventually improve life-chances in the latter to match those of the former (Schuurman 1993). With the disappearance of a conventional economy in some areas of the periphery, neither can it be taken for granted that an exploitative relation necessarily links the two. In other words, that a dependent periphery will, in some sense, be maintained to serve the interests of the core. Reflecting such changes, earlier modernisation and dependency theories have fallen from fashion.

Aid and security have long been associated. The relationship between them, however, has undergone significant change. During the cold war, when an inter-state system fashioned international relations, Western aid largely attempted to support an anti-communist alliance in the Third World (Griffin 1991). The end of the cold war has accelerated the decline of the inter-state system. It also revealed the extent of global economic polarisation. The relationship between aid and security has also shifted. Rather than alliances and antagonism between states, the focus is now on the character of social relations and divisions within states.

Disarticulation of the World-System

Several developments have shaped the reproblematisation of core and periphery relations. The membership of these systems, for example, has changed. While East Asia is entering core status, East Europe and the Commonwealth of Independent States (CIS) countries have moved toward the periphery. At the same time, the global economy has continued to polarise. Over the past thirty years, the ratio of income distribution between the richest 20 per cent of the world's population and poorest has doubled from 30:1 to 61:1 (UNDP 1996a). The geography of this polarisation has also become more regionally defined. It is mainly those areas outside the Western and East Asian core zones, that is, Africa, Latin America, the Caribbean, the Middle East, Eastern Europe and the CIS countries, where average indicators have been going backwards. Over much of this broad area, income levels and welfare spending is lower today than ten or even twenty years ago.

While the wealth gap has been increasing for decades, until the 1970s it was relative in character. In both the underdeveloped market economies (Cornia 1987) and the socialist alternatives (Arrighi 1991), real growth was taking place. Among other things, this relative improvement reflected a continuing need for Southern raw materials in core areas. Although terms of trade were declining, qualified development was possible (Adams 1993). Since the 1970s, the wealth gap has both accelerated and become absolute – a development associated with the actual collapse of formal economies and the disintegration of social and welfare services within the reconstituted periphery.

Besides its recent new members, what defines the current periphery as essentially new is the trend toward the regionalisation of the core economies. That is, the concentration of the conventional global economy within and between North American, West European and East Asian regional systems or blocs (Oman 1994). The increasing influence of the latter has helped shape the perception of the global economy, not as an undifferentiated system, but as one organised into distinct and competing species of regionally defined capitalism (Thurow 1992). Just as conventional economic activity has concentrated within the so-called Triad (UNCTC 1991), it has either shrunk or withdrawn from the non-bloc areas. Separated by a growing wealth and technology gap, one must now question whether a generalised relation of exploitation necessarily links core and peripheral regions. Rather than having an organic or integrated world-system, apart from a continuing need to secure a number of key resources or strategic areas, we have entered an era of global fragmentation and separate development.

The Western approach to the growing crisis in the Southern and Eastern periphery was, initially, to introduce structural adjustment and neo-liberal austerity measures (Walton and Seddon 1994: a move which demonstrated the limited economic sovereignty of the states involved. Aimed at improving competitiveness by lowering wages and cutting welfare spending, structural adjustment has tended to reinforce global polarisation and collapsing living standards. As a consequence, peripheral employment became increasingly informalised as parallel and extra-legal activities replaced the conventional economy (Tabak 1996). The more recent Western humanitarian and reconstruction interventions have highlighted the weaknesses of political sovereignty in the periphery. In many respects, these direct and operational interventions have taken place on ground prepared by structural adjustment.

The State and Contrary Regional Dynamics

The changing role of the nation-state has also helped reproblematise core and periphery relations. A number of commentators, especially in the West, have argued that the long trajectory of the modernising state is at an end (for example, Hobsbawm 1994a). While few would argue that both nationally and internationally the role of the state is changing, when one compares the core areas with the non-bloc regions a contrary dynamic is apparent. Within the core regional systems the process of competitive state formation has largely come to an end. Indeed, the main emphasis is on redefining sovereignty in terms of new systems of regional economic integration. Within the EU, albeit with hesitation, political unification is developing.

Regarding the crisis regions beyond the wealth gap, the forceful redefinition of political authority is still underway. Indeed, it would seem to be accelerating. Rather than new forms of regional integration, the opposite is occurring. Over large parts of the Southern and Eastern periphery, regional fragmentation and political separatism has grown. Either new states have been established or they have been redefined as ethnocentric or fundamentalist projects. Prior to 1989, state formation based on the principle of ethnic succession was uncommon. During the early 1990s alone, however, ten such states were established, almost all of them in Eastern Europe (Smith 1993). In some areas autonomous warlord structures have emerged within states. Where the resource base is insufficient for formal state re-assertion, as in parts of Africa, competing warlords have fashioned so-called failed or weak states (Reno 1995).

It is a fundamental contention of this paper that the contrast between integrating and fragmenting regions is a central problem for the new aid and security paradigm. Western aid policy is essentially state-centric. It is often said that the current phase of operational intervention is associated with the erosion of state sovereignty. It is also the case, however, that most interventions depend on negotiation and agreement with local political actors. In other words, while integration deepens in the core areas, Western intervention tends to reinforce the forces of political fragmentation and exclusivism in the periphery. Transitional ideology, that is, regarding such trends as a temporary phase on the road to liberal democracy, the birth pangs of a new beginning, tends to obscure this relation.

THE CULTURAL PLURALIST FRAMEWORK

How the West has understood the Balkan crisis has shaped the international response. The disarticulation of the world-system, and the eclipse in the West of the modernising role of the nation-state, have weakened the position of meta-theory and grand narratives. The new periphery, both ideologically and practically, has been re-engaged by the increasing predominance of a cultural-pluralist framework. Attempts to conceptualise the whole have been replaced by a rediscovery and celebration of difference and diversity. At the same time, the retreat from theory has been reinforced by a demand for practical relevance, that is, the futile task of attempting to reduce political problems to technical solutions. The growth and increasing influence of non-governmental organisations (NGOs) has been central to this change.

Two interdependent components define the cultural-pluralist framework: racial discourse and multiculturalism. The former has helped explain the Balkan crisis, while the latter has informed its practical engagement. Western racial discourse has been restructured to provide, among other things, a popular explanation for instability in the periphery.

New Barbarism

A radical reworking of Western racial ideology took place during the 1960s and 1970s. The result has been called by Barker (1982) the 'new racism'. This has effected a change from an earlier colonial discourse structured around hierarchical categories of alleged natural superiority and inferiority. Rather than hierarchy, it is difference, typically cultural difference, that is the key factor. This adaptation has made racism respectable by dispensing with the need to rely on outmoded notions of innate superiority. Like multiculturalism, new racism accepts that cultural difference is both natural and unavoidable. Because of the largely unreasoned character of these differences, however, contemporary racism urges caution and alarm: visible cultural differences within society inevitably lead to inter-ethnic violence, social breakdown and anomie (Barker 1982:13–29 and 38–53).

The utility of new racism is that you no longer need to think yourself superior, all you need to do is acknowledge the reality of cultural heterogeneity and its inner propensity toward social instability (Barker 1982:18). Contemporary racial discourse renders it unnecessary to rank peoples hierarchically. Since the 1970s, racial discourse structured around cultural difference has provided an influential platform in the West and has attracted supporters from across the political spectrum. This type of reasoning, for example, has formed the basis for calls to end immigration and promote repatriation. More recently, curtailing rights to political asylum in Western Europe have also been included.

New racist thinking also provides an explanation for the growing violence and instability in the West's hinterland. Developing during the 1980s, this variant has been described as the attempt to portray a 'new barbarism' in the West's new global hinterland (Richards 1995). In understanding the Balkans crisis, for example, racial discourse has tended to emphasise the innate, age-old and unreasoned aspects of cultural and ethnic identity. For new barbarism, the anarchic and destructive power of traditional feelings and antagonisms are unleashed when the state or constraining forms of economic regulation collapse.

Interestingly, there is an affinity with new barbarism and the primordialist and ethnocentric histories that the nationalist intellectual and political élites of the Eastern Europe and the former Soviet Union have manufactured (Tishkov 1997). Both accept the historical basis of cultural difference. New barbarism, however, turns the Eastern conception of the ethnos on its head. Rather than the primordialist project leading to fulfilment and liberation, for new barbarism the result is breakdown and chaos.

For new barbarism, instability in the Eastern periphery arises from the demise of the socialist party-state, which had suppressed deep-seated, and essentially irrational, ethnic tensions and animosities. Ancient rivalries were able to re-emerge into the light of day (Kennedy 1993). In the former Yugoslavia, for example, bottled-up tensions were released, allowing the 'Balkan mentality' a free rein (Kennan 1993). Such views have had a significant impact on how the collapse of Yugoslavia has been understood and responded to. It is the favoured explanation, for example, within Britain's Foreign and Commonwealth Office. Kaplan's (1993) book, tellingly entitled *Balkan Ghosts: A Journey Through History*, by painting a picture of innate and inbred hatreds, is also credited with dissuading the Clinton administration from its initial interventionist line on Bosnia.

The new barbarism thesis sees the contemporary world on the edge of instability and chaos. The urge to violence is a natural tendency, which can only be curbed by levels of development that a polarising world is now unable to deliver to all regions. Such views have been widely applied by journalists, government officials and aid workers within the Southern and Eastern periphery: a situation that attests to the wide resonance of new racist thinking. In the face of increasing global polarisation, contemporary racial discourse helps fuel the isolationist trend within the West.

The Multicultural Mirror-Image

Multiculturalism is the other key part of the cultural-pluralist framework. More specifically, it is the conventional critique of new racism. It emerged during the 1960s and 1970s in response to the changing nature of racial discourse (Duffield 1984). This common origin is reflected in the many pluralist assumptions that multiculturalism shares with new racism. While more optimistic in terms of outcome, multiculturalism similarly embraces categories of difference in preference to those of hierarchy.

Like new racism, multiculturalism regards society as synonymous with different ways of life or ethnic identities. These relations are of an enduring nature, and have the power to recreate themselves over time and in changed circumstances, including migration to culturally different societies. Multiculturalism is a historic by design rather than mistake. Social and cultural inertia is something that is actively maintained: it is what people themselves want and need. For multiculturalism, ethnic identity is a functionally useful relation. Because cultures endure and recreate themselves, it is natural that cultural differences are maintained. Assimilation, therefore, is not only impossible; it is undesirable. It is not a question of one culture being better or worse than another, they are just different. Pluralism is the normal state of the world (Norgaard 1994).

While there are numerous shared assumptions, the differences between multiculturalism and new racism are few. In fact, there is only one major contrast. That is, the place of violence within the system.

For contemporary racism, unrest stemming from ethnic heterogeneity is inevitable. For multiculturalism, however, this is not the case. Pluralism is normal, and with proper understanding, support and political structures it need not lead to violence (Rupesinghe 1996:11). From this perspective, new racism and multiculturalism are essentially mirror-images of each other, sharing many assumptions about the nature of society but differing on outcomes and necessary action. The dialectic between the two is a defining feature of the new aid and security paradigm.

Multiculturalism has shaped the social aspects of development and transition policy in the periphery. This includes the redefinition of development as the empowerment of cultural and gender differences and the growing interest in conflict resolution using models adapted from the

Western race relations industry (Voutira and Brown 1995). At the same time, the establishment of a plural and democratic civil society has been cast as both the goal and the handmaiden of market reform.

WORKING IN UNRESOLVED CRISES

The West's response to the collapse of Yugoslavia and the emergence of its successor states encompasses both the restriction of migrant and refugee flows, and the complementary development of new forms of aid and security intervention. Since the 1970s, there has been growing pressure in Western Europe to reduce immigration and restrict the right to political asylum, trends strengthened by the ending of the cold war. The outbreak of open conflict in Bosnia in April 1992, and the prospect of a massive refugee influx into Western Europe, prompted a further rapid tightening of asylum regulations (Helsinki Watch 1992). A Fortress Europe, however, would have been politically unfeasible without the aid industry's increasing ability to keep and support civilians within war zones.

This new capacity is reflected in United Nation's High Commission for Refugee's (UNHCR) changing case-load. For several decades, the number of people for which UNHCR is responsible has grown relentlessly. By 1995 it had increased to over 27 million. Since the beginning of the 1990s, however, the number of actual refugees, that is, people crossing an international boundary and receiving political asylum, has been decreasing. The continuing rise in the total case-load has been due to UNHCR's growing involvement with non-refugees. This new and burgeoning category now represents almost half of the overall figures. In terms of decreasing magnitude, it comprises internally displaced and war-affected populations within their home countries; people outside their home countries but without asylum status; and returnees to their home countries (UNHCR 1995). Reflecting the importance of the Balkan crisis to this change, in 1995 Bosnia's 1.7 million internally displaced represented more than 30 per cent of UNHCR's total case-load in this category.

The ability for aid agencies to work in live conflicts is a relatively new phenomenon. Indeed, until the end of the 1980s, it was uncommon. Prior to this period the UN, for example, intervened in relatively few conflict situations. When it did, it was usually under some form of existing ceasefire arrangement (Goulding 1993). The end of the cold war changed this situation radically. Shorn of super-power patrons, warring parties have been increasingly willing to reach agreement with aid agencies over the distribution of humanitarian assistance in areas they control. This is especially the case when such parties lack valuable niche commodities such as drugs, gemstones or hardwoods.

Developing in Africa from 1989, through a series of *ad-hoc* UN resolutions, negotiated access has allowed aid agencies to work on all sides of the line in a growing number of internal conflicts. Following the establishment of the 'safe haven' in Kurdistan, by the time of the outbreak of fighting in Bosnia in 1992, the aid industry had achieved a fair degree of operational experience in terms of a growing ability to mount humanitarian operations in war zones and thus contain large-scale refugee outflows (Duffield 1994a). This capacity has been complemented by a growing trend to repatriate refugees (forcefully if necessary) to their home countries as part of (or even ahead of) a political settlement. Indeed, the success of international 'humanitarian' operations has been increasingly judged in terms of the satisfaction of such criteria (Ferris 1996). As the role of nation-states has diminished, this has been achieved through a complex process of subcontracting welfare and security services to a range of new international actors (Weiss 1996).

Working on all sides of a protracted political crisis, unfeasible even less than a decade ago, have supported a rapid expansion of the aid industry. While overall development spending has been stagnating and declining, since the mid-1980s especially, relief and humanitarian expenditure have sharply increased. By 1993, the global total of about $3.2 billion and rising (excluding food-aid and the cost of military peace-keeping) represented a six-fold increase in less than a decade (IFRCS 1995). At this stage, the Balkan region was accounting for about one-third of global relief expenditure.

Access to the crisis regions, however, represents more than an opportunity for agency expansion: it has revolutionised the aid industry. Old mandates associated with non-interference and the inviolability of sovereignty, together with an international system shaped around the predominance of intergovernmental relations, have dissolved. They have been replaced by new forms of conditional sovereignty established by a range of non-governmental, regional and multilateral bodies forming agreements and partnerships with the political authorities in the periphery. Rather than governments and states, this network of supra- and sub-national organisations reflects the emerging pattern of global governance in an increasingly polarised world.

INTERNALISING THE PROBLEM

The organising principles of the new aid and security paradigm are *internalisation* and *relativisation*. These principles operate at several levels. The 1951 Refugee Convention, for example, while detailing the rights of asylum-seekers and the obligations of the host country, makes no mention of the sending country. The new paradigm places this rectification at its centre (UNHCR 1995). It would be misleading, however, to see this change as simply reflecting a better way of tackling the problem. Internalisation would not have been possible without the demise of alternative national political projects. Until the early 1980s, for example, erstwhile Third-World and socialist leaders could still effectively argue that refugee flows resulted from the heritage of colonialism and continuing global inequality (Suhrke 1994). The collapse of the Third World and, more recently, socialism as international political projects, however, has allowed the West to define the cause of instability in terms of defective internal relations and institutions. That is, poor economic management, environmental degradation and, especially, authoritarian and non-democratic political bodies.

Internalisation involves a redefinition of the notion of responsibility. Internal conflict, large-scale population displacement and refugee flows are now regarded as synonymous with so-called complex emergencies. That is, the outcome of weak state structures in combination with multiple economic, social and political pressures. It is important to note, however, that the new aid paradigm assigns a dual role to local political actors. While recognising that they have often been a contributory factor, they are also assigned the main role in normalising the situation. The character of internal social relations and political actors are simultaneously the problem and the solution. Warring parties, for example, as well as instigating humanitarian disasters have, through negotiated access, become the arbiters of international humanitarian relief.

In many respects, the focus on internal relations is a welcome development. One would expect that it would create the space for a deeper analysis and more informed response. Unfortunately, this has not happened. Rather than concrete analysis, the aid paradigm substitutes an image of the transitional society. Internal relations are assessed, usually negatively, in terms of their relation to an idealised conception of liberal democracy, a condition towards which, in any case, it is imagined that the societies concerned are haltingly moving. Rather than an analysis of actually existing relations, internalisation is associated with desired futures and what transitional societies should or ought to become. In this respect, in placing the main developmental burden on local actors, the new aid paradigm is essentially concerned with changing internal behaviour and attitudes (Pupavac 1997). Whether it relates to the role of women, how the economy works or attitudes towards one's neighbours, the emphasis is on changing what people do and how they think. A whole series of aid conditionalities, both formal and informal, are now geared to the perceived adoption of liberal-democratic values.

A major casualty of the duality of roles accorded political actors, by the new aid paradigm, has been the issue of justice. If aid agencies or

Western governments depend on the agreement of a particular authority to distribute relief or support a peace process, for example, then it is difficult to simultaneously prosecute that party for human rights abuse: justice becomes contingent and optional. At the time of writing, of the 75 war crime suspects being investigated by the Hague tribunal, only seven are in custody.[1] Moreover, it is widely held that the purpose of the war crimes tribunal has been sacrificed to the efforts of Western diplomats to secure the support of various parties and successor states for the wider Dayton Agreement.[2] For many, rather than a weakness, the contradictory duality within the new aid paradigm is the essence of access and the West's room for political manoeuvre.

Relativisation of Development

Relativisation relates to how development, and ultimately security, is now regarded in the periphery. During the 1980s, increasing global polarisation and regionalisation contributed to a growing developmental crisis. The imagined social convergence of the post-colonial period, with the exception of East Asia, was not happening. Reflecting the growth of multiculturalism within Western countries, the response has been to extend this framework to the new development and security arenas. For example, much of what has been called post-impasse theory (Schuurman 1993) traces a trajectory similar to that for racial discourse that was outlined above. That is, there is a rejection of categories based on hierarchy, including modernisation and dependency approaches, in favour of plurality and difference. Post-impasse theory largely appears as a rediscovery of diversity in the periphery and, indeed, a celebration of its existence (Booth 1993).

Reflecting this rectification, practical development has been redefined as a cultural-pluralist enterprise: the empowerment of cultural and gender differences in pursuit of behavioural and attitudinal change (Duffield 1996). Its proponents have championed this shift against the reductionism of earlier grand theories. At the same time, government-led infrastructural programmes of the 1960s and 1970s have been criticised as top-down and inappropriate. While some of this critique has substance, it could be argued that this response constitutes an accommodation with systemic crisis and global polarisation, rather than a fundamental challenge to it. Instead of modernist ideas of convergence or dependency models of exploitation, the multicultural rectification provides a conceptual underpinning for separate development in an era of global fragmentation and disarticulation. Images of empowerment and sustainability complement shifting the burden of transition to local actors and making aid conditional upon it.

The now outmoded terms of development and underdevelopment implied a view of progress that was absolute and measurable. Within the new aid paradigm, progress has become a relative concept. In practice, it is little more than whatever private aid agencies can actually do on the ground. Externally supported infrastructural or preferential economic programmes have been replaced by an internal focus on local partnership, empowerment and capacity-building geared to behavioural change. Despite the wider aims of development becoming difficult, if not impossible to evaluate (Keen 1993), budget-conscious donors have been more than willing to accept this essentially social redefinition of the problem. Not only has development changed its meaning; since the mid-1980s, the subcontracting of official aid programmes to NGOs has grown apace. As a consequence, and as is largely reflected in the burgeoning level of humanitarian assistance, an aid market has emerged where none existed before.

Compared with the infrastructural programmes of the past, the development projects that emerged during the 1980s provide little more than a basic level of welfare and social provision for targeted groups and communities. Ideally through sustainable, that is, self-help means, they aim to lessen the vulnerability of marginal groups to the rigours of their increasingly precarious existence. Through health, education, agricultural and employment projects, NGOs have established what Clark (1991) has called 'compensatory programmes' in societies often in the midst of systemic and protracted crisis. In this fashion, earlier notions of social convergence were transmuted during the 1980s into the provision of basic welfare safety-nets by private agencies.

From Relief to Reconstruction

Traditionally, relief and development were seen as distinct activities. The latter relating to the normal, long-term movement of societies (a position more recently taken up by the advocates of transition in former planned economies), while the former concerned temporary upsets and unpredictable external shocks. Within the new aid paradigm, following the redefinition of development in welfare and social support terms, relief and development have become increasingly blurred. This situation has been well reflected in the current debate on the so-called relief-to-development continuum (Buchanan-Smith and Maxwell 1994): a debate that is crucial in understanding how the development/transitional and security agendas have merged.

Rather than separate practices, conventional wisdom now holds that relief should be provided in such a way as to foster sustainable development and transition. Relief work, with its alleged tendency to ignore local structures is usually cast as the villain in this argument (Duffield 1994b).

Actual development, however, has increasingly situated itself to occupy a behavioural change and basic welfare, indeed, relief, position. Rather than relief giving way to development, the movement has been in the opposite direction. Given the decline in overall development funding, together with the high levels of infrastructural damage and social disruption in conflict affected areas, continuum thinking makes little sense without a relativisation of the reconstruction and development goal.

THE HUMANITARIAN PHASE IN BOSNIA

Prior to the outbreak of fighting within the former Yugoslavia in 1992, Western welfare and humanitarian provision as a response to political crises in the periphery had already achieved a certain organisational coherence. The fusion in Bosnia of aid agency negotiated access with, at least in theory, military protection for humanitarian logistics and civilian safe areas, represented a culmination of the major trends within the aid industry during the first half of the 1990s (Duffield 1994a). One could define this movement as that of UN-led military humanitarianism. It was complemented by the emergence of new multilateral humanitarian coordinating bodies – for example, the UN's Department of Humanitarian Affairs (DHA) and the EU's European Community Humanitarian Office (ECHO). At the same time, a number of European governments established their own operational humanitarian agencies.

During the course of the Balkan war, humanitarian provision followed a rough geographical division of labour. As with the present reconstruction phase, Serbia and the Serbian controlled areas of Bosnia were largely excluded. Croatia and Bosnia were the main recipients. Owing to the severity of the fighting, however, international NGOs were found mainly in Croatia. Moreover, the aid operation in Croatia and Bosnia was organised differently. In the former, ECHO was the main player in providing logistics and donor funding for NGOs. Within Bosnia, UNHCR played this role.

By the time of open fighting in 1992, having to negotiate access with warring parties had established the need for a UN lead agency. At the same time, the virtual collapse of the economy and devastating effects of the fighting were such as to demand a UN system wide response. In theory, the lead agency coordinated other UN specialist agencies in an agreed division of labour. In practice, only minimal cooperation existed between these traditionally independent and often competing bodies. At the same time, the increased expectations placed upon the UN served to illustrate its limited operational capacity. This encouraged a significant expansion of the aid market through the growth of UN/NGO subcontracting. That is, UN agencies handing over major aspects of their own donor-funded aid programmes to NGO implementers. In this respect, welfare subcontracting became more extensive and complex.

Reflecting contemporary practice in other so-called complex emergencies, UNHCR attempted to regulate NGOs through signed letters of affiliation. In exchange for agreeing to the principles of neutrality and supplying only non-strategic humanitarian assistance, UNHCR undertook to secure access and provide logistics for NGO run programmes. Affiliated NGOs received UN blue card IDs for their staff. On the basis of a regular cycle, UNHCR established joint plans of action and agreed with the warring parties the destinations, routes and timings of humanitarian convoys. Following agreement, military escort or other assistance, as necessary, was requested by UNHCR from UNPROFOR.

This arrangement gave the warring parties a good deal of control over the humanitarian operation. Not only did they regulate access; needs assessments, for example, were often conducted by the actual local authority that was responsible for distribution. At the same time, little, if any, end-use monitoring was undertaken by UNHCR. Aid diversion was widespread. Even official documents put this as between 35 and 40 per cent in central Bosnia (DHA 1993 Oct 8:16). At the same time, however, since most of the fighting was done by civilian militias, the distinction between civilian and combatant was rather academic. Even without diversion feeding a mother more for a son. Despite such considerations, however, humanitarian aid was a lifeline for the population contained in the ethnic enclaves and besieged towns.

This degree of access for international agencies was unique in the history of warfare. Humanitarian assistance tended to ebb and flow with the changing dynamics of the conflict. Even at the height of the blockade and bombardment of Mostar East, for example, UNICEF was attempting to support local teachers restarting primary education in the cellars of the ruined ghetto (Duffield 1994a). It should be noted, however, that most NGOs tended to concentrate in the more secure and accessible areas. With the exception of the French relief agencies, it was the UN that largely maintained the lifeline. The high level of current NGO activity in Sarajevo has developed since the end of the war.

The Expansion of the Non-Governmental Sector

Excluding the cost of UNPROFOR, during the war humanitarian expenditure in the Balkan region averaged $1 billion per year. This represented a major opportunity for NGO expansion. Most international NGOs began to arrive in the early part of 1993. While more existed on paper, at the height of the conflict there were about 40 actively operating in Bosnia.

For those international NGOs willing to be involved, especially in insecure areas, the financial rewards were great. Indeed, they were of a new order of magnitude. Mainly as a result of subcontracting part of UNHCR's massive Bosnia emergency shelter programme, the 1993 budget of the International Rescue Committee (IRC), for example, was $50 million (Duffield 1994a). This was greater than UNICEF's budget for the entire region. Unusual at the time, the emergence of the NGO mega-project is now an established feature of complex emergencies and, indeed, it has continued to characterise Bosnia's present reconstruction phase.

Another feature about the Balkan crisis was the impetus it gave to the creation of new NGOs, both international and local. With the exception of the French agencies, many established international NGOs were slow to respond. Bosnia represented a new challenge for such agencies. That is, an increasing need for international NGOs to work in regions which had no previous experience of non-governmental activity. At the same time, however, the proximity to Western Europe made it relatively easy for small relief organisations to become operational. Such agencies were usually formed specifically because of the collapse of Yugoslavia. Running periodic aid convoys to the more secure areas within the region was a typical activity. A few, however, developed into major players and, usually within the UNHCR negotiated framework, developed niche services in such things as logistics or child support. Born in war, these new relief agencies have a different temperament from the more established developmental NGOs.

New international NGOs (INGOs), however, emerged not only in the humanitarian sector. Support for conflict resolution, democratisation and civil society activities also developed. This, together with the formation of local NGOs (LNGOs), is discussed more fully below.

War as a Mental Health Problem

Bosnia has been a major site of internal displacement as a result of ethnic cleansing and fighting. About half of Bosnia's current population of around 3.4 million (down 1 million on pre-war figures) are internally displaced (Bojičić *et al.* 1995:7). The internally displaced have become absorbed into private residences and, to a lesser extent, camps.

The majority of NGOs that established themselves in Croatia and Bosnia were not major players in the relief operation. As noted above, most tended to concentrate in the more secure areas. While the work NGOs engage in is varied, a concentration on psycho-social projects is evident, that is, activities that can be described as attempting to help people recognise and overcome the trauma of war. This includes such things as counselling for the victims of rape and violence, training teachers to support traumatised children, projects for demobilised soldiers, and so on. In 1995, the EC Task Force noted 185 projects within the region being implemented by 117 separate organisations. Many of these were local NGOs.

The high level of NGO activity within the psycho-social field, together with evident enthusiasm among donors to fund this type of work, has attracted some criticism (Stubbs 1996; Summerfield 1996). The issue is not that war is distressing; or indeed devastating, in its effects: it is whether, for most people, distress *per se* is a psychological ailment needing treatment rather than part of a difficult, but normal, process of healing and accommodation (Summerfield 1996:14). Post-traumatic stress disorder (PTSD) was first diagnosed around 1980. Originally associated with extreme occurrences, PTSD has increasingly become synonymous with the everyday accidents and violence that characterise capitalist civilisation. As such, it has become the cornerstone of a burgeoning compensation industry.

From the trauma perspective, the individual is the main unit of analysis. The proposition is that painful events have a lifelong psychological effect. Its application to humanitarian emergencies is relatively new. War is regarded as having damaging and far-reaching psychological consequences for whole populations: a mental health emergency on a societal scale. It is claimed, for example, that in Croatia and Bosnia some 700 000 people are severely affected, with a similar number to a lesser degree (Agger 1995). Such assertions have helped fuel the growth of NGO psycho-social projects and treatment centres.

As Summerfield (1996) has argued, the trauma approach objectifies suffering and turns it into a clinical condition regarded as amenable to technical solutions. While wider social issues are sometimes mentioned, in the final analysis, it is an individual's attitudes and responses that are thought crucial. In other words, psycho-social work is a further example of how the West has attempted to internalise the Balkan crisis at the level of attitudes and behaviour. The war is reduced to its effects on individuals for whom technical palliatives are provided. To the extent that the individual's response then becomes the main object of concern, psycho-social work also contributes to the process of relativisation. For example, while not contradicting the need for justice and restitution, the concentration on the individual erodes this need by providing an alternative and spurious point of focus. As discussed below, the trauma approach has shaped much of the current work on conflict resolution and social reconstruction.

Demise of UN-Led Military Humanitarianism

UN intervention within the Balkan crisis contained a certain logic. In the face of growing asylum restrictions in Western Europe, it attempted to contain population movements and, in the context of ongoing conflict, support affected populations within the war zone. While appeasing the isolationist lobby in the West, this approach attracted widespread criticism. In particular, that humanitarian aid had replaced any meaningful search for a solution. At best, it lacked political vision and, at worst, the tendency for UN deployment to freeze the *status quo* was actually helping the war aims of aggressors.

The ultimate failure of the UN in Bosnia, however, related to the impossibility of its fundamental aim, namely of supporting war-affected populations within a live conflict through the consent of the warring parties. From the outset, some perceptive critics predicted that without first securing a cease-fire this approach was doomed to failure (Higgins 1993:469). The declaration of 'safe areas' in 1993, and the subsequent inability of the UN to protect them, tragically illustrated the problem. Within an ongoing war, consent is fragile and contingent. UNPROFOR failed because of the contradictory nature of its mandate: to help distribute relief as well as protect civilian areas. The UN could not guarantee the consent of the warring parties, nor could it prevent them from dictating the nature of the engagement. Lacking an appropriate mandate, equipment or command structure, UNPROFOR was drawn into situations for which it had no effective response (Brinkman 1996).

The experience of Somalia and Bosnia marks the demise of UN-led military humanitarianism. This has had wide implications for relief operations in the periphery. The high hopes and euphoria surrounding the end of the cold war and collapse of the USSR, has given way to a more cautious attitude. Rather than opportunities for deepening world government, external political instability now represents itself as a series of 'wars of choice' for Western powers (Freedman 1995). With a careful eye on the purse strings, involvement is increasingly calculated in terms of national, regional and strategic interest. Reflecting the disarticulation of the global economy, this calculus of interest has seen a growing distinction between strategic and non-strategic areas. Bosnia, for example, warranted a Dayton Agreement, while Albania was also judged worthy of a military humanitarian intervention (although few aid agencies regard the situation as a humanitarian emergency). The turmoil and suffering in Central Africa, however, receives scant attention.

Rather than developing military humanitarianism, in strategic areas it been increasingly accepted that military forces need to extricate themselves from the humanitarian agenda. They should be seen as setting the agenda and supporting the conditions for a more favourable political outcome. The rationale for this position stems from the argument that any form of military involvement will unavoidably become entangled in the political process (Freedman 1995). It is therefore only by making long-term changes to that process that military forces can secure both a role and the basis for their withdrawal. In Bosnia, during 1995, reducing the geographical exposure of UNPROFOR allowed a more robust pattern of NATO air-strikes, which, together with increased diplomatic pressure through American involvement, helped redefine the nature of Western engagement along these lines. This change of thinking focuses attention not on humanitarian relief but on addressing the 'fragility of local institutions, infrastructure and economic activity' (Freedman 1995). In other words, military intervention becomes an adjunct to the support of civil society. In December 1995, the Dayton Agreement was signed. UNPROFOR was replaced by the NATO-led Implementation Force (I-For). Unlike UNPROFOR, I-For had no humanitarian brief. Rather, by separating the warring parties and providing security, it was meant to provide a framework in which the Dayton Agreement could be realised. In this respect, the Organisation for Security and Cooperation in Europe (OSCE), formerly the Conference for Security and Cooperation in Europe, was invited to oversee the electoral process and help support the establishment of civil society as set out in Dayton. In all major respects, two regional bodies, that is, NATO and OSCE, have taken over from the UN in Bosnia. This development can be seen as a further deepening of internalisation. The failure of the humanitarian phase of Western involvement helped shape the current stage of reconstruction through regional bodies. As such, it has helped focus attention on the nature of the internal social and political relations within the Yugoslavia successor states. While many would regard this development as a success, there is a danger that the reconstruction phase may prove less open than the preceding stage. It carries a tremendous pressure to normalise the situation regardless of actually existing conditions.

The Merging of Development and Security Agendas

The conventional approach to internal war and political instability is, essentially, to see it as a problem of underdevelopment (Boutros-Ghali 1995): as something that results from poverty, economic hopelessness and political authoritarianism. Political violence is not regarded as a rational response to changing circumstances, that is, as a set of relations and strategies that can exploit and manipulate the modalities of global marginalisation to secure sectarian ends. To the contrary, these modalities are thought to be a cause and not a means. There is a difference. Rather than something that is capable of growing and adapting to outside influence, political crisis is viewed rather like an unfortunate social illness, which disappears with benign economic development and democratisation.

The Western approach, which sees conflict as transient and irrational, leaves much to be desired. It takes place with an almost total disregard of deepening global polarisation and any meaningful analysis of the emerging socio-political formations in the periphery. The basic model is to internalise the problem and encourage self-help solutions. In the economic field, structural adjustment backed by fragmentary welfare safety-nets is meant to equip weak economies for global competition. Within the political field, economic liberalism has been complemented by support for pluralism and democratic institutions. It is not that there is anything intrinsically wrong with pluralism and democracy, rather it is that, together with deregulation, it has become a single cure for all ills – something that is automatically prescribed with little regard for history, conditions or outcomes. It is a monist straight-jacket that prevents the development of more nuanced and locally informed approaches.

In Eastern Europe and the CIS countries, the term 'transition' has been substituted for the more South-oriented term 'development'. The structure of debate, however, is similar. Transition to a market economy is seen as dependent on the dual process of economic adjustment and the development of democratic institutions. As Schuurman (1993) has noted, this neo-liberal framework has not achieved a position of hegemony through some intrinsic power of analysis or proven track record: it is due to the collapse of alternative political projects and visions. As an approach, it bears some resemblance to former modernisation theory. Since it sees little role for the state, however, other than as a facilitator kept in check by plural civil institutions, it has less to offer.

Transition theory owes something to the perceived role of independent organisations and associations in the fall of communism (Hankiss 1990). The pursuit of human rights, support of democratisation and promotion of civil society have become central to both the development and transitional agendas. Given that democracy is also equated with stability, transition and security concerns have also increasingly merged. The security of Western Europe, for example, is now widely regarded as resting on the existence of plural democracies in the East. This process is well illustrated in the development of the OSCE. In many respects, changes with the OSCE have paralleled those of the UN during the first half of the 1990s. Notably, the move toward increasing operationality while focusing on the deficiencies of internal relations and institutions. The separation of the economic and human dimensions within the transition, for example, has established that internal affairs and the welfare of the individual are now legitimate international concerns (Guerra 1996:17–18). This represents a radical departure from the traditional state-centric approach to international relations and security issues.

In promoting plural civic institutions in the East, the West has advocated a multicultural model of openness and tolerance. Humanitarian aid is not enough. Assistance must extend to the re-establishment of effective government (Boutros-Ghali 1995:9). A comprehensive strategy has been advocated in which preventive diplomacy and confidence building are seen as part of a wider attempt to institutionalise democracy and pluralism as the best means of regulating ethno-nationalist conflict (Suhrke 1994:32).

The role of OSCE in Bosnia, in supporting democratic elections and a plural civil society, is an example of the pursuit of a comprehensive strategy. In many respects, such an approach can be seen as a response to one of the major criticisms of the humanitarian phase in Bosnia. That is, that it lacked a political vision. While this could be argued, a little care needs to be exercised. Much of the criticism levelled at Western policy was aimed at its failure to act against identifiable aggressors. In supporting the development of plural civil institutions and democratic elections, a political vision, as such, is still not being articulated. Like structural adjustment, it is more the case that a single abstract solution is being advocated to solve a concrete problem that is poorly understood. The mandate of OSCE, for example, in common with most negotiated programmes, expressly stipulates that its involvement is non-political and support is given to all groups within civil society, that is, to both winners and losers. Rather than a political vision, what is being established is a technical process. For most supporters of the transition argument, this technical process is sufficient to overcome the political problems of ethno-nationalism and social exclusion.

Civil Society as Service Delivery

The Balkan crisis was one of a series of recent major events that have helped to stimulate and change the non-governmental sector. Many new international NGOs (INGOs) were formed as a result. The crisis, together with the nature of the international intervention, also encouraged the growth of local NGOs (LNGOs) in societies where the voluntary sector had previously been limited and mainly confined to professional and cultural associations.

The concept of so-called civil society plays an important, indeed central, role in Western transition and security policy. Its under-theorisation and the absence of any shared or accepted meaning, especially among NGOs, is therefore all the more notable. Nonetheless, as Stubbs (1995) has pointed out, to mention civil society in some way, whether its strengthening, deepening or whatever, has now become obligatory in all NGO or research projects. This requirement, in the absence of concrete meaning, reflects the potent symbolic role of civil society. It becomes the idealised space between the family and the state: the arena of free association of citizens' groups and associations. It is the natural repository of plural and democratic values and, as such, a counterbalance to the state. It represents an idealised duality of society and state. Rather than existing in Western Europe or America, this notion of civil society was rejuvenated in the West's confrontation with the Europe's planned economies and, more recently, the ethnocentric and authoritarian political projects that have largely replaced them.

In the Balkan region, the growth of civil society has been closely associated with emergence of LNGOs and international welfare intervention. Indeed, reflecting the uncertainties with the concept, in practical terms civil society and the non-governmental sector have become interchangeable (Duffield 1996). In other words, while civil society may aspire to be an arena of free association and plural values, in its actually existing form, it is circumscribed by the service-delivery activities of competing private agencies. From this perspective, civil society is of recent origin. Indeed, it dates from the outbreak of war in 1992. Owing to the concentration of the international aid effort in Croatia during the stage of open fighting, LNGO-based civil society is more developed there. Since 1995, however, the LNGO sector has begun a period of rapid expansion in Bosnia.

Compared with the high hopes placed on it by the new aid paradigm, civil society, as based on LNGOs in the Balkan region, is a weak and divided structure (Stubbs 1996, Duffield 1996). An important aspect of this weakness is the dependence of LNGOs, especially in their attempts to broaden their activities, on INGOs and donor governments. This dependence has important financial aspects and these will be discussed below. Its ideological and political dimensions need to be mentioned first, however.

From Social Movements to Regulatory Agencies

As well as relief INGOs, the humanitarian phase in the Balkan crisis also saw the emergence of international NGOs more interested in supporting conflict resolution, the independent media and civil society: a group of activities that can be described as social reconstruction. Strictly speaking, many of these agencies were, initially at least, not NGOs. They had their origin, for example, in the West European social-democratic, women's and peace movements (Stubbs 1996; Duffield 1996). For such groups, the Balkan crisis and the depth of suffering it involved was a turning point. The end of the cold war and collapse of the Soviet Union undermined the dynamic and rationale of these social movements. The Balkan war, however, together with the indecision of donor governments and the UN, helped redefine their sense of direction.

Redefining the mission of Western critical social movements involved a process that drew together several of the themes discussed above, especially that of internalisation. Just as negotiated access opened the way for humanitarian agencies to work in ongoing conflict, the redefinition of security in terms of the nature and quality of domestic relations has provided new opportunities for those interested in social reconstruction. The changing OSCE framework and the delineation of a human dimension to peace and security has been welcomed by most NGOs. They have been able to expand their role from external lobbying and providing indirect support. The new human dimension, and especially donor willingness to fund activity in this sphere, means that such agencies can now become directly involved in social and political change in their own right.

In response to this opportunity, many Western social movements, for example, in Sweden, have formed INGOs to support LNGOs in social reconstruction work (Stubbs 1996, Duffield 1996). In most cases, this process of INGO formation has involved setting up organisations to act as sponsor, conduit and monitoring body for donor government funding. For many, this has been celebrated as the formation of transnational society and the emergence of a global civil society. If nothing else, it graphically reflects the changing architecture of the state in core and periphery regions. The opportunity afforded to the critical social movements has, however, involved a major transformation of their role. That is, from a critical social movement to technical regulatory agency. It is a transformation that involves contradictory tendencies. While INGOs proclaim their critical, democratic and empowerment activities, they simultaneously subordinate the implementing bodies that are subject to the deregulation of welfare and social security and the 'privatization of social and ecological problems' (Demirović 1996).

The changing nature of security is a good example of this transformation. During the cold war, when security was regarded as an interstate matter, Western social movements were often critical of governmental positions. Indeed, this role played an important role by helping to maintain public concern. The redefinition of security as a problem of internal relations, however, and the involvement of INGOs in strengthening pluralism and civil society, has radically changed this situation. Rather than being critical social movements, INGOs and their activities have become an organic part of Western security policy. Critical discourse has given way to a search for technical solutions. If one couples this transformation with the collapse of academic endeavour into the NGO agenda in an attempt to remain relevant (Edwards 1993), the movement is symptomatic of a general decline of independent and critical research in the West. The irony is that this reduction could hardly have come at a worse time.

An important aspect of the regulatory role of INGOs lies in the selection of what LNGOs to sponsor or support. Usually the criteria for selection are informal and rarely codified. They reflect the multicultural ethos of the Western liberalism which, as noted above, is seen as the blueprint for transitional political structures. If LNGOs, therefore, hope to receive external support it is better that they reflect this Western ideal: that is, to have an open or plural organisation, to be gender-relevant or, if such things are not physically possible, to at least clearly profess support for such values. This is not to argue that aid agencies should support LNGOs that preach ethnic separatism. Nor is it doubted that many LNGOs genuinely hold plural values. Rather, it is that the multicultural ethos has become an informal screening device. Moreover, LNGOs are advised to learn 'aid-speak' if they hope to succeed. Once INGOs are satisfied, however, that these loose criteria are met, they rarely enquire further.

Actually Existing Civil Society

LNGOs in Croatia and Bosnia are dependent on external support. By extension one could say the same of civil society. The nature of this support directly shapes some of the main contradictions within actually existing civil society. Donor governments and INGOs prefer not only to support those LNGOs that profess a multicultural and gendered ethos; they also tend to favour the more vocal and articulate. In other words, active and campaigning LNGOs. Within ethnically exclusivist states and, especially, as in the Balkan region, when the legal and fiscal status of the non-governmental sector is problematic, this support is tantamount to the encouragement of a *de facto* political opposition. This situation is reflected in the antagonism and suspicion which characterises state and NGO relations in Croatia and Bosnia.[3]

The propensity to fund active and articulate LNGOs tends to favour some organisations over others. Rather than a diverse range of organisations and bodies, this has encouraged fewer and larger LNGOs providing a relatively small range of services. For example, psycho-social support work in Croatia (Stubbs 1996). Moreover, this same trend has tended to encourage an urban and middle class bias among LNGOs. It should be noted that official donor aid, for example, IMF or World Bank assistance, is not directed toward LNGOs and civil society but to the governments in the region. In this manner, Western aid policy, rather than promoting openness, could be argued to be funding extremes (Duffield 1996): that is, encouraging the emergence of two opposed camps which communicate little and have even less regard for one another. In Croatia, at least, this trend has contributed to moderate opinion being squeezed out of actually existing civil society.[4]

In relation to social reconstruction, external support can be said to reinforce internal divisions. Important in this respect is the distinction between those INGOs originating from a social democratic tradition on the one hand, and the peace and women's movements on the other. While there are important overlaps, for example, support for conflict resolution; within Croatia and Bosnia, INGOs have usually encouraged like-minded LNGOs. The social democratic tradition, for example, has favoured independent trade unions, people's assemblies, and so on, which take a more direct, even traditional view of political action. On the other hand, INGOs from the peace and women's movements are likely to support the anti-political alternative, that is, the human rights, gender and ecologically aware networks that disavow the state and anything to do with it. These two traditions disagree on many important issues – not least, the nature and role of politics.

While the external funding regime tends to favour some LNGOs over others, it must be stated that the LNGO sector generally is weak and divided. In Croatia and Bosnia a few LNGOs can trace their origins to Yugoslavian cultural and professional associations. Most, however, emerged during the war in relation to peace and media campaigning, together with welfare and humanitarian provision. In adjusting to the present situation, LNGOs that wish to continue are faced with the need to deepen and professionalise their activities. They are handicapped in this by a number of factors. For example, international assistance for LNGOs is both transitory and uneven. By early 1996, INGOs had left Croatia, either to establish themselves in Bosnia, or to move to other theatres of operation. This departure served both to highlight the trend to encourage extremes and to arouse concern about the sustainability of the non-governmental sector. In Bosnia, while donor funding is currently more readily available, a long-term international interest cannot be taken for granted.

The LNGO sector in Croatia and Bosnia is intrinsically weak. Not only does it lack official recognition, but it also mainly exists through the efforts of volunteers. Paid staff are few, and of these, those that contribute to pension and insurance schemes are even fewer. The external funding regime has tended to encourage this situation. Donor funding usually covers only direct project costs. There is an expectation that overheads and other running costs will be met by the LNGO. Given the depth of the economic crisis and the lack of official support for the non-governmental sector, this is a big assumption, and tends to reinforce the voluntary and under-resourced character of LNGOs. While private welfare provision and a strong civil society could be argued to be central to Western policy, in practice, no one is prepared to meet its real costs.

The precarious financial position of the non-governmental sector is a factor that promotes competition between LNGOs for donor funding.

Rather than treat civil society as an arena of open exchange, restricted funding makes for secrecy and discourages collaboration. Funding sources are often seen as things best kept confidential. Even when LNGOs form networks, when different agencies are funded by different donors this can work against cooperation. There are a number of such LNGO networks in Croatia and Bosnia. Rather than improving coordination, such networks have been encouraged by the NGO registration procedures. It is easier for an LNGO to obtain government registration if it can claim to be an affiliate of an already registered agency.

Social Reconstruction and Conflict Resolution

Actually existing civil society is fraught with problems of both a conceptual and a practical nature. Nonetheless, great development and security hopes are riding on it. In Bosnia and Croatia, the most immediate challenge of civil society is helping to reintegrate returning refugees and internally displaced peoples as part of the process of peace and reconciliation.

In Bosnia, in particular, this represents a massive problem and one on which the Dayton agreement could easily fall. There are around a million refugees living outside Bosnia, most within other European countries, and about 1.7 million, or half the remaining population, internally displaced within it. Without a significant return and reintegration, most local commentators are of the opinion that Bosnia will not be able to exist as an independent country (Forum of Tuzla Citizens 1995). Apart from anything else, the refugees contain a disproportionate number of skilled and professional people. Attempts at reintegration, however, are tantamount to reversing much of the ethnic cleansing for which the war was fought.

NGOs are attempting to play a role in trying to reduce tension and promote social reintegration. Many LNGOs are active in attempting to build confidence between communities. It is also the case that INGOs have often added conflict resolution work to the range of services that they offer. There are a number of levels at which this type of activity is taking place, for example, conferences and networking between the urban and intellectual elites of the successor states. At a local level, some LNGOs are supporting exchanges to build confidence between adjoining communities. INGOs have also begun to train LNGO staff and other professional groups, such as teachers and social workers, in methods and techniques of conflict resolution.

I-For, and subsequently S-For, through increasing the scope for free movement within Bosnia, has made many of these measures possible. While some local improvements have been made feasible by increased movement between entities, the general approach to conflict resolution and peace-building needs some comment. Following the psycho-social work on trauma, conflict resolution among both INGOs and LNGOs is heavily influenced by psychology. Like trauma, it usually centres on the individual. One begins with the individual, and, by building confidence between individuals and then groups, peace-building moves outwards and upwards.[5] From this perspective, conflict is seen as resulting from a breakdown in communication between individuals and groups. In a period of tension, misunderstandings develop and compound each other until breaking point is reached (Greek *et al.* 1995). In contrast to new barbarism, however, the essentially multicultural solution is implied in the analysis: exchanges, workshops and training programmes to give individuals and groups both the opportunities and tools to improve communication.

The attempt by INGOs in Bosnia to train professional groups in conflict resolution techniques is typical of this approach. Such groups are regarded as 'opinion formers' within the community and therefore able to exert a moderating influence. In the case of American INGOs, the reliance on problem-solving techniques developed in the business world is noticeable (Duffield 1996:38). The approach involves variations on the teaching of 'life-skills'. For example, how to create a partnership atmosphere between rivals; redefining problems as joint problems; clarifying perceptions; developing power 'with' rather than 'against' scenarios, etc.[6] The methodology of many LNGOs within the region, including church-based groups, is essentially the same (for example, Greek, *et al.* 1995).

The logic of seeing political violence in terms of the individual and communication breakdown is that ethnic cleansing and the war become a form of mistake, something that started in a series of misunderstandings that were allowed to get out of hand. This approach ignores the issue of the war economy and the rationality of conflict, or, moreover, that the primordialist projects of the successor states were consciously orchestrated by the intellectual and political elites. In other words, it cannot see war and protracted crisis as a means to an end. The conflict resolution approach is not only breathtakingly naïve, it is also insulting in its ignorance to those many people who have suffered during the conflict. If conflict resolution is so far off the mark, one may wonder why does it currently attract so much donor attention?

Conflict resolution is essentially non-political: the epitome of the technical fix. By focusing on the individual it does not challenge the *status quo*. In this manner it answers an essential requirement of the new aid and security paradigm, namely, that international intervention is only with the agreement of local political actors. Moreover, it is cheap while promising a good deal. For LNGOs working in an authoritarian environment, conflict resolution also has advantages. It attracts external funding while not threatening the ability to continue working. By focusing on the individual, the approach also allows aid agencies to blame the victim if things go wrong: they must not have paid enough attention in class. In February 1997, for example, in one of the worst pogroms since the end of the war, elderly Muslims were forced from West Mostar by Croatian police, despite 'millions of dollars and dozens of projects' having been deployed to bring the two communities together.[7]

The Absence of Conditionality

What practical success this technical and multicultural focus of the new aid and security paradigm can achieve is questionable. Even the apparently political focus of such institutions as OSCE, however, are weakened by the difficulty of operationalising conditionality within the new paradigm. Based on an agreement with the Bosnian government, OSCE is attempting to provide a neutral but supportive framework in which the competing forces of civil society can participate in the democratic process. The element of conditionality within the OSCE framework relates to its potential for mobilising international pressure if human rights or electoral issues are not as they should be. In theory, nascent civil society is afforded some protection.

Reflecting the new paradigm, the OSCE approach is based on the assumption that Bosnia, together with the other successor states, is in the process of transition to a liberal democracy. Ethnic exclusivism and the war are unfortunate but temporary steps in this transition. There is an inbuilt tendency within this position to give the state the benefit of the doubt. Western governments, moreover, do not want to be permanently involved in the region. In other words, there is pressure to 'normalise' the situation as quickly as possible. This relates to the contradictory effects of the aid programme mentioned above. That is, official aid supports the states, while welfare and social reconstruction assistance is encouraging the formation of a *de facto* LNGO opposition. Pressure to normalise the situation, however, has tended to leave isolated and vulnerable those among this opposition who are seeking justice and genuine political change. In giving the state the benefit of the doubt, Western governments have weakened what credibility the OSCE framework had. Accusations of abuse and misconduct in the September 1996 elections, for example, have been played down in favour of *realpolitik* and support for state partnership.[8]

This contradiction indicates the gulf at the heart of the new aid paradigm. While seeking technical and multicultural solutions on the ground, politicians are either unaware, or do not want to know, about its potential to encourage a *de facto* opposition. In the attempt by diplomats to secure regional alliances in support of wider peace strategies, this local

opposition is continually undermined and weakened. Part of this difficulty lies in the split between development and political functions among
Western governments. While the new paradigm might be forcing development and security issues to merge, in practice they remain largely the
separate and mutually suspicious worlds of the career diplomat and aid
worker. In short, while the new aid paradigm has cast a strong civil society as essential for a transition to liberal democracy and Western security, international intervention has, so far, produced an essentially weak,
divided and vulnerable non-governmental sector – a sector, moreover,
that is concerned mainly with the impossible task of reducing political
problems to technical solutions.

CONCLUSION

Emerging out of the novelty of the immediate post-cold-war situation,
the humanitarian phase in international relations is now over. The end
of the cold war allowed a temporary period in which a critical analysis of
the character of internal relations within the periphery was possible. Such
an analysis is vital if the emergence of countervailing political projects
are to be encouraged. While imperfect, the demise of UN-led military
humanitarianism marks the closure of this window of opportunity. In both
Africa and Europe, regardless of actually existing conditions, the reconstruction phase has been ushered, indeed, forced in. What ever the underlying conditions, the situation has been decreed to be normal and aid
workers and political actors left to take their allotted positions on the
development and transitional ladder.

The new aid and security paradigm has an historical momentum and
inner logic. It is an attempt to internalise the problems of political instability in an increasingly divided world. Of itself, the shift of responsibility
to local actors is no bad thing. The dominant move toward internalisation, however, also involves relativisation. Rather than political analysis,
the problems of the periphery are lost in pluralism and reduced to technical issues. It is only in this manner that the increasing global polarisation can be rationalised. Thus, while the new aid and security paradigm
has a certain dynamic, it is also flawed and dangerous.

The basic question is this: are the ethnic and politically exclusivist states
that are emerging in the periphery a phase along the path to development and liberal democracy, or, alternatively, are they new social and
political formations adapted to exist on the margins of the global economy?
The new paradigm would hold with the former view. If it is wrong, however, it would mean that politicians, policy makers and aid workers are
not even asking the right questions, let alone providing the answers. Is

this the reason why, despite the increasing intervention in protracted crises and multiplication of the actors involved, so little real or original knowledge is being produced? The plural and technosist hegemony is all the more worrying in this respect.

The extent of this hegemony is reflected in the now obligatory requirement to make recommendations on how the situation can be improved, the implication being: unless you know a better way of doing it, keep quiet. This attitude needs to be challenged. There are no technical solutions for political problems (Edkins 1996). It is only as an ethical and political project that the issues of polarisation, exclusion and instability can be addressed. This project, moreover, links together both the core and the periphery. The trend toward social polarisation is general within the West and its sphere of influence. So too is the changing role of the state and the privatisation of welfare and security. In many respects, internal and external social and public policy reflect each other. In other words, if one is being realistic, it is only when the West begins to put its own house in order and reduce internal inequalities that one can expect a meaningful change in the external aid paradigm.

Resistance to providing dubious recommendations, to make the new aid paradigm more technically effective, does not extend to the research agenda. Both the line of closure and the insistence that, in the last analysis, the problem is political, indicates the nature of such an agenda. In the first place, it must seek to expose at every turn the conventional view that the current situation in the periphery is somehow normal. Attention must be directed to the nature of parallel or war economies and their relationship to politics and external assistance. This would include how commercial assistance, humanitarian aid, privatisation and democratisation have been appropriated by political elites and reworked as new systems of political exclusion and ethno-centric expression. In other words, political projects in the periphery have to be studied and analysed with far greater attention than they currently receive.

At the same time, if the problem is political and not technical, then the whole issue of the changing nature of politics in the present stage of the world-system comes centre-stage. At a time of increasing global polarisation and the decline, at least in the West, of the nation-state the political position of NGOs and the critical social movements must be examined. While often cited as the basis of a new transnational society, the trend for incorporation and the reappearance of such movements as regulatory bodies also seems real. The problem that a radical research agenda must face is that the declining role of the state has given rise to a new system of global governance. A system, moreover, that might use the populist environmental, gender and rights language of the alternative, but could be just as restrictive as the system it is replacing. Redefining progressive

146 *Lunching with Killers*

politics when transnational linkages are growing, at a time when state authority is being redefined both upwards and downwards, is the challenge of the moment.

Notes

1. Julian Borger, 'Dayton's First Year Reveals Cracks in the Fragile Facade of Peace', *Guardian*, 4 December 1996, p. 12.
2. John Palmer, 'War Crimes "Downgraded"', *The Guardian*, 5 December 1996, p. 13.
3. Ian Traynor, 'Soros Buys Hatred in East', *Guardian*, 20 January1997, p. 8.
4. Interview with Nenada Vukman, Croatian League for Peace, Zagreb, 2 October 1996.
5. Interview with representative of the ICVA, Tuzla, 6 October 1996.
6. Interview with Jacqueline Kearns, Psycho-Social Program, World Vision International, Sarejevo, 10 October 1996.
7. Julian Borger, 'Croatian Police Force Out Muslims', *Guardian*, 12 February 1997, p. 2.
8. Julian Borger, 'West "Covering Up Mass Fraud in Bosnian Polls"', *Guardian*, 24 September 1996, pp. 1, 11.

6 Nothing from Nothing is Nothing: Privatisation, Price Liberalisation and Poverty in the Yugoslav Successor States

Boris Young

The Yugoslav successor states now share the problems of other, formerly communist, states as well as the consequences of some particularly unpleasant wars. They must all find a way to overcome their internal imbalances, develop effective and efficient production, and establish a place for themselves in highly competitive and often protectionist world markets. To do so, the Yugoslav successor states are effectively limited to two major models on which to reorganise their economies. One of these, the neo-liberal model based on neo-classical economics, is largely geared to the needs of international capital markets. It is also the official ideology of globalisation promoted by international financial institutions such as the International Monetary Fund (IMF) and the World Bank. So, in the Yugoslav successor states as in much of the rest of Eastern Europe, the tendency has been to replace the political monopoly of the communist party with the conceptual monopoly of the market (Amsden *et al.* 1994, Sadowski 1991, Toye 1987). By way of contrast, successful East Asian efforts to enter the world market have not been so ideologically limited and have included the construction of institutions and organisations capable of promoting and directing investment, trade, technological development and expansionary macroeconomic policy, often through the state (Amsden 1989, Wade 1993, Wade 1996). This other main model – the model of the production and trade-based economy demonstrated by the Asian High Performance Economies (HPAEs) less concerned with neo-liberal ideology than with results – is heavily oriented to successful export production rather than to the needs of international capital.

The neo-liberal 'market friendly' model favoured by the international financial institutions, which set the pace for other agencies and governments assisting in reconstruction or aid in the former Yugoslavia, is based on 'getting the prices right'. This approach has been used in the rest of Eastern Europe with mixed results. Rather than finding a comfortable niche in the global economy East European economies continue to suffer serious 'transformation recessions' with shrinking output, uncertain exports, disrupted industrial supply networks, plummeting incomes, high unemployment levels, weak currencies and rising levels of absolute poverty (Kornai 1994). In many countries, including all the Yugoslav successor states, as production plummeted and regional markets collapsed, entrepreneurs took advantage of local conditions for short-term, often speculative, profits in black and transient luxury markets rather than in longer-term productive investment. As conditions worsen, there is a growing suspicion that something has been seriously wrong with the prescription offered by Western economists. Exploring this problem, this chapter sets out to review the experience of Latin America.[1]

IDEOLOGICAL ERROR

At the beginning of the transition in Eastern Europe, Lawrence Summers, then chief economist for the World Bank, commented that there was a high degree of consensus among economists about the essentials of market reform (Summers 1991, OECD 1991). Much of this consensus was on the need for the sort of shock therapy associated with the writings and policy prescriptions of Harvard's Jeffrey Sachs, and focused on the steps necessary to eliminate the old system and liberate the market forces assumed present but helpless under the old order (Sachs 1990, Lipton and Sachs 1990). While there was never any clear specification about measures by which to develop transitional economies, the consensus seems to have held, by implication, that sudden 'marketisation' would lead directly to sustained growth. The belief was that foreign investment and capital would support and promote privatisation and the development of modern efficient business enterprise, while small-scale manufacturing and service enterprises would absorb excess labour shed by privatised enterprises. All of these firms and their activities were to be disciplined by freely operating market forces. At the same time, anti-inflationary policies and devaluation were to provide a basis for dynamic entrepreneurs to establish a competitive presence in international markets. The source of this competitiveness was to be the low wages of its skilled workers[2] (Taylor 1987).

Very few of these expectations have been met. Eastern Europe has seen a persistent drop in living standards and economic output. Foreign investment has not arrived in the volume required nor had the effects predicted. Instead, the whole of post-communist Europe has become a backwater of the world economy, its industries shut down, its currencies worthless, its economies gutted, its societies strained to breaking point. Things have gone so obviously wrong that a United Nations–European Commission study found that these policy prescriptions '[M]ay reflect either a misunderstanding of the microfoundations or unforeseen external shocks. But there is a good case for the cock-up hypothesis: that those devising policies and forecasting their outcomes simply got the policies wrong' (Nuti and Portes 1993).

This may be because the World Bank and the IMF are currently run by a breed of economists dissatisfied with the failures of past well-funded projects to generate economic growth or transitions to a market society in many recipient countries. Market-based society, in their view, reflected the natural order and only needed to be freed of superfluous political shackles to bring about stable and growing economies (Lal 1983, Little 1982). Prices were the major tool in this liberation. If prices could function freely and without impediment then markets would naturally tend towards equilibrium. In neo-classical theory, prices are how the market manages to coordinate myriads of transactions and relationships. Prices are also the primary means by which the market manages to transfer information quickly and efficiently. Thus, the establishment of market equilibrium and 'clearing' markets not only depended on getting prices right but was in fact synonymous with such a policy (Toye 1987).

The only problem with the price-is-right approach is that empirical evidence does not support it. The application of the price approach to policy in Latin American reforms was uniformly disastrous. On the other hand, the east Asian HPAEs succeeded by deliberately getting the prices wrong (Amsden 1989).

The Latin American Example

In Latin America, the neo-liberal variant to neo-classical economics was used with some ferocity in the early 1980s, especially in Chile, Argentina and Uruguay (Ramos 1986, Foxely 1983). It is no accident that at the time of such applications each of these countries was under the heel of particularly nasty despotisms. Only a centralised state with no inhibitions about using coercion could have implemented the reforms that 'Chicago school' neo-classical economists favoured (O'Brien 1984, Sheahan 1980).

Latin America, unlike much of the rest of the world in which these kinds of 'marketizing' reforms were tried, had a long tradition of extensive marketisation. Many of the assumptions built into neo-classical economics had some sort of empirical referent here, so why did they not work as expected? After all, much of the impetus for applying the neo-classical model had come from conditions that on the whole were common to the less-developed world. These included idiosyncratic tariff systems, which might have saved on foreign exchange but had great long-term social costs; exchange rate controls; price controls which discouraged basic production; and subsidies including credits for specific industries and sectors which encouraged excessive capital investment and excess capacity construction. All of these conditions also held, or in some cases still hold, for the Yugoslav successor states.

It was forgotten that there were other conditions that had to be observed when talking about free market equilibrium. One of these conditions was that macro and micro economics are not the same thing. The clearest example of this was to search for equilibrium in specific markets rather than recognise the interconnection of the economy – that is, partial equilibrium rather than general equilibrium. None of the four major markets constituting the national market in any of the Latin American societies were in equilibrium during the time of maximal neo-classicism. The goods market was never in equilibrium because income was distributed upward to producers and away from consumers. This meant that goods prices did not come down with any great alacrity. Inflation was therefore followed by recession and stagnation. The labour market was not in equilibrium even as wages dropped to unheard-of levels. This was largely the case because unemployment was the result not of excessive prices demanded for labour but of lack of productive employment and consumer demand. The financial market was not in equilibrium as interest rates rose to ludicrous levels, reflecting very high demand for credit, related not to growth in the economy but largely to speculation. The foreign exchange market was never in equilibrium, because changes in currency valuation not only encouraged speculation, and in some cases capital flight, but also caused transitory surges of capital flows, sending shock waves into the economies and causing the prices of locally produced goods to fluctuate wildly (Ramos 1986).

Equilibrium and market clearing are not, despite neo-classical belief, the same thing. Different equilibria are possible but few of them are optimal. Neo-classical economists believe that it is prices that will always adjust and not some other aspect of exchange such as quantity (Wells 1991). As Keynes so clearly saw in an earlier period, it is perfectly possible for an economy or market be in equilibrium while stagnant.

The East Asian Example

By way of contrast, the huge success of East Asian economies appears to have been brought about largely because they pursued a policy of deliberately getting the prices wrong (Amsden 1989, Wade 1989, 1992). In this sense, East Asian economies – Taiwan, Korea, Hong Kong and, in its own way, Japan – followed policies in line with Keynesian (and Kaleckian) thought, in which prices were consequences of costs of production and policy, rather than being entirely set by the market.

The policies followed by these economies, according to Wade and others, targeted certain key industrial sectors and industries. Once targeted, these industries or sectors were the recipients of preferential financing and directed investment, often at very high levels. Selected enterprises then competed with each other for sales and effective production, but within the context of a state-set export plan. Although these companies had a fairly high level of international exposure, state policies existed that spread risks and allocated resources, especially investment funds (Amsden 1989, 1994a, Wade 1989, 1992, 1993).

These policies were centred on controlling the financial system – in particular, on capturing and subordinating private financial capital to planned industrial needs, maintaining a stable long-term price, interest, and exchange rate, by fiat if necessary, dampening the effects of foreign competition on the domestic economy, organising and ordering the use of foreign exchange, promoting organised technological acquisition and, of course, promoting organised exports (Amsden 1989, Wade 1993).

Certainly the success of the HPAEs can be traced to help from the US market and the fall-out from a quarter century of military and commercial involvement in Asia, but this was not the deciding factor. More interestingly, the East Asians pursued a concerted policy of economic growth and industrial development based on exports, while the Latin Americans did not or could not. In so doing, the Asians violated nearly every tenet of the neo-classical prescription. Rather than being freed, prices were kept stable. Tariffs on imports were kept high to protect domestic industries and the domestic market. Exchange rates were controlled and, although the local economies participated in the international economy, the international economy did not participate overly in the local economies. Rather than eliminating regulatory control over interest rates and credit, the state actively manipulated and controlled them. Domestic collusion that, from a theoretical perspective, obstructed the operation of market relations except for independent labour unions, were positively encouraged. Not only was the state central to coordination and organisation of the economy, but it exercised its functions through the manipulation of subsidies. In fact, subsidies, fiscal and monetary policy were all means to a particular end, namely economic growth and export expansion (Amsden 1989, Wade 1989, 1993, 1996).

As a consequence, the HPAEs were able to coordinate market segments such as labour, foreign exchange, goods, and finance. The state played an active and controlling part in the economy (Amsden 1989, 1994b, Wade 1996). Prices in these economies were useful, but certainly neither central nor controlling. Unlike either Yugoslavia or Latin America, the East Asian economies became the envy of all others, by ignoring neo-classical doctrine and idealist economics, in favour of results.

BEFORE THE FALL: THE YUGOSLAVIAN EXPERIENCE

Such an ideological predisposition might conceivably be excused as igno-rance in Poland or other economies in the Soviet sphere, but not in Yugoslavia. There, two major reform efforts, one in the period 1981–3 and the other in 1990 under then premier Ante Marković, offered clear evidence that the transition was going to be considerably more complex than claimed by the price-and-privatisation school.

The Yugoslav project after the Second World War was based on in-dustrialisation of a largely agrarian economy, soothing the ethnic con-flicts manifested during the war, and maintaining the political monopoly of the Yugoslav Communist Party (later the League of Communists of Yugoslavia).[3] Industrialisation, in Yugoslavia as in other socialist coun-tries, was the key to the whole project and capital investment was the key to industrialisation. Heavy capital investment from Western sources flowed in for years, in part to keep Yugoslavia out of the Soviet camp and in part because the country was seen as a stable investment. By the 1980s Yugoslavia had become a semi-industrialised country and was ex-porting chiefly machinery and machine products, including the much maligned Yugo car, and the output of a very active arms industry. It was also exporting construction and technical expertise to much of the devel-oping world, including the oil-producing countries. It was a national economy very open to the world economy, with its industrial base highly dependent on foreign imports (Woodward 1986).

Despite claims to 'market socialism', the Yugoslav economy was not based on the market or the operation of market forces. Instead, economy and society ran by capital investment, usually as access to development or commercial credit or foreign exchange. Enterprises and regions were then responsible for jobs, social services, housing and pensions and health care. Allocations were made by project and region as patronage through the agency of the LCY and its local representatives, in order to promote industrialisation, create and incorporate a working class from a largely agrarian population, and undercut the appeal of 'ethnic' forms of social mobilisation (Schierup 1992, Young 1992).

This program, sometimes called 'workers' self-management', worked well if not smoothly, but constant infusions of capital or credit were re-quired and the various regions soon developed interests of their own. In the resulting politics, the LCY became less a national party then an agglomeration of regional parties representing regional patrons and their interests (Dyker 1990). By 1981, the Yugoslav current accounts balance and overall balance of payments (BOP) deficits, at a time when loans needed to be rescheduled, brought them to the attention of the IMF. The Yugoslavs considered their deficits to be temporary problems to be solved by a short term reorientation of resources from domestic investment to export. The IMF considered them signs of structural inefficiency of the Yugoslav economy.

Both external and internal conditions were also unfavourable during the early 1980s. World trade was down, largely because of very high interest rates, and several Latin American countries were threatening to default on their loans. Solidarity had been banned in Poland, and the Soviet Union had invaded Afghanistan. Lending to Eastern Europe or any communist country was a difficult proposition (Fallon and Shirreff 1982). Worse than that, an ideological revolution had taken place, in both the IMF and the World Bank, favouring highly conservative economic ideologies (Sadowski 1991).

In order to arrange any kind of financing or refinancing to keep its economy going, Yugoslavia had to submit to IMF-sponsored reforms under the new stabilisation and structural adjustment conditions (Nelson 1986, Taylor 1988). These reforms required currency devaluations, a massive redirection of resources away from domestic capital investment and to external creditors, removal of subsidies for salaries and operating costs, freeing interest rates and similar reforms.[4] The result was chaos, not because marketising reforms were not fully implemented but because they were wildly inappropriate to actual Yugoslav conditions. The dinar became nearly worthless and increasingly slighted in favour of the Deutschmark or the US dollar. Liquidity disappeared, prices soared, wages fell, industry faltered, living standards dropped and a serious political crisis set in (Samary 1995).

More seriously, the economies of republics and localities fragmented as patronage ties that had been inclusive now became exclusive. In the face of declining financial resources, stagnant capital investment, a federal government that was no longer allocative but promoted austerity, and a fragmented communist party, the Yugoslav project faltered. Regional or republican ethnic chauvinism became more pronounced as an alternative means of justifying localistic claims on resources and especially finance in an increasingly hollow economy (Samary 1995).

By the early 1990s, the situation was, if anything, worse. Eastern Europe, the Soviet Union, Iraq and Kuwait, all major trading partners during the 1980s, were no longer so. Eastern Europe had bailed out of the communist experiment in 1989. The Soviet Union fell apart in 1991. At the same time, Kuwait was invaded and gutted by Iraq. Iraq was isolated and broken by the US and allies. The Yugoslavs were left holding the bag while facing the prospect of a protectionist European Union after 1992 ending at their border.

It was at this time, in the face of economic disaster and rising ethnic nationalism in Serbia, Croatia, Slovenia and Kosovo, that the government of Prime Minister Ante Marković, with the backing of international financial agencies, chose to implement another austerity and marketisation reform plan including privatisation (Yugoslav Survey 1990). In a capital-starved economy, price liberalisation and privatisation is no recipe for stability. It is instead a signal for a bitter struggle to amass and control resources by elites. With the addition of currency devaluation, subsidy removal, wage decline, and falling levels of employment, such reforms open the way for a Hobbesian struggle between the desperate and the doomed.

Secession from Yugoslavia was now not just possible but mandatory (Samary 1995). The economic costs of secession were nonetheless very high but unevenly distributed among all the former Yugoslav republics in lost trade, lost production, subsidised resources, market losses, high unemployment, and monetary revaluation, not to mention appalling wars (Uvalić 1992).

AFTER THE FALL: THE YUGOSLAV SUCCESSOR STATES

In the face of the spectre of Latin America, the questionable effects of neo-liberal policies in the rest of Eastern Europe, and the experience of former Yugoslavia, it might be expected that policies of privatisation, price liberalisation, limited capital investment, low wages and austerity would be reconsidered. Unfortunately, current evidence shows no sign of a retreat from ideological free-marketism on the part of international financial agencies. The record of policies in the Yugoslav successor states, especially since the Dayton Agreement brought putative peace to the region and opened the way to normalisation of local societies, is not encouraging. Privatisation requires capital and there is precious little of it to be had.

Ironically, the Yugoslav successor states may not be able to reap any of the benefits of the neo-liberal approach for the same reasons that they cannot adopt the HPAE approach: their politics and especially their state sectors are too weak. None of the new states, except possibly Slovenia, can consistently supply even the minimum public goods, such as law and order, contract enforcement, public safety or a stable banking system, that the neo-liberal theory requires, let alone the kind of interventionism, labor discipline or industrial policy required by the HPAE model.

In fact, the Yugoslav successor states are less concerned with theoretical purity than with doing whatever is necessary to attract and extract capital. They are, thus, doing separately the same thing they were doing collectively when they were still republics of old Yugoslavia. To that end, new central banks have been created but, in a capital shortage economy, have only a tenuous grip on monetary or fiscal policy. The needs of finance, as embodied in the central bank, and the needs of industry for increased operating credit are constantly in conflict. At the same time, policies of privatisation and price liberalisation taken to reach some point of competitive advantage in world markets do not work because there is insufficient capital to privatise the economy. Nor will half-measures such as distributing vouchers to the population serve to raise any new capital. Despite price liberalisation there are still few markets for products of any of the former Yugoslav states except possibly some raw materials such as food crops, lumber or minerals. Without such markets there is no advantage to Yugoslavia's pool of skilled but cheap labour.

Now that Yugoslavia has disintegrated, its successor states must decide how to compete and survive as small economies on the edge of the European Union, largely redundant to the world economy, often in political uncertainty, damaged by war and suffering enormous capital shortages. The economic costs of secession were unevenly distributed but very high in lost trade, lost production, lost markets, lost subsidised resources, and high unemployment among all the former Yugoslav republics (Uvalić 1992). Worst of all, none of the new Yugoslav successor states started clean: all were saddled with varying portions of the Yugoslav international debt as determined by the IMF.[5]

Nor have any of the new states managed to escape either the macroeconomic crisis or the stagnation trap largely responsible for the fragmentation of the old Yugoslavia. The high inflation rates, an unsustainable balance of payments, and huge fiscal imbalances characteristic of a macroeconomic crisis are all still there, as are the slow growth, high unemployment rates and declining living standards characteristic of a stagnation trap (Solimano 1994).

SLOVENIA

Slovenia is generally recognised as the most successful of the Yugoslav successor states and the one in which the neo-liberal program has been most fully implemented. Slovenia established an independent central bank fairly quickly, promoted unstinting 'hard money' policies, restructured its external debts, and kept wages from rising too much. It has managed to reorient its trade towards Europe and away from the Balkans even though much of that trade goes to the Central European countries such as Hungary and the Czech and Slovak Republics. Slovenia may soon be admitted to the European Union as well, although on what basis is not yet clear (Kraft 1995).

The price for this success has been a drop in industrial output and relatively high and persistent unemployment. The economy is short of capital, there is no massive foreign investment but there is a large foreign debt. As of late 1995 this debt was about US$2.96 billion of which 98 per cent is long-term debt. Overall, Slovenia owes about US$500 million to various international financial agencies, about $200 million in sovereign debt to the Paris Club group of lending governments, and about US$430 million to the London Club group of commercial lenders. In addition, to cement its ties to world financial markets, Slovenia also had to assume its share of the foreign debt of the former Yugoslavia.[6]

To service these debts as well as to improve local living standards, Slovenia must expand its own economy and promote foreign trade. At this point, however, there is a conflict between the imperatives of the IMF/World Bank neo-liberal model. On the one hand, the Slovenian central bank has maintained a very tight monetary policy in part to keep inflation down and maintain the stability of a Slovenian toler that has been fully convertible only since September 1995. In pursuit of this policy, the bank has also maintained very tight restriction on the influx of foreign capital. This has put it into direct conflict with the insistence by business and industry on the need for external capital to maintain and expand the economy.

In the absence of foreign capital, privatisation, like the Slovenian economy, must run on limited domestic capital. Despite the privatisation of many former state enterprises, including the partial privatisation of Ljubljana airport, privatisation is in trouble. Most companies being privatised have no assets to privatise. By the end of 1996, the Slovenian stock exchange had only 25 fully listed companies with another 27 trading over the counter, but lacked liquidity to expand further no matter what is privatised. There is simply not enough domestic capital.

Privatisation also promotes increasing concentration of existing capital, as when the Kolinska food conglomerate acquired the Rogarski Vrelci mineral water company from the state enterprise Rogarska Slatina and inherited a sizable portion of the Slovenian mineral water market. The absence of domestic capital was underscored when profitable Kolinska itself was privatised and found there were no takers for its shares on the Slovenian exchange. Instead of a windfall for capitalists, there was widespread worry that the volume of Kolinska shares would soak up scarce capital and drive down the prices of other shares.

By the end of 1996 the social and political tensions brought on by the marketisation program could no longer be ignored. Stagnant wages and employer pressures to cut back on permissible strikes and work benefits had led to waves of strikes and work stoppages. By the November elections, the Liberal Democrats under Janež Drnovšek had been forced to slow economic reforms and promise a 14 per cent wage increase. Even so, the Liberal Democrats maintained their position as the strongest political party by a very narrow 27 per cent of the vote. To govern, they will likely have to ally with the People's Party, formerly the Slovenian Farmers Union, which held 20 per cent of the vote. Such an alliance may be stormy, since the People's Party opposes much of the neo-liberal program and has promised investigations into irregularities in privatisation. The pace of both privatisation, which was already in the doldrums, and further marketisation is likely to slow down even more. This raises the question of whether the neo-liberal program has been played out in Slovenia, and if so, what will take its place and who will be its protagonists?

CROATIA

At first glance Croatia seemed to be well placed to try an HPAE approach to global integration. Because of war conditions, the state is still a prime economic agent and most industries are dependent on patronage links and state contracts. Official prices were set more or less directly by state decree. Wages were low even though strikes and strike threats were frequent. Large enterprises organised along wartime (and earlier) patronage networks exerted much influence on economic policy. This was especially true for the state oil company INA, which was widely regarded as a sinecure for HDZ loyalists. INA also served as a useful conduit for foreign exchange and military supplies, including weapons, during wars in Slavonia and Bosnia (Kraft 1995). Even though Croatia entered the IMF and the World Bank in 1992 it did not immediately promote the standard reform package. Despite stabilisation measures taken to offset raging inflation in 1993, the National Bank of Croatia still has only limited independence

Following the Bosnian-Croat federation agreement in late 1993 and the subsequent large-scale entry of the United States into the Balkan equation, marketisation increased. Still, powerful opposition to the standard IMF model existed largely among manufacturing enterprises, the agrarian sector, and within the government. These put forward a program of public spending and domestic investment in infrastructure and especially in road improvement that would address unemployment and use local skills, especially among demobilised troops.

The US presence as well as that of I-For and various UN missions eased, overall, Croatian foreign exchange difficulties as did the influx of foreign currency from emigre sources. While the kuna is regarded as overvalued at K3.7 to DM1, it was holding stable at the end of 1996. As a sign that Croatia had arrived, a McDonald's restaurant opened in Zagreb in early 1996. Problems, due to outstanding debt, low foreign capital investment, little domestic capital, low wages and living standards, and high unemployment, persist.

Capital and State

Despite these potentially favorable conditions, Croatia is more likely to follow the Latin American than the HPAE path for two major reasons. The first is the structural weakness of the state and the second is the need for large capital influxes currently available only from the IMF and World Bank and geared more to the needs of international financial markets than domestic production

Croatia's apparent political stability is an illusion. In practice, the Croatian state is held together through the person of Franjo Tuđman. While Tuđman is in power, the HDZ can afford to ignore evidence of political opposition or any divergence of interests within the HDZ itself. Thus, issues such as the victory of anti-HDZ opposition candidates for control of the Zagreb city council and for seats in parliament can be dismissed by fiat, but there is no way of knowing for how long. It is unlikely that these conflicts or the ones in Tuđman's own circle of mostly emigré advisors, and so a major crisis of the state, can be avoided for long after Tuđman.

At the same time the most important divergence of interests is probably that between domestic industries and other reconstruction efforts and the demands of the international financial agencies for greater marketisation, privatisation, and globalisation of the Croatian economy. Domestic political forces also tend to follow this division with established industries favoring reconstruction and a greater role for the state while newer smaller enterprises fighting for market space as well as the fledgling commercial banking sector back greater marketisation.

Capital

The struggle for capital, and its political implications, becomes clear when considering the 1996 Croatian state budget plan. Out of an overall 36 billion kunas (about DM10 billion) the government plans to spend 33 billion, mostly on reconstruction and roads, while military spending is cut by about 15 per cent. Some 29 billion in revenue was to come from taxes while the rest was to be financed by loans, the sale of Eurobonds, and the proceeds from the privatisation of state assets. The fledgling commercial banking sector and some smaller enterprises charge that the plan is full of irregularities and unwarranted assumptions about revenues and production. Although these forces favor a shift of resources away from the military, they favor a shift to investment rather than direct reconstruction. Rather than spending K1.2 billion on roads they favor support for privatisation and small company development. The opposition uses the rhetoric of privatisation and marketisation to promote their own interests and expand their control over existing assets through privatisation of state resources. Advocating marketising reforms marks them out as allies of international financial agencies and so legitimates their claims on any future foreign capital inflows.

An uneasy balance is maintained in the 1997 proposed budget, but it has caused problems in Croatia's relations with the IMF. The government will funnel resources from a slightly higher level of public spending to ailing industries like shipbuilding and textiles, but will also cut tax rates and aid the banking industry.[7] This last is an attempt to improve access to consumer and business credit for the middle class and hard-pressed smaller businesses. There are also provisions for slightly increased wages and social spending. All this on top of some K4.3 billion (more than DM1 billion) in capital investment.

Debt

The Croatian national bank and the IMF are opposed to this new budget because of the problematic assumptions about increased state revenues even after tax cuts on which the budget is based and because of fears of increased external debt. This last fear is not unfounded. Debt provides much of the capital on which economic development and reconstruction are based, while overall exports stagnate and foreign markets remain scarce.

Croatia has agreed to pay its 29.5 per cent (about US$1.36 billion) share of the former Yugoslavia's still outstanding US$4.4 billion debt by turning it into state bonds. There is also about K4 billion (about US$730 million) currently due to the Paris and London clubs of government and commercial lenders, in addition to some US$103 million in road and reconstruction loans from the World Bank as well as an earlier US$31.5 million. The Croatians successfully floated a DM200 million Eurobond issue in October and plan to float another DM320 million denominate in kunas. Croatia has apparently even managed to acquire an international bond market rating of BB+ which it hopes to bring up to BBB soon. This is pretty near the bottom, but it is an achievement that the country managed any rating at all.

All of these debts have to be paid sooner or later and the government is buoyed up by the reported revival of the Adriatic tourist industry, which allegedly brought in some US$2 billion in hard currency during 1996. However, there does not seem to be any great increase in trade nor any major market for Croatian goods in the European Union's markets. As a consequence Croatia may well attempt to recapture its Yugoslavia-era markets in Eastern Europe. It is unclear whether this includes the rest of the former Yugoslavia or not. This seems to be a step towards acceptance of the US-backed Southeast European Cooperation Initiative, which Croatia and Slovenia had earlier refused, preferring to focus on Mediterranean and Central European markets.

A major impediment to the implementation of any such regional economic sphere, aside from the obvious political ironies, is the current dispute between Croatia, Macedonia and Slovenia on the one hand, and the Federal Republic of Yugoslavia (FRY: Serbia and Montenegro) on the other over about US$5.5 billion in ex-Yugoslav assets in currency and property outside ex-Yugoslavia (Bosnia traded claims against the FRY on this matter for political recognition by Belgrade). There is also some speculation that these assets have already been used by Belgrade to finance the Bosnian war and domestic affairs (Salay 1992).

Trade

Although there have been some joint deals signed, as with Agip, the Italian oil company, for joint exploration in the Adriatic and near Istria, and with German and Austrian banks, to reconstruct Adriatic hotels, official Croatian trade is in the doldrums. According to IMF figures the Croatian current accounts deficit for 1995 was about 9 per cent of GDP. Part of the reason for this lies in the current unavailability of commercial insurance or reinsurance, from Lloyds or any of the usual London insurers, on trade with any of the Yugoslav successor states except for Slovenia. Still, an apparent bright spot in all this is the Croatian pharmaceutical company Pliva. Although this company sells well abroad and its shares trade at DM550 per share on the admittedly limited Zagreb Stock Exchange, it is in direct competition with the Slovenian pharmaceutical company Krka and the Serbian company IGN-Galinka.

Trade also occurs on the black market throughout the former Yugoslavia, but except for the FRY few data exist (Yugoslav Survey 1995). Anecdotal evidence suggests a thriving commodity trade in gasoline, construction materials and, most recently, drugs (Veit 1996).

Privatisation

Given the lacklustre performance of Croatian trade, and presumably industry, the only alternative means of raising capital is to privatise existing economic assets. Privatisation, however, has not had much success in Croatia, again largely because of the lack of domestic capital or foreign investment. Interest rates in 1996 were officially 25 per cent, but ran closer to 50 per cent on the black market, usurious even by commercial bank standards. Official interbank rates ran anywhere between 15 to 30 per cent. The fact that there is a black market in capital, usually in foreign exchange, indicates that the official state institutions, especially the Croatian national bank, are not in full command of the economy. There is, consequently, little interest in privatisation of industry, which requires private capital investment. At one such privatisation auction held in early 1996 in Zagreb, only one broker bothered to show up. Perhaps in an attempt to achieve its goal of becoming a Balkan Switzerland, Croatia is planning to privatise the chocolate producer Kras.

MACEDONIA

Market reforms got off to a slow start in Macedonia despite the leadership of Kiro Gligorov, who had been a leading exponent of marketisation in the ex-Yugoslavia. The need to keep ethnic tension between Slav-speaking Macedonians and Albanians within some limits, a lack of international recognition, a boycott by Greece, and the embargo on Serbia and Montenegro limited Macedonian trade opportunities. An independent central bank was established in part to curry favor with international financial institutions and the US, but it had small foreign exchange reserves and could not find many foreign bankers who would take its paper seriously (Wyzan 1994).

Despite several stabilisation packages in 1992, inflation continued at double-digit levels. As a counter-measure Macedonian authorities followed a tight money and credit policy, introduced new currency (the denar) and delayed payments of wages and pensions. Macedonian unions opposed these measures as well as privatisation and austerity programs which then came to nothing. In December 1993, an IMF-sponsored stabilisation measure was introduced with the usual requirements, and inflation seems to have been restrained.

Overall, Macedonian living standards declined after the collapse of the old Yugoslavia as trade fell off and federal subsidies stopped arriving. Although basic prices appear to be controlled at the time of writing, Macedonia also lacks capital for privatisation. This seems to have been a major obstacle to further marketisation, despite efforts by the IMF to educate local élites through seminars with representatives from Chile and other survivors of IMF marketisation plans.

Macedonia plans to privatise and liberalise most of its economy, but there is strong opposition from workers and managers in state industries. Opposition comes also from the agricultural sector, often state enterprises, which demand protection and support especially in the face of a 44 per cent drop in budgeted funds in 1995 over the previous year. In particular, it is the milk producers who want protection from imports, and wheat farmers have sued the government for underpaying on guaranteed wheat prices.

Although Macedonia may have profited from the presence of US forces and its low-key ties to various Western agencies, capital investment has been nearly non-existent. Capital generally has been in very short supply as more than 2500 companies became insolvent in 1995. Of these 416 were state enterprises and more than 2100 private enterprises. From this total, 1600 had not been able to pay their employees for at least 60 days. The total number of workers affected was more than 75 000 of whom 70 000 were in state companies. In other words, most of the new private companies were tiny and no doubt suffered from the same capital anaemia that sank their cousins in the other Yugoslav successor states. Overall production was down 10 per cent in 1995 over the previous year. In a triumph of wishful thinking over reality, the Macedonian stock exchange opened on 28 March, 1996 with an overall pool of 60 internationally licensed traders. On its first day of operation the Macedonian exchange was patronised by nine brokerages, and conducted 25 transactions for a total of 395 shares and a total worth of $15 000 (Geroski 1996) – a nice gesture but hardly an engine of capitalism.

As with Croatia, the dynamic element of the economy may be the black or grey market, officially estimated at US$300 million to 500 million. Anecdotal evidence suggests this is mostly commodity trade, Serbian sanction-busting, weapons and drugs. The Macedonian government has found it necessary to announce restrictions on arms sales and imports and, presumably, trans-shipments.

Perhaps because of this bifurcation between the official and unofficial economy, and the subsequent shifts in control of capital, Macedonian politics were very lively in 1996. President Gligorov has been the victim of a car bombing but survived. Gjuner Ismail, speaking for the government, has decried political oligarchies and their corrupting effects on Macedonian, Saso Ordanski has been dismissed from his post as head of Macedonian Television over complaints against similar forces and Prime Minister Cervenkovski does not enjoy the confidence of the Liberal Party, and has refused to include them in his government. By November 1997, the ruling Social Democratic Alliance of Macedonia (SDAM) was only slightly ahead of the right-wing VMRO-DPME in by-elections for city officials. Plainly, both in the area of the economy and politics, Macedonia is facing major changes soon, but in what direction is difficult to predict.

THE FEDERAL REPUBLIC OF YUGOSLAVIA

Although Serbia and Montenegro are not yet officially the wards of the IMF, they too suffer from similar troubles. Because of the embargo, the official economy has effectively ground to a halt. Living standards are in free fall, and industrial output is not far behind. Wages bear no relationship to living standards, unemployment is widespread and there is a notable absence of capital. The National Bank of Yugoslavia's (NBY) dinar auctions are regularly under-attended and under-subscribed because of lack of capital as well as lack of confidence. As in most of the rest of the former Yugoslavia the Deutschmark is the favoured currency. Anywhere from a third to a half of the overall national social product is derived from the black economy despite the efforts of the authorities to bring that economy under control (Yugoslav Survey 1995).

That effort, however, raises the possibility of serious conflict within the FRY. If the black economy is to be replaced by a more standard model then capital will be needed in large quantities, and as in all other Yugoslav successor states capital is in short supply. To attract foreign capital or aid from international financial agencies the usual privatisation and price liberalisation reforms will have to be implemented or at least attempted. In turn, that will require some semblance of financial control by the central bank.

Not only does this cut into potentially or currently lucrative black market operations; it also undermines the supply relationships worked out by industrial conglomerates to keep production going. Much of this production, in the metallurgical industries and coal production, is unlikely to be acceptable to the EU, because of existing capacity in the EU and in Eastern Europe and also for ecological considerations. FRY coal is soft lignite and highly polluting, while the metallurgical industries are not only highly polluting but also lagging well behind EU technical standards. Neither is likely to draw foreign capital nor any remaining domestic capital in any privatisation scheme. The lines of political division have been demonstrated by the opposition of industrial groups to the tenure of FRY central banker Dragoslav Avramović, who was forced to resign for advocating privatisation.

At the same time, it is unlikely that the FRY economy can stay in isolation forever if only because the political consequences of normalisation dwarf in comparison to the political consequences of total economic collapse. In addition, there appear to be growing tensions between the two components of FRY, with Montenegro increasingly unwilling to tie its economic fortunes to developments in Serbia. Again, the issue appears to be access to capital.

The State

Starting in the fall of 1996, street demonstrations against the regime of Slobodan Milošević in Belgrade and later in Niš have brought on a crisis of the state. These demonstrations came about as the work of a new opposition coalition, Zajedno (Together), shortly after Avramović's dismissal. Avramović was even offered the leadership of the group but turned it down after rumours of initial acceptance. As expected, the early backing for these demonstrations came from students and the urban middle class impoverished by the isolation of the FRY, in practice Serbia. Later, they were joined by pensioners, the army, some industrial enterprises and, recently, perhaps even segments of élite police units. The crisis of the state seems even more developed in Serbia than elsewhere among the Yugoslav successor states.

On the other hand, the crisis may be more over personalities than organisation. If Avramović is correct and the country is down to about $400 million in foreign exchange while inter-enterprise debt roughly equals the total money supply, then foreign capital is crucial.[8] Milošević may be sacrificed without any major structural changes in the state. Since many government officials also head industries, political change and privatisation on the Eastern European model may not be as traumatic or as much of a change as expected. Such a change might well mean an influx of capital and the effective transfer of real political power to whomever controls the economy. Alternatively, a change in regime followed by a capital influx might well leave the FRY, or at least Serbia, with a coherent political and economic oligarchy on a road closer to the HPAE model. Although speculative, this may well be on the minds of some within the FRY élite such as Oskar Kovač, who have gone on record as opposing precipitous privatisation while stressing the centrality of Serbia as a transport hub between Europe, the Black Sea region and the Middle East (Kovač 1996, Minić 1996). Yet again, it may also be that the FRY élite has no long-term plan and is simply grasping at straws before it is swept away.

Kovač's proposals hinge on the willingness of foreign capital to invest in the region. To further this end, the semi-official position, also championed by Kovač, is the creation of a common economic space among the Yugoslav successor states, in effect reunifying the region torn apart by the wars of secession, and if not recreating Yugoslavia then at least raising its shadow. At first glance this concept may seem more than a little disingenuous, given the bloody history of the last few years, but it does make a certain amount of sense in the age of globalisation and the unlikelihood of entry into the EU for any of the Yugoslav successor states except perhaps Slovenia. Serbia as the FRY and Croatia have been improving relations recently, if only formally, and the common economic space has been proposed by both the US and the EU. In light of stagnant exports Croatia may not be as hostile to the idea as it once was.

Critical Conditions

All of this speculation is moot if the FRY's, essentially Serbia's, economy collapses before major political changes take place or if no influx of capital occurs despite any political changes. By official estimates the FRY lost half of its GDP in every year that sanctions were in place.[9] Even after the sanctions were lifted, the 'outer wall' of sanctions, effectively blocking capital import, remains. Until the FRY agrees to assume responsibility for its share of the liabilities of the former Yugoslavia, pays off its outstanding debt and agrees to drop its claims to be the sole legal successor of the former Yugoslavia, that wall will probably remain.

Otherwise, the FRY economy is largely stagnant with very high unemployment and very low capacity utilisation. There is a consistent 30 to 40 per cent cash shortage in the country with currency hard to get as well as being pretty much useless. Workers, police, and the army have not been paid regularly and have become restive. Annual per capita income has fallen to about US$1500 from a prewar level of about US$2700, putting the FRY near the bottom of the Eastern European transition economies. Trade is down as well, with the trade deficit standing at over US$2 billion. While the largest imports have been the traditional raw and semi-finished materials, exports have been largely of food and agricultural products. Most of this import and export trade was with Russia, Germany and Italy. Had 1996 not been an exceptional harvest year, even this might not have been possible.

Although the FRY (Serbia) has large lignite coal deposits, there is not enough money to operate either the mines or the electrical plants. Electricity from Bulgaria and Romania had to be imported to meet shortfalls in domestic and industrial needs. Between January and November 1996 the FRY also imported nearly US$500 million in oil and oil products.

Overall unpaid liabilities between enterprises have grown to the point that the National Bank of Yugoslavia (NBY) has plans to turn all outstanding enterprise credit into state bonds. Initially this would have turned 2000 billion dinars of bad debt into short-term securities. These securities with high interest rates might be paid off in printing press dinars but at least they would preserve the illusion of a working economy. Domestic banks, however, fear that the scheme will land them with a lot of bad paper.

Despite all this, official figures still have the social product rising for the third consecutive year and further growth is expected for 1997 even though industrial growth is below projected levels. The draft budget for 1997 is 70 per cent higher than 1996 at about 9 billion dinars, although budget revenue will probably level out at 5 billion to 5.4 billion dinars assuming a 13 per cent growth rate in an economy with a current official 1996 growth rate of about 7 per cent.

Privatisation has also been bruited about, but there are deep divisions in the élite over this issue. Despite this and despite the difficulties of privatisation in a capital-starved economy, very radical plans are afoot, at least on paper, to privatise Montenegro's electrical and power industry along with the flagship of Serbian industry, the Zastava industries producing cars, metal products and, mostly, armaments. At the time of writing no actual activity has taken place.

BOSNIA-HERZEGOVINA

The situation in Bosnia is perhaps even more complicated than in other parts of the former Yugoslavia. Not only is there enormous war damage, especially in cities and industrial centres, but also there is no possibility for the reconstruction of a national all-Bosnian economy. The Bosnian-Croat federation is held together largely by American bayonets and reconciliation with the Bosnian Serb Republic seems unlikely in the extreme. More than elsewhere, the need for large-scale investment and employment has a political as well as a humanitarian and economic imperative. Conservative estimates place Bosnian needs at around US$5 billion over four years, and various amounts have been pledged, but there is some question as to the actual availability and use of funds (World Bank 1995). Most of the aid has been channelled into the Bosnian-Croat federation and very little into the Republika Srpska, largely because that entity refuses to abide by aspects of the Dayton Agreement. Competition for scarce resources, an initial cause of the Bosnian war, may well be the cause of the next one as well.

Aside from immediate reconstruction aid, overall plans for the economic recovery of Bosnia run along a by-now familiar pattern. The first imperative is to bring Bosnia into the IMF/World Bank fold by negotiating an acceptance of Bosnia's share of the former Yugoslavia's debt. The second is to reorganise the Bosnian economy on the basis of privatisation and freed prices. The third is to limit the role of government to its night watchman role of ensuring property rights, a sound currency and the enforcement of contracts (World Bank 1995). In other words, use the same nineteenth-century model of capitalism that has worked rather badly for the rest of Eastern Europe. There is legitimate question as to whether such policies can work at all under present Bosnian circumstances and if they do work whether they will lead to recovery or to fragmentation and collapse. These questions would exist even if Bosnia was favoured by a large influx of investment capital but become even more pressing given that it is not.

A reasonably autonomous national bank, the National Bank of Bosnia-Herzegovina (NBBH) has existed since 1993 and a new currency, the Bosnian dinar pegged to the DM, has emerged as a unit of account as well as of many transactions. Curiously, it is currently headed by a foreign national, in effect placing Bosnia outside of the Republika Srpska into what amounts to an IMF protectorate. Despite the flight of many professionals into exile or refugee status, Bosnia still has a highly skilled and literate labor force disciplined by war to work hard for next to nothing. Construction skills are particularly well developed and widely dispersed (Mossberg *et al.* 1994, Iwansson 1996). No doubt there is also great skill in the commodity trade. These are all good signs for immediate reconstruction and recovery, but there is some question as to whether they are the proper skills for what will have to be an enormously and internationally entrepreneurial economy.

A recent suggestion to remonetarise the Bosnian economy is to sell rather than give away food and other aid. Since a large portion of the population in need of such aid is likely to be destitute, this plan will work only under one or both of two conditions. One is that the formal claims people have against the state or banks for assets dating prior to the war, or from back wages or benefits, are fully honored. The second is that people spend wages from employment in a functioning productive economy. The first is unlikely, given the World Bank's suggestion to write off these obligations as dangerous to monetary stability. Presumably, without a working economy such monetarisation would lead to a flight away from the Bosnian dinar and to an accepted currency such as the Deutschmark.

To promote a working economy, current World Bank reconstruction plans call for privatisation of industries and utilities as soon as possible, after immediate post-war reconstruction (World Bank 1995). As we have seen, privatisation requires capital and there is precious little capital in Bosnia. More importantly, private economic development satisfied ideological requirements on the basis of neo-liberal doctrine. Yet, the market that is supposed to coordinate such divided efforts does not now exist in Bosnia nor is it likely to be spontaneously generated.

Perhaps worse, a cantonisation policy and a Bosnian-Croat federation make such coordination even more difficult. Communications utilities as well as energy utilities cannot easily be made to work on a small scale, and in any case, duplication in each canton is economically insupportable. Even productive and trading enterprises profit from economies of scale in as small an area as Bosnia-Herzegovina. It is likely that if such a policy were actually put into effect Bosnia would become a Croatian hinterland.

Tensions between the Bosnians and Croatians exist on a number of other levels as well. Neither side has forgotten that appalling atrocities were committed, most notably, but not solely, around Mostar, a city still under dispute. Although the economic recovery plans for Bosnia provide for a port at or near Ploce on the Croatian coast, there is strong political resistance to this development in the Croatian half of the federation. If the Serb-held portion of Bosnia manages to merge with Serbia, it is highly likely that the Croatian portion will merge with Croatia. This will leave the Bosnian-government-held regions of Bosnia isolated and economically untenable. Even should this not be the case, economic union between the two halves of the federation is unlikely since neither the kuna nor the dinar are likely to be accepted by the opposing economy no matter how official decrees run. If a third currency is used, such as the Deutschmark, Bosnian monetary stability will evaporate.

A series of impoverished mutually suspicious cantons with duplicate facilities or worse, no facilities, is a recipe for chaos, not economic development. If Bosnia, whether as part of a federation or alone, must also be internationally competitive and earn its keep through exports, the situation becomes even worse. Judging by the experience of its neighbours, the possibilities for favourable Bosnian international trade, even with low-wage labor, is negligible.

CONCLUSION

The major question facing the Yugoslav successor states is how best to integrate into the world market. The same problem faced the former Yugoslavia, and a wrong answer was directly responsible for its collapse. Unfortunately, present indications are that the same policies which brought about the fragmentation of the old Yugoslavia are being continued by Yugoslav successor states. Policies of stabilisation and marketisation, strongly promoted by the International Monetary Fund (IMF) and the World Bank, usually by privatisation of productive resources and insistence on freeing prices, and on cheap labor, without regard to actual local conditions, will almost certainly do more harm to already battered societies.

Both the IMF and the World Bank operate under the assumption that there is no alternative to immediate and drastic marketisation, sometimes abbreviated as TINA ('There Is No Alternative'). Yet, marketisation and privatisation in post-communist Europe has largely been a disaster, both for the economies and for the societies undertaking it. Even official success stories like Poland suffer enormous social dislocation and disintegration of the productive economy. A different model is offered by the integration of the HPAEs, which followed a set of development policies almost entirely opposite to the current orthodoxy (Wade 1992, Amsden 1994a).

The Yugoslav successor states now face integration into the world economy on terms that are probably worse than those they could have got as part of the old Yugoslavia. Small economies, comparatively large debt burdens, weak exports, a lack of investment or venture capital, declining living standards, high unemployment, often unstable currencies, and declining production characterise all of these states to one extent or another. In the face of these burdens, the international financial community, especially the IMF and World Bank, insist on policies that are based on privatisation in the absence of capital, freeing prices, in the absence of working markets, and the comparative advantages of cheap labor when there are no jobs and no export opportunities. Neo-liberal ideology has overtaken contrary examples of successful economies using exactly those policies that the IMF and World Bank decry: directed investment, preferential credit, an export and industrial policy, and economic coordination rather than last century's laissez-faire. Plainly, it is in the interest of the international community to integrate the Balkans into a common economic framework, but to do so successfully production must be coordinated with finance, and local needs must take precedence over the demands of the neo-liberal model.

POSTSCRIPT (SPRING 1998)

The financial crisis that has hit the East Asian HPAEs is a tribute to the efficacy of their development models. It is a crisis of profit taking in world financial markets speculating on highly developed economics; a crisis of form rather than content. Already, these same HPAEs, even venerable Japan, are showing signs of recovery because their underlying productive economies are sound. Rather than an argument against the East Asian model both the crisis and its brief duration are testaments to the vitality and strength of the economies based on deliberately 'getting the prices wrong'. These economies now have the luxury of indulging the whims of currency speculators and ideologues, a luxury that the Yugoslav successor states do not share.

Notes

1. Unless otherwise noted all economic data is taken from *New Europe*, various issues.
2. Of course this was pretty much what the communist project was formed to avoid.
3. Korošić (1988) points out that industrialisation was the actual programme of 'really existing socialism'.
4. Ramos (1986) codifies these as (1) freeing prices to reflect opportunity costs, (2) reducing tariffs, establishing realistic exchange rates, and opening the local economy to international competition, (3) promoting a domestic capital market by eliminating regulatory control over interest rates and prices, (4) promoting free entry and exit of capital, (5) preventing domestic collusion that would obstruct the operation of market relations, (6) reducing the role of the state in the economy, (7) eliminating all subsidies and fiscal deficits and controlling money supply growth to assure stable prices.
5. Although overall Yugoslav foreign debt was about $16.5 billion at the time of dissolution, much of this was the contractual responsibility of the constituent republics following the economic reforms of the 1970s and 1980s. Only about $6 billion was federal debt, and the IMF divided this debt (as well as other assets and responsibilities) in the following proportion: Bosnia Hercegovina 13.2 per cent, Croatia 28.49 per cent, Macedonia 5.4 per cent, Slovenia 16.3 per cent, and Federal Republic of Yugoslavia (Serbia/Montenegro) 36.52 per cent (IMF Survey 11 January 1993).
6. Slovenia appears to have assumed about 18 per cent of the old Yugoslav federal debt, slightly more than its allotted share of about 16 per cent.
7. The banking sector is currently slated to get some 820 million kuna (roughly DM220 million) while there are to be no taxes on foreign pensions, salaries below 800 kuna or on private farm land and a profit tax rather than a VAT.
8. See *Euromoney* (1996), Country Risk issue, September.
9. See *Euromoney* (1996), Country Risk issue, September.

7 Globalisation, Governance and the Political Economy of Transition

Branka Likić-Brborić

Eastern European countries have once more become the object of massive social engineering, still waiting for the bright future that somehow always happens somewhere else. Contrary to the optimism of the initial approaches to transition that reflected the textbook notion of the capitalist economy, in which the change in property rights is the magic means, the experience of reforms in Eastern Europe has shown that privatisation has become the source of political and economic problems that cannot be solved from the top down. Furthermore, the evidence provided by the results of the standard approach to economic reform strongly suggests that the process of transition from a command to a market economy has taken place differently in different countries, different sectors, and different enterprises. It is necessary to account for these differences, and it is possible to do so if one starts from the importance of history, which can provide valuable clues regarding the particular choice of the strategy and model for transition and privatisation in a particular country.

This chapter outlines how the awareness of alternative choices to the dominant neo-liberal shock therapy approach, including the important so-called contingency and industrial policy approaches, has gained ground. Furthermore, both the transitional debates and the ensuing alternative approaches to transition and development are related to a wider context of modern–post-modern controversies and to the search for an alternative way between absolutism and relativism, universalism and particularism. A wider heterodox institutional framework, which provides an alternative approach for pursuing 'economics as a policy science', is thus advocated (Hodgson *et al.* 1994:411).

Since this latter approach is based on an instrumental value principle that does not prescribe an ideal economy, it is more appropriate for a problem-oriented analysis and examination of the systemic change that has taken place in the former socialist economies (Hodgson *et al.* 1994:411). According to the arguments put forward here, 'transition to market economy' implies a process of institutional disembedding and re-embedding that ushers in a wider and changing context due to the pressures of internationalisation and global restructuring towards more post-Fordist forms of organisation based on new technologies (Jessop 1995). This approach provides insight into the *path-dependent* (that is, contingent on particular historical legacies and institutional frameworks) manner in which the current changes have been determined by both past experiences and the character of ongoing learning processes.

But since this issue has been largely ignored by the standard approach associated with orthodox economics, the institutional approach is brought to bear on the particular case of the dissolution of Yugoslavia, especially to illustrate the width of the span between differing paths of extrication from socialist self-management within the various successor states and in Eastern Europe in general. A brief reference is made to Bosnia-Herzegovina's violent transition, which Bojičić and Kaldor discuss in detail in this volume. This tragic case may be taken as epitomising the most adverse qualities of the 'destructive destruction' that has been present to varying degrees in most countries in transition, of which the former Yugoslavia as a whole stands out as the most conspicuous and calamitous example. However, the analytical endeavour of the present essay is focused chiefly on the contrasting alleged success of Slovenia. Finally, contingencies and perspectives for certain international initiatives concerned with the establishment of new and wider frameworks for cooperation in the Balkan region are briefly discussed.[1]

CHANGING CONCEPTIONS ON TRANSITION[2]

A huge body of literature, particularly after 1989, explores various themes connected with transition to a market economy, such as macro-economic stabilisation, liberalisation, privatisation, restructuring, corporate governance, institutional change, 'safety-net', and so forth. Every issue is examined and debated either in the light of the mainstream economic paradigm (including the neo-classical, Austrian, and new institutional views), or in the light of a broad radical or critical alternative paradigm (including the Marxian, post-Keynesian or institutional views). Although all those involved in the debates agree that the present moment conveys a major political as well as economic change (Winiecki 1992:71), especially in respect to the issue of privatisation, there were initially two major divergent approaches to the choice of the most appropriate strategy for transition, namely, the *shock therapy* approach and the *gradualist* approach.

The first approach is based upon the simple assumption that the shock treatment conducted by a strong state can rapidly induce change in the economic behaviour of the agents. The proponents of this approach focused on immediate macroeconomic stabilisation, liberalisation of prices and foreign trade, and privatisation by fiat, thus conflating means and ends. Gradualists, on the other hand, concentrated on institutional change as a timely and complex process, since they assumed that the behaviour of the agents can only be changed through the process of trial and error. They envisaged a piecemeal engineering of transformation, a weak state and a spontaneous privatisation through the entry of new agents (Poznanski 1995).

The common point of debate in this regard concerned the means to attain the goal of pure market capitalism and the rate of change, not that vision itself. Various scholars, experts and institutional actors were involved in the debate, such as the developed states, the states in transition and international financial institutions. In the initial phase not all particular (national and group) interests could be distinguished, since their latent differences were largely masked by an overt common affiliation to the dominant discourse tied to the neo-liberal idea of the general interest and harmony to be achieved through the functioning of free market forces. Given the pervasive intellectual and political climate, which was predicated on a vision of perfect market capitalism, the hierarchical and situated character of economic knowledge and discourse (Strassman 1996:13–19), and the dominant economic terminology applied to changing geopolitics (Jessop 1995), it is not surprising that the political actors in both East and West initially 'agreed upon' the choice of shock therapy as the standard prescription to guide the ongoing change.

The Standard Model: Neo-Liberalism and Shock Therapy

Harvard professor Jeffrey Sachs strongly advocated the programme for rapid transformation, the shock therapy model, which was presented in his article 'What is to be done?' in the *Economist* of 13 January 1990.[3] As the first two steps, Sachs (1990:19) proposed that:

– Eastern Europe must reject the idea of market socialism, based on public ownership or worker self-management, and go straight for a Western-style market economy (the alternative models of Western Europe capitalism are here deemed identical);
– Western Europe has to provide debt relief and finance the restructuring.

This model required immediate macroeconomic stabilisation, liberalisation of most prices and the privatisation of state-owned enterprises (Lipton and Sachs 1991:24). It also implied the fragmentation of the Comecon region, since Sachs did not take individual states as his object of discussion but rather the entire region of post-communist East and Central Europe (Gowan 1995:6).

Privatisation, which according to Lipton and Sachs (1991:24) is primarily seen as a problem of the rapid transferring of state-owned property to private hands in an equitable and fiscally sound way, plays a critical role in attaining the two fundamental goals, namely, the efficient operation of the resulting private enterprises and the development of efficient capital markets. 'Privatisation means creating anew the basic institutions of a market financial system, including corporate governance of managers, equity ownership . . . mutual funds, and investment trusts' (Lipton and Sachs 1991:25).

This standard approach to economic reform was supported by the Americans, G7, and the major international financial institutions, that is, the IMF, the World Bank, and their experts.[4] The alternative European (Franco-German) strategy for the reform of the East European bloc countries based on a gradualist approach that would keep the Comecon region economically together was rejected, but it later reappeared with the EBRD (European Bank for Reconstruction and Development) and was also supported by the UN/ECE.[5]

The core output was to be the creation of a universal free trade regime and the correct institutional and economic conditions for attracting foreign direct investment (Gowan 1995:9). The vision was one of an undisturbed global capitalism. At the basis of shock therapy was the notion of a single and lasting change in the political system expressed by the political will for, and dedication to, transition, the building blocks being stabilisation, liberalisation and privatisation, which together were to construct the new system from scratch. The main agent of change was the state, which had to pursue the goal of the free market and foster foreign investment and foreign trade through legislation and practice.

Policy-makers in the countries in transition had to concur with this position and follow a uniform set of domestic policies in order to meet conditions of the international financial institutions and of Western governments, which were to provide both capital and markets (World Bank 1991:30). This implied the active promotion of the neo-liberal policy manifesto and the implementation of a particular economic theory, even though these were later proven to be irrelevant for addressing institutional change and informing strategic behaviour.

In so far as the breakup of the Soviet Union was sudden and unexpected, the standard reform prescription was not an elaborated solution suitable for the formidable task of reforming the socialist economies. It rather comprised an extension of the logic of development policies as they were redefined during the 1980s in the form of structural adjustment programmes, especially in respect to their application in Latin America. The Washington consensus, which consisted of ten policy reforms listed by John Williamson in 1989 in the belief that 'Washington' would accept them as necessary for Latin America (Williamson 1996:1), thereby became the dominant political programme and the dominant discourse for the economic reforms in East and Central Europe as well (Eatwell *et al.* 1995:55).

Lessons from the Yugoslavian Tragedy: The Contours of a Differentiated Approach

Although the standard approach was imposed on almost all the countries in transition, the neo-liberal blueprint has now become exposed to growing criticism, particularly after experience has shown the failure of speedy reforms and the downfall of misplaced expectations.[6] Alternative visions based on different theoretical approaches and different methodological and epistemological foundations are gaining ground. This is an issue in need of further scrutiny.

Unfortunately, as has been argued, the initial transitional debates resulted in the choice of a kind of blueprint, that is, an 'end-state' which governs the ongoing change, regardless of the domestic factors that have proven to be important determinants of the paths of extrication from socialism.

But as result of acquired transitional experience and changing relationships between ideas and interests in policy-making, other approaches emphasising pragmatism and contingency have developed and have been taken into serious consideration by various institutional actors. However, the legitimacy of these claims, which were inspired by both critical theory and practically driven thinking, could not be fully affirmed before the collapse of a number of the states undergoing transition, of which the former Yugoslavia is the most catastrophic example. Williamson (1991) warned of the lessons for political economy that would have to be learned from the Yugoslav experience.

In the same year an uneasy process was begun of building closer transatlantic economic relations between the EC/EU and the US, whose global competitiveness was later to be boosted by NAFTA (North American Free Trade Agreement), in order to find new bases for maintaining cooperation beyond the old NATO security framework and anti-communism. Subsequently, the Clinton administration's commitment to American competitiveness within the global economy was based upon a recognition of 'the usefulness of the European Union as a partner in battling for market access outside the transatlantic realm' (Rashish 1995:7). Although devoted to the long-term goal of liberalisation, the Clinton team consisted of people who were much more inclined towards the idea of finding a cooperative framework both domestically and internationally in so far as the neo-liberal project had been shown to be socially worn out and dangerous, even in the US. All this paved the way for a more constructive American approach to transition that was informed by American pragmatist traditions (e.g. Salvadori 1963:384), here exemplified by the *contingency approach.*

The contingency approach draws on the consideration of capital and labour structures, national history, and economic development goals when choosing an appropriate model of capitalism. Brouthers and Lamb (1995:357) develop this approach on the work of Lodge (1990) and Thurow (1992) both of whom claim that national ideologies which emerge from each country's unique history, together with the political social, cultural and institutional contexts, determine strategy, goals and policies. Brouthers and Lamb (1995:358–63) thus take the following examination of types of ideologies as a starting point:

- *Individualism* stresses the freedom of the individual to make decisions that are in his/her personal interest, as well as 'the right of business to develop and implement strategies that reflect the shareholders' desire to maximise profits'. In an individualistic society, that is, a market economy, most appropriately illustrated by the United States, where a tension exists between workers and employers, the role of government is limited to protecting property, enforcing contracts and promoting vigorous competition. Regulation of the market is permitted only in the case of 'market failure'.
- *Communitarianism* emphasises the role of government as a vision-setter in a production-oriented economy, of which the most typical example is Japan. Relations between individuals are governed more by consensus than by contract, and employees are taken to be the most important stakeholders in a business, followed by customers, with shareholders a 'distant third'.
- *Middle ideologies* situated between the above two ideological extremes value both individualism and communitarianism. Economies based on these ideologies, industrial democracies, of which Germany is the most typical example, are characterised by capital markets and government-regulated labour markets.

The contingency approach draws on the idea that there is no single best capitalist economy, and that one should not force uniform individualistic ideologies upon economies in transition, the latter having been implied by the shock therapy model. Hence, Eastern European countries' decisions to adopt a particular type of capitalist economy must be made with respect to their internal structures, national histories, citizens' preferences, ideologies, and economic development goals. This approach, which suggests that many East European countries should consider adopting the industrial democracy type of economy (Brouthers and Lamb 1995:361), also exemplifies the current phase in the process of global economic and political restructuring, with the question of the leading role of the USA, Japan, and the EU temporarily settled (Jessop 1995:681).

This in fact corresponds to the emerging European industrial policy approach advocated in *Transformation and Integration: Shaping the Future of Central and Eastern Europe*, the report of the Forum Economic Programme Group that was initiated in November 1993.[7] The report, which is premised on the principles of political economy, maintains that inequality is inherently inefficient and that some type of mixed economy must be the objective of institutional change. It proceeds from the disastrous social costs of transition and proposes social and economic policies for reversing the direction of this process (Eatwell *et al.* 1995:59). Against the background vision of a 'fully integrated Europe, without new poli-tical and economic divisions', the authors of this report declare that its objective 'has therefore been to assist the political process that can lead to a social market economy, sustained growth and full employment, an equitable income distribution and basic social services' (Eatwell *et al.* 1995: *Preface*).

This report was positively reviewed in the World Bank's *Transition*, which is a sign of change in the Bank's general attitude towards development initiatives and issues (Schrenk 1996:10–12). This wavering in the Bank's neo-liberal stance can be traced to *The World Bank Participation Sourcebook*, where participation is defined as a process through which stakeholders influence and share control over development initiatives and the decisions and resources that affect them (World Bank 1996b:3–4). Such decisions are deemed to be more feasible and sustainable than those made by experts.

The Revision of a Dogma: New International Learning Processes

The Bank's own experts have recently questioned neo-classical dogma regarding the equality/growth trade-off. For example, Bruno and Squire (1996:6) have shown that unequal asset distribution impedes growth, even though their research did not find such a strong association between income inequality and growth.

One can only speculate on the ultimate sources of the Bank's changing attitudes and on the role played in this regard by the political position of the Clinton administration, the US being the Bank's largest single shareholder. But one thing is certain, namely, that all the actors had to undergo a learning process requiring time and experience that implied disappointment with the given solution and a rebound effect.[8] The post-socialist countries themselves are now forging new national and regional solutions for the social and political problems implied by transformation, along with new means for coping with these problems.

But 'the owl of Minerva only flies at dusk'. The unconditionality of neo-liberal shock therapy and its rhetoric was unopposed both by the weakened social-democratic parties in the West, which were capable of offering no viable alternatives at the time, and the bankrupt socialist parties in the East. It took several important years for dissonant and critical positions to take shape and for their warnings to be articulated in alternative political programmes, such as that of the Economic Forum.[9] Most of these positions were inspired by the pragmatism and eclecticism of the successful strategies of the East Asian economies, where state involvement has played a crucial role. Nevertheless, the damage had already been done by virtue of the fragmentation of the region and the austerity measures that had been implemented in many countries.

Unfortunately, only a few of the Central and Eastern European countries have regained pre-transition income levels, and most of them are 'still struggling to catch-up with the past' in order to be able to 'catch up with the future' (Koch-Weser 1996:11). The reference here is to the socialist past, whose results were to be erased in the reconstruction of the capitalist modernisation project with the same eagerness that had been characteristic of the earlier socialist modernisation project to expunge the pre-socialist past.

NEO-CONSERVATISM, ITS CONSEQUENCES AND ITS CRITICS

By addressing different theoretical approaches to the problem of transition 'from plan to market', I want to argue that transitional problems can be neither envisaged nor resolved by textbook economics. Transition implies a contest for entry into and control of new markets by different economic agents within a changing geopolitical context. There are no feasible blueprints for this. The one that had been imposed is now being altered and adjusted within the process of institutional change and learning by all of the actors and stakeholders involved. The explanation of this process entails an analysis of economic changes as they are determined politically, ideologically and historically in the real world of global competition, where all actors are not equal in pursuing their interests. The process of transition thus implies changes in institutions as normative, regulative, and cognitive systems.

This also implies that the contemporary quest for a socio-economic system is embedded not only within the process of global geopolitical and economic restructuring, but also within the concurrent quest for a philosophical system. The latter has been, as Best suggests (1995), predicated on 'the politics of historical vision'. Contrary to the alleged binary distinction between critical theory as political and positivist theory as objective and apolitical,[10] the crucial difference is rather 'between overt and covert politics, between open and suppressed normative-political commitments (Best 1995:xvi). Best thus proposes a rather rough division of prevalent visions into *conservative*, *liberal* and *radical* approaches. While the conservatives reject modernity and seek the renewal of tradition, the liberals, ensuing from the *philosophes*, utilitarians and political economists, embrace modernity, Enlightenment ideas, individualism and capitalism (Best 1995:18). The radicals, namely socialists and anarchists, also embrace the Enlightenment and individualism, but their dialectical vision views capitalism as an obstacle to the development of the liberatory aspects of modernity (Best 1995:18).

The rival theories in development economics have been shaped by competing liberal and radical visions respectively.[11] With the exception of dependency theory, which does not consider history to be a linear process, all of these approaches share a common view of history as progress towards a final goal. This implies the definition of development as a change in a particular direction, a notion heavily determined by Eurocentric and ahistoric positions. Alternative models of development have, in turn, been informed by refurbished modernist challenges to the economic superiority of the West in terms of growth rates presented initially by the Soviet Union and later by the Japanese, East Asian and Chinese economic success stories. Consequently, development studies were seldom those of particular histories, economies and policies, which also implied a lack of institutional analysis.

Already in the early 1980s, with the deepening of the world socio-economic crisis and poverty, the awareness grew of the need 'to pass beyond these paradigms and, in particular, to break free of their implicit belief in the natural progress of history' (Wilber and Jameson 1984:20). However, rather than shifting towards more attentive forms of institutional and cultural analysis, the mainstream intellectual climate and Western *realpolitik* throughout the 1980s and the early 1990s came to be dominated by a peculiar merger of neo-liberalism with conservatism. Habermas (1981), for one, warns of this pervasive 'neo-conservative' climate in the Western world that is perpetuated by an alliance of post-modernists with pre-modernists. This project, which is critical of cultural modernism, furthers a type of capitalist development with simple economic growth as its objective at the same time as it propels a seemingly endless fragmentation and disorientation of the public communicative sphere of the life-world.

Laissez-faire Globalisation and Fragmentation of the Life-World

But warnings from critical social scientists could certainly not stem the tide of the neo-conservative project of 'modernisation'. The standard approach to transition prepared by Western experts was but the expression of the inner logic of this project. At the end of the 1990s we, unfortunately, both live and observe the devastating effects of the various programmes that have arisen according to this logic.

We have seen the IMF, the World Bank and the OECD, the most important institutional actors shaping development policies globally, pursuing a rampant *laissez-faire* approach. This has taken place in conjunction with the preceding shift to the Right in US and British politics and the diffusion of their peculiar merger of neo-liberalism with a traditionalist conservatism, which is objectively supported by post-modern relativism, into other OECD countries during the 1980s. This neo-conservative reaction, as Habermas qualifies it, centres around the argument that the crisis of the 1970s in the West was caused by high domestic wages due to the excessive power of workers and by the high prices of raw materials. The latter claim induced a redefinition of development policies that imposed 'double squeeze' conditions upon Third World countries, that is, unfavourable terms of trade and a heavy burden of debt service (Preface in Marglin and Schor 1990:xi). The resulting structural adjustment programme defined the economic policy of export orientation and liberalisation such countries had to follow in order to obtain loans from the IMF and World Bank. This was a policy that blocked development for years to come and which, indeed, seemed to confirm the arguments of the dependency theorists. Similarly, 'Second World' (real-socialist) countries, exposed to the same kind of double pressure, were 'Third-Worldised' (Frank 1992:43), plunging into deep economic, social, and cultural crisis that was structurally embedded.

In so far as the legitimacy of the visions informed by critical theory was eroded by the failure of the Soviet socialist project to reform and deliver freedom, the world for a certain period of time was left with only one choice, namely, the positivist vision of endless capitalism and the 'end of history'. This vision was informed by neo-classical economics, promoted by neo-liberal rhetoric and politics, and was closely related to the rigid stance of the administration in Washington, DC, the latter having been inspired by George Bush's vision of a New World Order that would be constructed upon the premises of the free market, individualism, rationality and, paradoxically, freedom of choice.

The West itself is still adjusting its industrial relations systems and the welfare state in order to comply with the interests of business both at home and abroad, regardless of diminishing democratic aspirations. Neoliberal cum conservative political forces in the US and Great Britain chose to break the existing social pact with labour, which added another feature to the process of global restructuring that had already been begun and which was characterised by the shift from import substitution to export-led growth, from state ownership and the regulation of prices to privatisation and liberalisation, and from an organised labour force to a flexible labour market with a strong gender dimension (Moghadam 1992: 10–12). Moghadam (1992) thus describes how the neo-liberal ideology and discourse of efficiency, productivity and flexibility, merging with a conservative and traditionalist discourse of domesticity, championed the idea of global harmony, even as it created the world of political instability, regional differentiation, job destruction and income inequalities embodied in its regime of flexible accumulation.

With the breakup of the Soviet Union, the radicalisation of the process of transition in the former socialist economies was a logical consequence of the previous shift to the Right and geopolitical restructuring that was accompanied by the redefinition of the very notion of freedom in terms of the freedom of business (Panitch and Miliband 1992:11). These changes were coupled with the strengthening of conservative values centring on an idealised image of the family and cultural traditionalism, trends that were indeed supported by the allegations put forward in the decentring, fragmentative and culturalising discourses inherent in the booming postmodernism within philosophy, science and cultural politics.

Retrieving an Attentive Universalism

However, we are now encountering a growing quest to retrieve and remould universalising criteria of reason and truth, and the social sciences in their search for truth are currently returning to different versions of a hermeneutic vision of social reality and truth as constructed 'in dialogue and interpretation' (Best 1995:17). Thus Best, rereading Marx, Foucault and Habermas as critical social theorists who break with the positivist historigraphic tradition based on the strict disconnection of fact and value, suggests a return to the analysis of history in order to question forms of domination, injustice, coercion and inequality (Best 1995:261). At the same time he points to the need to deal with the regressive political implications of post-modernism, namely, a new racism, a new fascism and a new barbarism, which unrestrained pluralist and multicultural discourses bring about.[12] Guided by a hermeneutic and pragmatic vision of social reality, we could instead understand and practice post-modern theory not as a break with modern theory but rather as a continuation of certain of its critical aspects (Best 1995:262–3).

There is at present a promising trend to reconstruct developmental logic along these same lines in that development theory and discourse have relaxed their over-fixation with the positivist notion of growth as expressed by the simple measure of per capita GNP.[13] Consequently, as the discussion above has indicated, mainstream economic reasoning can hardly remain immune to the general problems and disputes imposed upon the social sciences in general, even though the neo-classical paradigm has for some time enjoyed an image of disinterested and objective science and has dominated political and social concerns. Just as was the case during the Great Depression of the 1930s, political and social problems brought about by the application of simple economic recipes to the inherent disorder of the modern world demand a broader approach to economic problems. Today, at a time of convulsive systemic change, global restructuring and great uncertainty, an appropriate approach must redefine the notion of economic rationality and involve an institutional analysis that is both complex and holistic, as well as attentive to issues of history and of social and cultural evolution.

ELEMENTS OF A HETERODOX FRAMEWORK FOR INSTITUTIONAL ANALYSIS

The importance of institutions for the explanation of economic processes is hardly disputed today. Among the adherents of neo-classical economics, so-called 'new institutionalism' has been attempting to advance the neo-classical methodology of economic rationality toward the domains of other social sciences. Similarly, the aim of inquiries based on transaction costs and property rights constraints considerations, namely, the property rights school, transaction costs economics, new economic history, law and economics, and others (Eggertsson 1990:6), was to design an ideal set of institutions and incentives in order to promote economic growth. The concerns of an emerging heterodox institutionalism, however, lay beyond these transaction costs and property rights analyses and the benchmark of universal methodological individualism. Those concerns have, rather, been informed by the 'old' institutionalism of Veblen and Commons, but also by Myrdal and Galbraith (Hodgson 1988:20–1), in their critique of neo-classical economics both for its methodological individualism and also for its quest for optimum equilibrium solutions that 'foreclose(s) the operation of real world processes of working things out and tend(s) to substitute economists own conception of institutional organisation and individual preferences for those of economic actors' (Samuels 1995:572). But although institutionalists, just as mainstream economists, address the problem of the allocation of resources, they disagree with the reductionism of the idea that the market is the guiding mechanism of the economy and that scarce resources are allocated by the market. Instead of focusing on the market, they believe that 'the real determination of whatever allocation occurs in any society is the organisational structure of the society – in short, its institutions' (as quoted in Samuels 1995:571). The central problem for contemporary heterodox institutionalism is thus the 'organisation and control of the economy as a system encompassing more than a market' (Samuels 1995:571).

Proponents of institutionalism claim there must be transparency in value objectives, and they call for a policy of economic pluralism and intellectual democracy. This implies the participation of broad categories of the population in the establishment of values (Samuels 1995:574–5; Hodgson 1988:252). Together with post-Keynesianism, a subset of Marxism, a subset of mainstream economics, and certain neo-Austrians, institutionalism belongs to the domain of political economy. Since it is informed by a vision of the economic process as an integral part of a broader sociopolitical process, it adopts a modern realist philosophy that implies both 'world realism' and a process 'truth realism' (Dow 1990). Sofianou advocates a stance critical of the 'anthropocentrism' both of the positivist empiricism of neo-classical economics and of the idealism that shapes post-modernist influences on economics. Sofianou maintains that empiricism conflates the world with our knowledge of it, while post-modernism conflates the world with our language about it (Sofianou 1995:377), thus dissolving the subject–object distinction and eliminating any notion of choice. She argues that choice presupposes agency, agency presupposes intentionality, and intentionality presupposes some sort of structure on which it can be based as well as our knowledge of this structure (Sofianou 1995:382). Sofianou thus concludes that the existence of relatively enduring structures is necessary for freedom to be possible.

According to Hodgson, an institution is 'a social organisation which, through the operation of tradition, custom and legal constraint, tends to create durable and routinised patterns of behaviour' (Hodgson 1988:10).[14] Institutions thus consist of 'cognitive, normative and regulative structures and activities that provide stability and meaning to social behaviour. Institutions are transported by various carriers – cultures, structures, routines – and they operate at multiple levels of jurisdiction' (as quoted in Scott 1995:xiii).

A regulative approach, which sees behaviour as guided primarily by self-interest and expedience, is thus juxtaposed to the normative and cognitive approaches, which take collections of norms and knowledge systems into consideration. On a more general level, Campbell (1997) claims that the symbolic acceptability and legitimacy of different institutional forms is just as important as their efficiency in determining their emergence and survival. By the same token, he defines evolutionary change as a process based on 'interaction, interpretation and bricolage – three mechanisms that reveal the enabling, as opposed to the constraining, effects of institutions' (Campbell 1997:26). Within this framework it is possible to correlate inclusive and less exchange-based forms of interactions, both with more cooperative frames of interpretation and also with a kind of bricolage (the process of solution development) that is based on tacit knowledge and the process of social learning.

Institutionalism is, in fact, a very heterogeneous approach that is far from having a set definition, but it is very illustrative of the intellectual and philosophical climate that has appeared beyond the modern–postmodern and capitalism–socialism concerns. Moreover, it is very convenient for the constructive analysis of various transitional experiences.

In accordance with this general approach, I shall attempt to analyse aspects of the Yugoslav experience. More specifically, the following analysis is based on the premise that the choice of transition models in the former Yugoslavia and in its successor states, along with the ensuing national and regional strategies, were determined by:[15]

• the path dependence and the paths of extrication from state socialism, that is, the institutional and historical legacies and resources, since the starting point was not an institutional void or some type of *tabula rasa*;
• the political constellation of newly elected governments, along with the related question of the internal legitimation and character (inclusive or exclusive) of the political systems;
• the fluid geopolitical context, with international organisations, Western governments, and transnational corporations as influential players that propose blueprints and formulae for external legitimacy.

YUGOSLAVIA AS AN ABORTED MODERNITY PROJECT

Not many years ago the Socialist Federal Republic of Yugoslavia was looked upon as a case of a successful middle way of development.[16] The initial economic success of this reductionist modernisation model, which was based on the assumption that industrialisation would solve all problems, led to various forms of differentiation. The latter in turn challenged the system, the legitimacy of which was based on the alleged solution of both national and class problems. The power of the Yugoslav League of Communists and its patriarchal way of governing was called into question by the student movement and the Praxis philosophers, but also by influential liberal-managerial groups within the republics and among the federal political establishment, who had developed upon the social and economic basis of Yugoslav decentralised workers' self-management and market oriented reforms. Similarly, the legitimacy of the central administration was questioned by ethno-nationalist movements in Croatia, Slovenia and Serbia that often sprang forth from factions within the communist organisations at the republican level.

The institutional changes of 1965–75 resulted in the transfer of decision making processes to regional levels through the Constitution of 1974 and the curtailment of the power of management by the Associated Labour Act of 1976, which set forth the design of a contractual socialist economy (Mencinger 1991:75). Allegedly intended to promote economic efficiency through workers' self-management and to increase governmental legitimacy and meet democratic demands through self-government, these changes in fact provided the opportunity for regional leaders to forge independent power-bases and exercise a pervasive bureaucratic control over the economy. Diana Plestina (1992) demonstrates how this fact, in combination with external pressures originating in the crisis of capitalism, fostered *ad-hoc* solutions that led to competition for scarce resources and intensified political divisions.

Similarly, Schierup (1992) describes how the economic pressures of the 'debt trap' led to reperipherialisation and a process of rebureaucratisation and retraditionalisation of society at the level of the republics that became dominated by local bureaucracies without grandiose visions of internationalism.[17] In addition, Young sees Yugoslavia as having been a rent-based nested hierarchy of patron–client linkages in which the institutional divisions between state and market and between politics and economics required for market-based society had not developed (Young 1992:274–5). Ethnic violence is thus seen as having been brought about by ill-considered market reforms and the political drift that resulted from 'the application of neo-classical nostrums, particularly the curtailment of demand and the elimination of governmental regulation and control of economy' (Young 1992:274–5).

In the long and uneven process of reform to a market economy, the tensions between ideals and reality again led to a lowering of democratic aspirations under pressures from market rules and forces (Baumgartner *et al.* 1979). Finally, the economic, political, social and moral crisis of the 1980s was, according to the position maintained in the present discussion, the result of a political failure to meet the 'plethora of differing historical and political visions' brought about by the dynamic forces of modernity (Best 1995:17). Political élites were forced to proceed towards more fundamental reforms, such as property rights reforms, thus replacing both the rhetoric and ideology of workers' self-management by the rhetoric and ideology of free market and efficiency. The top-down application of the regulative formula for the immediate deconstruction of the formal rules of the game gave way to varieties of informal socio-economic and socio-cultural institutions that were determined by different regional survival strategies.[18]

Thus, although the 'heterodox' shock therapy imposed by the last Yugoslav government, which had also been advised by Professor Jeffrey Sachs, could be called successful if measured in its own terms in that foreign exchange reserves had increased to US$8 billion, the dinar was kept convertible, and inflation was curbed, it nevertheless actually radicalised disintegration tendencies. While the earlier inter-republican conflicts that had been controlled by the dominant consensus among political leaders were triggered by the distribution of foreign loans, market shares, and rents, this time it was differences concerning the distribution of the costs of economic reform and debts that accelerated the centrifugal forces of the vicious circle. Not only were common survival strategies now exhausted, they became transformed into protectionist economic policies that resulted in reduced mutual trade,[19] ethnic mobilisation, and, finally, violent disintegration. This is a process that still dangerously haunts the whole Balkan region.

This discussion points to one common variable in the various accounts of the complex problem of the aborted Yugoslav modernisation project, namely, the political élites and their cultures, ideologies and practices, which have been developed in differing historical and geopolitical contexts.[20] This is the point of departure in Susan Woodward's (1995a) examination of the Yugoslav political economy and the paradox of socialist unemployment, in which she demonstrates how common development and reform strategies led to competing visions of the state – the *Slovene* model and the *Foča* model – and to the dissolution of Yugoslavia when applied to particular histories within a changing international context.

The Slovene model of administration and economic strategy was long characterised by an effective governmental apparatus, a local tradition of self-government, civilian control of all economic affairs, and a commitment to national liberalisation whose origins can be traced to Austro-Marxist influences.[21] The Central Committee of the Communist Party of Yugoslavia established governing rules in line with Slovene ideas that were based on sound economic principles, cooperation, and self-governance. However, their application in a region destroyed by the Second World War, where the army and the poor competed for supplies, implied the use of different means, namely, 'persuasion, rather than a money price' (Woodward 1995a:60–1). It is these different means that determine the nature of the Foča model.

Even though differing regional combinations of these two extremes can be identified within the territories of the former Yugoslavia, it is the idea of a decentralised state that strongly distinguishes Slovenian political traditions from those in Croatia, Serbia and Bosnia, which are basically authoritarian and self-enforcing.

The Republic of Bosnia-Herzegovina, marked by a particularly stubborn merger of neo-Stalinism and a traditional patriarchalism, stands out as the ideal typical example of the Foča model. This part of the former

Yugoslavia also epitomises the débâcle and institutional void that has resulted in post-socialist countries from the dogmatic application of the shock therapy model, capable of offering no alternative to post-modern ethnic deconstructivism. The economic crisis of the 1980s reaffirmed patterns of domination and patriarchal bureaucratic practices disguised in the robes of particular national interests.[22]

The brief period of 'democratic' pandemonium before nationalistic parties won the elections in Bosnia-Herzegovina was not utilised by urban civil society to instill their values or to devise a realistic path of political and economic reconstruction. The forces of post-modernism, traditionalism, and a neo-conservatism imposed from the outside led intellectuals and the media alike into a spider's web spun by political élites and populist movements in the search for particular identities and easy economic spoils that had no clear political, democratic, and historical vision. This state of affairs was mirrored in the resulting terrible devastation of human, material, and moral resources. But even without a war it would have been difficult to reverse these negative trends. Measures imposed by various stabilisation programmes during the 1980s had caused a grave deterioration in the economy of the republic while simultaneously undermining both the social position of the middle class and its influence on the political process (UNDP 1996b:296–7). Today, following the Dayton Agreement, the World Bank's reconstruction programme (World Bank 1996c) for Bosnia-Herzegovina offers no substitute for the plethora of conflicting historical visions and national political programmes of an exclusive character that have had such devastating results, since it neither addresses social issues nor expresses the need for a 'strategic framework for reconstruction, reform and economic management' (UNDP 1996b:274).

WHAT COULD 'CREATIVE DESTRUCTION' BE? THE SLOVENIAN EXPERIENCE RECONSIDERED

If it is at all possible against the background of the 'destructive destruction' of Bosnia-Herzegovina to speak of a Schumpeterian 'creative destruction', then it is instructive to examine and analyse the Slovenian example, which stands out as one of the most promising among the formerly socialist countries in transition.[23]

Slovenia is usually considered to be a strong and successful reformer in spite of the high transition costs caused by loss of markets and resources through secession and long and exhausting debates regarding the choice of privatisation model. For this reason, it is valuable for other economies in transition to explore whether her 'success' can be ascribed to the external factors determined by her favourable geopolitical position, or whether it depends on political vision, internal expertise, experience, and other historical, cultural, and ideological advantages. Furthermore, workers' management and participation is still a very interesting subject at the level of organisational studies in the search for a more efficient form of organisation due to the challenging competitiveness of the Japanese firm and the pressures of globalisation (e.g. Blinder 1990, Prasnikar and Svejnar 1993). Because of the Yugoslav wars, it is possible to assess and follow the transformation of this model within a long-term perspective only in Slovenia.

The Slovenian Path of Development Within Yugoslavia

Owing to the impotency of the Kingdom of Yugoslavia to solve regional disparities, Slovenia initially held a privileged position in the Second Yugoslavia because she had inherited a strong industrial base and a pool of industrialised workers and a corresponding level of socio-economic development. In addition, the anti-centralist and liberal orientation of her political leadership placed Slovenia in the leading role in the Yugoslav pursuit for a more efficient economic organisation through the institutionalisation of the ideas of workers' self-management and socialist self-government.

For example, the Slovenian prime minister, Stane Kavčić (removed from office in 1972), was the first major Yugoslav political leader to be devoted to economic efficiency, market solutions, decentralisation and support for initiatives to forge close economic ties with Western Europe and to advocate the 'shareholders' model of self-management. Similarly, certain Slovenian social and economic thinkers emerged as the primary critics of 'social ownership' as 'non-property' in that neither the state nor the workers' collectives were owners or responsible subjects and managers were merely executive organs of workers' collectives.[24]

Consequently, managers' powers were not curtailed as much in Slovenia as elsewhere during the 1974–6 so-called anti-technocratic reforms, and the expertise of financial and bankers' views was valued more, since the managers were recruited mainly from industry. This is in contrast to Serbia or Bosnia-Herzegovina, where managers were less interested in production or design because they were primarily politicians (Lydall 1989:112). It was thus not by accident that the most efficient firms were located in Slovenia, and that no gigantic, politically determined and eventually failed investment projects were assigned to Slovenia. All the other republics had at least one such symbol of political megalomania.

Slovenia left behind the perils of the dissolution of Yugoslavia without totally falling back onto pre-socialist political practices, but built rather upon the structures and relatively positive experience acquired through the operation of a decentralised economy based on social property, self-management and partial reliance on the market mechanism.

At the beginning of the 1990s, the two million Slovenians comprised just 8.5 per cent of the total Yugoslav population, but they produced 20 per cent of the Yugoslav GNP and 30 per cent of the overall exports, also holding a 12 per cent share of the Yugoslav external debt, while the unemployment rate was only 5 per cent (Štiblar 1993:9). Although Slovenia suffered a drop in real GDP by 22 per cent in the period 1987–91, her real GDP per capita in 1990 of US$8658 and her economic structure in 1991 (agriculture 5.6 per cent, services 51.6 per cent, and industry 42.8 per cent) clearly placed her in the category of post-industrial countries (Zapp 1993:62–3).

The path taken early on by Yugoslavia from a command to a market economy, and particularly the positive Slovenian socio-economic development beyond the features of a shortage economy,[25] have shown a number of advantages in the present transition process in comparison with the other socialist countries. Bearing all this in mind, it is not surprising that foreign expert advice was not appreciated at face value. Indeed, all three ingredients of the standard approach, namely, macroeconomic stabilisation, liberalisation and privatisation, were called into question.

Macroeconomic Stabilisation

The DEMOS coalition won Slovenia's first multi-party elections in April, 1990.[26] The new government was formed in May, and one of the first items on its agenda was the preparation of the macroeconomic programme, including both fiscal and monetary reform. Macroeconomic management has been relatively successful, especially considering Slovenia's initially very low official foreign exchange reserves and the lack of external financial support (OECD 1997:39, Pleskovic and Sachs 1994). The role of the foreign experts in these processes is controversial. Mencinger, for one, argues that this success has been due to the fact that Slovene policy-makers did not fully implement the stabilisation programme proposed by the foreign experts Sachs and Associates (Mencinger 1996:416). Contrary to their recommendation that a nominal exchange rate and a nominal wage be introduced, thus pegging the new currency to the German mark, the ECU, or a basket of currencies, a rapid conversion of dinars to the new currency and a floating exchange rate were pursued in line with the advice of Slovene economists.[27]

However, Slovenia also experienced a typical transformation crisis with a cumulative fall in GDP of 14.5 per cent in 1991–2 and an increase in unemployment to 14.4 per cent in 1993–4. This negative trend began to be reversed in 1993, but this positive change seems to have become possible only after the resolution, through long and exhausting debates, on the issue of the privatisation of state enterprises, a matter that 'caused major dissent within the government, divided politicians and has become the root of political instability' (Mencinger 1992:30).

THE PRIVATISATION DEBATES

Because of the obvious need both to revise federal laws and develop Republican legislation concerning privatisation, the DEMOS government prepared the first draft of a privatisation law, known as the Korze-Mencinger-Simoneti code, in November, 1990, which was approved on an initial reading by all three chambers of the Slovenian parliament for further legislative consideration.[28] This law envisaged a 'gradual, decentralised and commercial' privatisation (Mencinger 1996:418), a conception that was partly a revision of the federal law adapted to Slovenian circumstances. According to Mencinger (1992:30–1) these included the relative independence of enterprises, the regional dispersion of industry, the existing industrial structure, close links with foreign firms, the financial means of the population (an estimated US$2.5 billion was held in foreign banks or 'under mattresses' and an additional US$1.2 billion was frozen within the banking system), and the old Slovenian contention that economic ownership, particularly the role of management, should be strengthened.

Accordingly, the government's function was to be restricted to defining the rules of privatisation and supervising their implementation through the Privatisation Agency and the Development Fund, the latter making assistance available to large loss-makers. Although there was to be no free distribution of property, certain discounts to citizens and employees were allowed for. Firms were also supposed to initiate privatisations in which managers, workers, citizens, and both foreign and domestic legal buyers, could participate. Particular importance was given to leveraged management/employee buyouts that resembled American employee stock ownership plans (ESOPs).

Although the draft law was passed by all three chambers at the end of March 1991, the Privatisation Law itself was blocked by criticism from both Left and Right and was never brought up for vote. While the Slovenian labour unions demanded the free transfer of more than one-third of a firm's value to both active and retired employees, the former (pre-Second-World-War) owners claimed full compensation for their previously nationalised companies, including lost profits (Zapp 1993:67). The right wing of the DEMOS coalition brought anti-communist rhetoric into the critique of the proposed law and also prepared an alternative proposal, the Sachs-Peterle-Umek code. Both Jože Mencinger, the deputy prime minister for the economy, and Marko Kranjec, the minister of finance, resigned in May 1991, after Jeffrey Sachs visited the Assembly in order to promote his well-known idea of 'centralised, mass and distributive' privatisation, which was presented as the final draft of the previous privatisation proposal. According to this idea, the nationalisation and conversion of large enterprises into joint-stock companies was envisaged while the smallest enterprises would be able to privatise spontaneously. The method of free distribution of shares to all citizens through financial intermediaries such as banks, pension funds, and mutual investment funds, also controlled by government officials, was proposed.

The Yugoslav Federal Army withdrew from Slovenia in July 1991, after the short war, and the new constitution was decided. It became a hot late summer and fall for the Peterle government when his privatisation proposal was criticised by organised managers, trade unions, economists, and government officials. Peterle, a Christian Democrat himself, disregarded both Slovenian liberal political traditions as well as the legacy of the national circle of professional economists concerning the search for active and responsible owners.

After Slovenia was officially recognised by the EC on 15 January 1992, and then in April of the same year by the US, 'the window of opportunity' for the Peterle government closed, the DEMOS coalition split and Peterle was forced to resign after a no confidence vote. J. Drnovšek, the liberal prime minister of the new government installed in April, 1992, showed a will and ability to compromise, thus allowing for a cooperative political framework inclusive enough for many different interest groups to articulate their positions. The Law on Ownership of Socially Owned Companies, passed on 11 November 1992, and amended during the course of 1993, was a middle solution, containing elements of decentralisation and gradualism on the one hand and distribution of ownership certificates to all citizens on the other.[29]

Even though actual privatisation started slowly, it was expected to have been completed by the end of 1997 for all 1545 eligible enterprises (OECD 1997:92).[30] Among the various methods utilised in the process of ownership transformation, the most common have become 'the internal buyout' of shares and the mandatory transfer of 40 per cent of shares to institutional owners. In general, managers and employees hold a maximum of 60 per cent equity in 78 per cent of privatised companies, while holding a majority in more than 85 per cent (Mencinger 1996:422–3).

But restructuring costs have been considerable. Already by the middle of 1992, approximately 98 large companies with aggregate losses of over DM 1 billion and employing almost 10 per cent of the labour force were transferred to the Development Fund (Mencinger 1996:422), and around 50 per cent of managers were replaced in the period 1990–2. The rate of unemployment has remained high, young and old workers and ethnic minorities being the main losers (Vodopivec 1996), but the position of women has improved with restructuring towards the financial sector both in terms of female–male wage differentials, which were relatively high even before transition (0.88 in 1987 and 0.90 in 1991), as well as in terms of a lower probability to become unemployed (Vodopivec 1996:111, 115). It has been argued that this may be attributable to the fact that the Slovenian government did not blindly follow the neo-liberal transition recipe (European Forum 1995:27).

The Transformed Economic System and Transitional Strategy in Slovenia

As consensus on the issue of privatisation was being reached, Slovenian business people, professionals and politicians came to adopt the position that the government must take a more active strategic role in order to facilitate transition and integrate Slovenia into the EC (Petrin 1995:20–1).[31] A strategic industrial approach was advocated in order to enhance production efficiency since research had shown that Slovenian productivity was two to three times lower than that of Western competitors (Petrin 1995:33). The protection of national interests was emphasised in so far as this strategy did not rely on a crucial role for foreign direct investment (FDI), even though a liberal legal framework for it had been set up.[32]

The emerging Slovenian economic system appears to be a mixture of the German bank system with its workers' participation, the American stock market with its investment funds and bankruptcy rules, and the Japanese model of informal networks (Simoneti 1994:42). But the particular results of the privatisation process in fact conform to a marked degree to 'the legacies of self-management and dispersed decision-making' (Mencinger 1996:425). Uvalić (1994:37) emphasises the remarkable pragmatism and inventiveness of Slovenia in respect to the official introduction of a system of codetermination similar to the one in Germany, in addition to the fact that the introduction of a system of profit-sharing is being considered by many firms.

The continuity in path dependent change should not of course be overstated, given that workers' self-management was transformed into management over workers in line with the overall privatisation shift 'from politico-ideological workers' participation to managerial centred employee involvement' (Bar-Hayim 1996:191). Nevertheless, the Slovenian experience appears to follow the heterodox institutionalist frame of reference, which suggests how the legacies of the past and the perceived international economic and political position may be moulded together within a political process that define a viable economic system and a successful strategy for transition. In the particular case of Slovenia, one can discern the positive role played by a modern cooperative and pragmatic political culture, the product of a path-dependent process of cultural and communicative modernisation defining an effective democracy, which both inspired and continually reshaped top-down reform and transition recipes throughout the history of the Second Yugoslavia.

In summary, this story of Slovenia's transition does not imply that the typical economic problems and social tensions related to the application of the standard recipe were avoided. It is argued, nevertheless, that adjustments to the particular domestic circumstances were necessary in order 'not to kill the patient'. Slovenian experts had recognised early on, and discursively promoted, a model similar to the above-described contingency approach that was oriented towards integration into the EU based on middle ideologies. Furthermore, both formal and informal political institutions, along with the dominant political vision, have proven to be sufficiently inclusive and transparent for offering a broad framework in order to comply with the many different interests that have been articulated in the long process of defining the legal framework for privatisation. Finally, this approach can be perceived as a 'country-specific', (Mencinger 1996:425) 'non-ideological', and 'practical' model of transition which is a stimulating alternative to *shock therapy* (Zapp 1993:57).

However, the actual delay in Slovenia's full integration into the EU and NATO may be related to new initiatives for the regionalisation of the Balkans, which have been greatly influenced by external political and economic pressures. Slovenia might be compelled to supplement its initial transitional strategy and national policy, which were aimed at mediating international competitive pressures through public governance with efforts to participate in the process of development of new forms of cooperation in the region of the Balkans (Kumar 1997:138). This at present unpopular redefinition of the strategy may provide dividends in the long run in light of the very small size of the Slovenian market.[33] Despite its relatively successful transition experience, Slovenia in 1998 has not yet returned to pre-transition levels of industrial production (EIPF 1997:6), and pressures from product markets and further liberalisation are expected to intensify.

CONSTRUCTING A NEW REGIONAL FRAMEWORK

It is now widely admitted that multilateralism, that is, the expression of pluralistic tendencies in international relations that arose in the post-cold-war structural vacuum, failed to play a constructive role in controlling the explosiveness of the Yugoslav crisis and of other emergencies elsewhere on the periphery (Lucarelli 1995, Jakobsen 1994). Hettne maintains that a new and different form of regionalisation, termed 'new regionalism', is emerging in today's multipolar world order and may likely structure the potential basis for a qualified multilateral system.[34] Such a system may be able to inform and guide efforts aimed to break the vicious circle of underdevelopment that is usually accompanied by regional conflicts and insecurities. This New Regionalism is thus defined as a response to the security and developmental problems that occur with changing core-periphery relationships.[35] It is also an attempt to shape and control globalism from below and through cultural diversity, and is characterised by 'the higher degrees of regioness and the explicit political ambitions to achieve that aim'.[36]

Unfortunately, South-Eastern Europe, and the Balkans in particular, with its geopolitical position between East and West and between the formerly great empires of Austria-Hungary and Ottoman Turkey, inherited not only cultural diversity but also a history of violent political conflicts and social disintegration. For such reasons it can hardly be defined in a positive sense as a region with the potential to become 'an actor in its own right and with an agenda of its own' (Hettne 1997:35). But it is on the basis of these very differences that various and overlapping EC regional initiatives began to thrive at the end of 1980s as the promised way to European integration, which has been the more or less common goal of all the states in the region.[37] In the absence of historical distance, one can only speculate on the role of these initiatives in accelerating the disintegration of the former socialist Yugoslavia, already subject to intense ethnic, cultural and political differentiation.[38]

The most recent of these regional initiatives have arisen against the threat of a further destabilisation and isolation of the region. In the absence of stronger internal cohesive forces, the dynamism of the process of regional reintegration is highly dependent on economic, political, and even military external pressures. Adamović (1997:12) lists these initiatives as follows:

• the EU initiative for the economic reintegration of the former Yugoslavia;
• the EU Mediterranean Regional Seas Programme;
• the South-East Cooperation Initiative (SECI);
• the Black Sea Economic Cooperation initiative;
• the Sofia Declaration;
• Danubian Europe.

There are also a number of other overlapping initiatives for the reintegration of the region, and it is perhaps now likely that they will in fact play an integrative role in light of the interests of the EU and the constructive steps taken in that direction in 1996.[39] While it is obvious that this positive turn in external attitudes towards the region was greatly influenced by the perception of the dangers facing the European project, even more important is the qualitative change in American-European relations, which finally resulted in 1995 in a discussion of a possible Transatlantic Economic Area and of the concept of a Transatlantic Marketplace (Rashish 1995:2). This framework, in turn, made possible other regional initiatives. In December 1995, the 'Process of Stability' and 'Good-neighbourly Relations' was launched in Royaumont, and the July 1996 Sofia meeting resulted from the Bulgarian initiative for a Balkan Conference on Stability and Cooperation in South-Eastern Europe. While these initiatives address political and ethnic problems in South-Eastern Europe, the EU initiative and the SECI, the American initiative, have common social, economic and environmental concerns and are opposed to the discussion of specific political, historical and ethnic differences (SECI 1997:1).

The EU initiative is more concentrated on the five countries of the former Yugoslavia and addresses the revival of economic cooperation and infrastructural reconstruction. The conditional bilateral agreements and programmes of financial support for promoting legal–institutional adjustment and the transfer of knowledge (the PHARE programmes and the EIB loans) are proposed as methods for implementing regional cooperation (Minić 1997:76).

The SECI, which was announced in Geneva on 6 December 1996, is geographically very ambitious and includes twelve states: Albania, Bosnia-Herzegovina, Bulgaria, Croatia, the Federal Republic of Yugoslavia, Greece, Hungary, Macedonia, Moldavia, Romania, Slovenia and Turkey.[40] It is in fact the most ambitious initiative concerning the region in so far as it includes within its framework almost all other initiatives and involves virtually all actors in the region besides the national states, such as the United Nations Economic Commission for Europe (ECE), the Organisation for Security and Cooperation in Europe (OSCE), the World Bank, the European Investment Bank, the European Bank for Reconstruction and Development, etc. The SECI named the former Vice-Chancellor of Austria Dr Erhard Busek as a 'high level personality' with general responsibility, and an agenda committee was set up to initiate and organise joint projects and meetings. The agenda included infrastructure development, trade facilitation, energy, oil, gas, electricity, research and training, information exchange and media, communication, conferences, privatisations, technology transfer, economic potential, investment opportunities, legal structures, credit insurance schemes, tax advantages, banking and other issues. In respect to the twelve projects developed by the UN/ECE experts, it gave priority to the following six and established agreement concerning the host countries and international bodies responsible for the respective organisational efforts (SECI 1997:2–5):

- Trade Facilitation – Greece;
- Identification of Bottlenecks along Main International Corridors in the SECI Region and Short-term Measures to Remove Them – Bulgaria;
- Financial Policies to Promote Small and Medium Enterprises through Microcredit and Credit Guarantee Schemes – Romania;
- Energy Efficiency Demonstration Zones Network in South-Eastern Europe – Hungary;
- Interconnection of Natural Gas Networks, Diversification of Gas Supply, and Improvement of Security of Supply in South-Eastern Europe – Bosnia-Herzegovina;
- Danube Recovery Programme – ECE/Danube Convention Secretariat.

Not of least importance is the fact that the intention of the SECI is to promote the stable climate necessary for Euro-Atlantic industries to invest in the region, and a Business Advisory Council consisting of government officials is to be established to carry out this function. Consequently, the ultimate aim of the SECI is 'to create and implement viable mechanisms which would preclude military or political solutions to regional contrarieties' (SECI 1997:6).

BEYOND ECONOMISM: STRATEGIES FOR TRANSITION AND RECONSTRUCTION

Addressing transitional problems entails the analysis of economic changes as the latter are determined historically, politically and ideologically in a real world where all actors are not equal in the pursuit of their interests. Another part of the picture is an articulated, realistic political vision of capitalism accompanied by a strategy appropriate for realising that vision (Hardt 1996:240). If there is anything in common in those few cases of successful economies in transition that have shown some signs of recovery (Slovenia, Czech Republic, Hungary and Poland), it is the fact that each had such a vision and strategy. The common goal has been membership of the EU, but the strategies have differed according to their contingency upon particular economic, political, historical and ideological premises.

It is beyond the scope of this enquiry to speculate whether the early application of alternative approaches would have produced different results. Given the dominance of neo-liberalism both in the West and in the East during the early stage of transition, it is difficult to identify the existence of such a possibility from the standpoint of economic history. Without the acquisition of practical experience, the *laissez-faire* eschatology could not have faltered. By the same token, positions that recognise the need for industrial policy in transitional strategies have been steadily reinforced. Furthermore, in the current structural transformation of the world order and of the world economy, both the countries in transition and the developed countries have recognised the urgency of forging regional cooperation for development. This dialectical process of transformation with as yet uncertain results, namely, the new regionalism, is shaped by concerns that are beyond the scope of only economic cooperation, such as democracy, security, social policy and environment. Hopefully, today's capitalism has learned some lessons from history. The freedom of business is conditioned on stability and on a responsibility for human development. These can only be achieved by pursuing a path dependent on an inclusive political framework and a broader, critical historical and political vision that has been evolved beyond opposing modes of thought. Once again, the character of transitional and developmental strategies is conditioned by a nexus of economics, polity and society within a wider geopolitical context.

Notes

1. The author is especially grateful for the comments and suggestions provided by Carl Ulrik Schierup. She also benefited from discussions with Veljko Bole, Neven Borak, Branko Horvat, Franc Križanić, Jože Mencinger, Janež Prasnikar and Dragoljub Stojanov. The usual disclaimer applies. The financial support provided by the Swedish Institute and Department of Economic History, Uppsala University is gratefully acknowledged.
2. This discussion partly draws on Branka Likić-Brborić (1997).
3. Gowan (1995:4) lists other names for this same model, such as shock treatment, radical economic reform, Big Bang, and the 'three zatsias'.
4. The term 'standard reform prescription' was used by Stanley Fischer (1994:237). See also Peter Murrell (1995:164–78) and Brouthers and Lamb (1995).
5. Ivo Fabinc (1992:33) quotes the statement by Jacque Attali, President of the EBRD, at the First Annual Meeting of the Board of Governors, Budapest, 13–14 April 1992, indirectly warning about Mafia capitalism as the destructive result of shock therapy. See also Gowan (1995).
6. However, some still insist on viewing these as successes (e.g. Balcerowicz 1993:27–8). For a brief retrospective look at the first five years of reform and an account of the dramatic divergence between expectations and reality, see ECE (1995:9–16).
7. The European Forum is predicated on a broad Western European Social Democratic approach. See Eatwell *et al.* (1995:Preface).
8. In the sense as discussed by Hirschman (1982:12).
9. One example of such alternative positions is that of the AGENDA Group, initiated by Egon Matzner and Amit Bhaduri, which first gathered at the Austrian Academy of Sciences in Vienna in October 1991. Many scholars of

various provenence, from both East and West, were active in drafting documents critical of neo-classical dogmas; they included Jan Kregel, Leo Specht, Joze Mencinger, Tadeusz Kovalik, Jozef Pajestka, Roberto M. Unger, and others (Perczynski *et al.* 1994:vii). Unger is also known as one of the co-authors of the Latin American alternative to neo-liberalism. See Ciro Gomes and Roberto Mangabeira Unger (1996).

10. The term 'vision' has attained two meanings which articulate two different approaches to history. The first is a traditional empirical or descriptive approach, and it therefore is positivist since it separates facts from values and claims that theory should be a free observation of historical reality without any intent to change it. The other is a 'critical' approach, and it is normative or prescriptive in nature since it links historical analysis with political vision in order to understand and challenge the sources of domination and promote the cause of human freedom. See Best (1995:xv).

11. This includes those based upon the orthodox paradigm (the *laissez-faire*, planning, and growth-with-equity approaches), as well as those based upon the political-economy paradigm (the Marxist and dependency approaches). See Wilber and Jameson (1984:6).

12. See Duffield in Chapter 5 in the present volume on this point.

13. See UNDP (1996b). The idea of an automatic transposition of growth into a higher standard of living is questioned and qualitatively different development measures, such as HDI (human development index), GDI (gender development index), and GEM (gender empowerment measure) are elaborated.

14. Douglas C. North distinguishes between institutions, as formal and informal rules of the game, and organisations, as players. Together they structure human interaction. He introduces history into his analysis of change through the concept of path dependence, meaning that 'the consequence of small events and chance circumstances can determine solutions that, once they prevail, lead one to a particular path' (North 1992:94). The constraining character of institutions is represented by the concept of lock-in, which indicates a solution difficult to exit from once it has been reached.

15. See Stark (1992) and Bartlett (1992) for a discussion of a similar methodological approach.

16. Before the relaxation of the cold war, Yugoslavia, together with Egypt, India and Indonesia, came to be known as the non-aligned Third-World countries in that they pursued a politics of non-alignment between the West and East. The failure of this pursuit led to the redefinition of the phrase in terms of under-development. See Stavrianos (1981:33–34).

17. For an analysis of the reality and theories of the Yugoslav crisis, see Schierup in Chapters 1 and 2 in the present volume.

18. The Programme of Economic Reform and Measures for its Implementation in 1990 was proposed in mid-December, 1989. In the following June a comprehensive privatisation programme was launched that envisaged the possibility for workers to purchase internal shares at a discount. The Law on Social Capital followed amendments to the constitution which, together with the Enterprise Act and the Law on Use and Circulation of Social Capital, outlined the framework for the introduction of capitalism in 1988–9 and envisaged pluralism in the market, ownership and politics.

19. Borak (1992:123) refers to the list of 71 regulations as revised by the Chamber of Economy of Yugoslavia that had a disintegrating effect upon the Yugoslav economic sphere. Slovenia and Macedonia each passed 17, Croatia 16, and Serbia 13, but Bosnia-Herzegovina only 3.

20. See Putnam (1993) for a similar explanation of regional differences concerning institutional performance in Italy. See also Murrell (1995:177).
21. (Woodward 1995a) Slovenia has a two-hundred-year-long experience of effective local self-government that dates back to the reforms of Maria Theresa and Joseph II in the eighteenth century (Mencinger 1996:416).
22. Again, see Duffield in Chapter 5 in the present volume for a discussion of this issue.
23. Kozul-Wright and Rayment (1997:653) take the Czech Republic, Hungary, Poland and Slovenia as examples where a 'legitimate institutional structure' is now emerging.
24. The property rights controversies have been openly and explicitly discussed in the former Yugoslavia, where a school of 'economic ownership' was developed that included scholars such as Bajt, Horvat, Maksimovic and Gams (Bajt 1993:85).
25. Sirc (1997:110–54) questions the story of Slovenia's success through a comparison of Slovenia with South-Western European economies. He is also very critical of Slovenian independence in respect to its very high costs.
26. DEMOS consisted of six parties ranging across the political spectrum whose only common denominator was the ambition to achieve Slovenian independence.
27. The Slovenian experts were Veljko Bole, Minister of Finance Marko Kranjec, Deputy Prime Minister Jože Mencinger, Ivan Ribnikar, and members of the Board of the Bank of Slovenia. See Pleskovic and Sachs (1994) and Mencinger for differing interpretations of their actual contributions to the relatively successful monetary conversion.
28. According to the old constitution, the Slovenian Assembly consisted of the Socio-Political Chamber, The Chamber of Communes or Municipalities, and the Chamber of Associated Labour, the latter comprising representatives of the various branches and organisations of the economy who were elected by working people. All three Chambers had to review and approve of legislative proposals in a three-step procedure consisting of two preliminary readings and a vote on the final draft.
29. By the terms of this law, 40 per cent of the social capital should be transferred to public funds as follows: 10 per cent to the Restitution Fund, 10 per cent to the Pension Fund, and 20 per cent to the Development Fund, would be freely distributed to all Slovenian citizens in accordance with their ages. The employees would be entitled to free distribution of a further 20 per cent of the social capital through shares in their enterprises, and the remaining 40 per cent value of the equity was left for commercial privatisations through management–employee buy-outs, public tenders, public auctions and public offerings of shares.
30. The obligatory procedure requires a company to submit a privatisation plan to the Privatisation Agency for approval. After the subscription of shares issued to the owners, the Agency gives final agreement. The Court Registry of Companies finally completes the procedure.
31. The World Bank mission to Slovenia 1992–3 also supported this initiative.
32. See OECD (1997:106). Kozul-Wright and Rayment (1997:657) discuss the importance of a state's development vision and the need for a strategic approach to FDI in respect to a more critical understanding of the activities of TNCs.
33. Both Slovenia and Croatia have insisted on taking the position of observer in various regional initiatives concerning the Balkans. However, the Slovenian government signed an agreement in March, 1997, to participate in the SECI, even though it did not disseminate this information to the wider public.

34. Contrary to the old regionalism, this new regionalism has been forged more spontaneously in the world of multipolarity. It is more open than the old because cooperation includes other actors beyond the relations between nation states, and it is also a more comprehensive process inasmuch as it considers economic, political, social, cultural, and environmental issues beyond security and free trade objectives. See Hettne (1997:25–6; 28–9).

35. One may speak here about core regions (Europe, North America and East Asia); intermediate regions (Central Europe, Latin America and the Caribbean, South-East Asia, the 'European' Pacific [Australia and New Zealand] and the South Pacific); and the Periphery (the post-Soviet area, the Balkans, South Asia and Africa). See Hettne (1997:27).

36. Hettne (1997:29) defines globalism as a qualitative deepening of the process of internationalisation that strengthens the functional dimension of development, weakens its territorial dimension, and tends to result in the dominance of the world market over local production with an increase in consumerism.

37. Examples include the Central European Initiative and Alpe-Adria, which respectively included only the western republics of the former Yugoslavia and excluded the others. The functional regioness of the Danube cooperation initiative excludes Slovenia.

38. See also Minić (1997:74) and Adamović (1997:10) on this issue.

39. As Minić (1997:75) has pointed out, all of these constructive initiatives to include former Yugoslavia into a wider cooperation framework were proposed even before the violent disintegration of Yugoslavia, among others by Ante Marković, the last prime minister before the breakup, and intellectuals such as Branko Horvat. For information specific to the European initiative, see CEC (1996).

40. The invitation extended to the Federal Republic of Yugoslavia has been temporarily withdrawn.

References

Adam, H. and H. Giliomee (1979) *Ethnic Power Mobilized: Can South Africa Change?* New Haven and London: Yale University Press.

Adamović, Ljubiša (1997) 'Ekonomska reintegracija Jugoistočne Evrope: Američki projekat SECI, regionalni pristup Evropske unije i druge inicijative', *Međunarodna politika* 1055:6–16.

Adams, Nassau A. (1993) *Worlds Apart: The North–South Divide and the International System*. London: Zed Books.

Adanir, Fikret (1989) 'Tradition and rural Change in Southeastern Europe during Ottoman Rule', in Daniel Chirot (ed.), *The Origins of Backwardness in Eastern Europe: Economics and Politics from the Middle Ages until the Early Twentieth Century*. Berkeley, Los Angeles and Oxford: University of California Press.

Aggarval, V. (1985) *Liberal Protectionism: the International Politics of Organized Textile Trade*. Berkeley: University of California Press.

Agger, I. (ed.) (1995) *Psycho-Social Projects Under War Conditions*. Zagreb: European Community Task Force.

Agrell, Wilhelm (1994) *Från början för sent. Väst och de jugoslaviska nationalitetskrigen*. Falun: Natur och kultur.

Albrow, Martin (1996) *The Global Age*. Cambridge: Polity Press.

Amin, Samir (1994) *L'Ethnie a l'assaut des Nations*. Paris: Harmattan.

Amin, S. (1996b) 'Towards a Strategy of Liberation', *Al Ahram Weekly*, 28 December 1995–3 January 1996.

Amin, Samir (1996a) *Capitalism in the Age of Globalization. The management of Contemporary Crisis*. London and New Jersey: ZED Books.

Amsden, Alice H. (1989) *Asia's Next Giant: South Korea and Late Industrialization*. Oxford University Press.

Amsden, Alice H., Jacek Kochanowicz and Lance Taylor (1994) *The Market Meets Its Match: Restructuring the Economies of Eastern Europe*. Cambridge, MA: Harvard University Press.

Amsden, Alice H. (1994a) 'Can Eastern Europe Compete By Getting the Prices Right? Comparisons With East Asia', in Andrcs Solimano, Osvaldo Sunkel and Mario Blejer (eds), *Rebuilding Capitalism: Alternative Roads After Socialism and Dirigisme*. Ann Arbor: University of Michigan Press.

Amsden, Alice H. (1994b) 'Why Isn't the Whole World Experimenting with the East Asian Model to Develop: Review of The East Asian Miracle', in *World Development*, 22(4, April).

Andersson, Benedict (1983) *Imagined Communities*. London and New York: Verso.

Andersson, Benedict (1992) 'The New World Disorder', *New Left Review*, no. 192:3–13.

Arendt, Hannah (1970) *On Violence*. San Diego, New York, and London: Harcourt Brace.

Arrighi, G. (1991) 'World Income Inequalities and the Future of Socialism', *New Left Review*, no. 189:39–65.

Bačković, Enver (1995) *A Marshall Plan – Dream or Reality?* Sarajevo: Futura, 3.

Bahro, Rudolf (1978) *The Alternative in Eastern Europe*. London: New Left Books.

Bajt, Alexander (1993) 'The Property Right School: Is Economic Ownership a Missing Link?' *International Review of Law and Economics*, 13:85–97.

Balcerowicz, Leszek (1993) 'Common Fallacies in the Debate on the Economic Transition in Central and Eastern Europe', EBRD, *Working Paper* no. 11. London: European Bank for Reconstruction and Development.

Banac, Ivo (1992) *Eastern Europe in Revolution*. Ithaca and London: Cornell.

Bar-Hayim, Ariad (1996) 'From Workers' Participation to Employee Involvement. A Comparison of Two Paradigms', a paper presented to the workshop: 'Privatization of Social Services and Its Alternatives', Bled, 26–29 September.

Barker, Martin (1982). *The New Racism*. London: Junction Books.

Bartlett, David (1992) 'The Political Economy of Privatization: Property Reform and Democracy in Hungary', *East European Politics and Societies*, 6(1):73–118.

Bauman, Zygmunt (1989) *Modernity and the Holocaust*. Cambridge: Polity Press/Blackwell.

Bauman, Zygmunt (1992) *Intimations of Postmodernity*. London: Routledge.

Bauman, Zygmunt (1993) 'Racism, Antiracism and Moral Progress' (mimeo), Leeds.

Baumgartner, Tom, Tom R. Burns and Duško Sekulić (1979) 'Self-management, Market, and Political Institutions in Conflict: Yugoslav Development Patterns and Dialectics', in Burns *et al.* (eds), *Work and Power*. London: Sage: 81–138.

Best, Steven (1995) *The Politics of Historical Vision: Marx Foucault*. New York and London: Habermas, The Guilford Press.

Bianchini, Stefano (1993) 'On the threshold of "An Epochal Transformation"', *Balkan Forum* 1(3):103–120.

Bilandžić, Dušan (1981) 'O osnovnim tendencijama društvenog razvoja', *Naše Teme*, 25 (12):1859–70.

Binder, L. (1971) 'Crisis and Political Development', in Binder L. *et al.* (eds), *Crisis and Sequences of Political Development*. Princeton University Press.

Birnbaum, Pierre (1992) 'Nationalism: A Comparison Between France and Germany', *International Social Science Journal*, no. 133:375–84.

Blinder, Alan S. (ed.) (1990) *Paying for Productivity*. Washington: Brookings Institute.

Bloch, Maurice (1976) 'The Past and the Present in the Present', *Man* 12:278–92.

Bojičić, Vesna, Mary Kaldor and Ivan Vejvoda (1995) 'Post-War Reconstruction in the Balkans. A Background Report Prepared for the European Commission', *Working Papers in Contemporary European Studies* no. 14, Sussex: Sussex European Institute, University of Sussex.

Booth, David (1993) 'Development Research: From Impasse to a New Agenda', in Frans J. Schuurman (ed.) *Beyond the Impasse: New Directions in Development Theory*. London: Zed Books.

Borak, Neven (1992) 'An Outline of a Current State of Slovenian Economy', *Development and International Cooperation*, VIII(14–15):121–33.

Bougarel, Xavier (1996) *L'Anatomie d'un conflit découverte*. Paris.

Boutros-Ghali, Boutros (1995) 'An Agenda For Peace: Preventive Diplomacy, Peacemaking and Peace-Keeping (A/47/277-S/24111, 17 June 1992)', pp. 39–72 in *An Agenda for Peace*. New York: United Nations.

Bowman, Glen (1994) 'Xenophobia, fantasy and the Nation: The Logic of Ethnic Violence in Former Yugoslavia', in Goddard, Victoria A., Josep R. Llobera and Cris Shore (eds), *The Anthropology of Europe. Identity and Boundaries in Conflict*. Oxford: Berg.

Brass, Paul R. (1991) *Ethnicity and Nationalism*. New Delhi, Newbury Park, and London: Sage.

Brecht, Bertolt (1967) *Gesammelte Werke* 12. Frankfurt am Main: Suhrkamp Verlag.

Bremmer, Ian and Ray Taras (eds) (1997) *New States, New Politics. Building the Post-Soviet Nations*. Cambridge University Press.

Brenner, Robert (1989) 'Economic Backwardness in Eastern Europe in Light of Developments in the West', in Daniel Chirot (ed.), *The Origins of Backwardness in Eastern Europe: Economics and Politics from the Middle Ages until the Early Twentieth Century*. Berkeley, Los Angeles and Oxford: University of California Press.

Brinkman, Major G.J.W. (1996) 'The Complexities of Actual Involvement From a Military Point of View: Rules of Engagement', paper, Symposium on the Politics of Humanitarian Intervention, The Hague: Institute of Social Studies, 23 February.

Brouthers, Lance Eliot and Charles W. Lamb, Jr (1995) 'National Ideology, Public Policy, and the Business Environment: A Contingency Approach to Economic Reform in Hungary, Poland and Eastern Europe', *International Business Review*, 4(3):355–72.

Bruno, Michael and Lyn Squire (1996) 'The Less Equal the Asset Distribution, the Slower the Growth', *Transition*, 7(9–10):6.

Buchanan-Smith, Margaret and Simon Maxwell (1994) 'Linking Relief and Development: An Introduction and Overview', *Institute of Development Studies Bulletin*, 25(4):2–16.

Camilleri, J.A. and Falk, J. (1992) *The End of Sovereignty? The Politics of a Shrinking and Fragmenting World*. Aldershot: Edward Elgar.

Campbell, John L. (1997) 'Mechanism of Evolutionary Change in Economic Governance: Interaction, Interpretation and Bricolage', in Lars Magnusson and Jan Ottosson (eds) *Evolutionary Economics and Path Dependence*. Cheltenham and Brookfield: Edward Elgar, 10–33.

Carlo, Antonio (1972) 'L'esperienza jugoslava – dal collettivismo burocratico alla ristaurasione del capitalismo', *Terzo Mondo*, no. 18.

Castells, Manuel (1989) *The Informational City*. Oxford: Blackwell.

Castells, Manuel and Emma Kiselyova (1995) *The Collapse of Soviet Communism: A View from the Information Society*, Exploratory Essays, no. 2, Berkeley: University of California Press.

CEC (1996) *Prospects for the Development of Regional Cooperation for the Countries of the Former Yugoslavia and what the Community Could Do to Foster Such Cooperation*. Brussels: EU, Commission of the European Communities.

Chepulis, Rita L. (1984a) 'A New Form of Seasonal Labour With Particular Reference to the Textile/Clothing Industry in SR Croatia', research paper, Oslo University.

Chepulis, Rita L. (1984b) 'The Economic Crisis and Export-Led Development Strategy of SFR Yugoslavia: In Between Possibilities and Limitations', Paper for the: Mediterranean Studies Seminar: Models and Strategies of Development, Dubrovnik, IUC, April.

Chirot, D. (ed.) (1989) *The Origin of Backwardness in Eastern Europe. Economics and Politics from the Middle Ages until the Early Twentieth Century*. Berkeley: University of California Press.

Clark, J. (1991) *Democratizing Development: The Role of Voluntary Organizations*. London: Earthscan Publications.

Cohen, J. *et al.* (1975) 'De-Parsonizing Weber: A Critique of Parsons' Interpretation of Weber's Sociology', *American Sociological Review*, 40, April.

Cohen, Robin (1987) *The New Helots: Migrants in the International Division of Labour*. Aldershot: Gower.

Cole, J.W. (1985) 'Culture and Economy in Peripheral Europe', *Ethnologia Europaea*, 15:3–26.

Čolović, Ivan (1994) *Pucanje od zdravlja*. Belgrade: Beogradski Krug.

Cornia, Giovanni A. (1987) 'Economic Decline and Human Welfare in the First Half of the 1980s', pp. 11–47 in G.A. Cornia, R. Jolly, and F. Stewart (eds) *Adjustment With a Human Face*, 1. Oxford: Clarendon Press.

Ćosić, D. (1993), 'Addressing the Self-styled Bosnian Serb Assembly at Pale', *Vesti*, 7 May.

Cox, R. (1995) 'Critical Political Economy', in Hettne, Björn *et al.* (eds) *International Political Economy. Understanding Global Disorder*. London and New Jersey: Zed Books.

Cuthbertson, Ian M. and Jane Leibowitz (1993) *Minorities: The New Europe's Old Issue*. Prague, Budapest, Warsaw, New York and Atlanta: Institute for East-West Studies.

Cvjetičanin, Vladimir *et al.* (1980) *Mješovita domaćinstva i seljaci-radnici u Jugoslaviji*. University of Zagreb.

Cvjetičanin, Vladimir (1988) 'Motivacije mješovitih domaćinstava i njihovih alternativno zaposlenih članova', *Sociologija Sela*, no. 99–100:115–30.

Dallago, Bruno and Milica Uvalić (1996) 'The Distributive Consequences of Nationalism: The Case of Former Yugoslavia' (mimeo), research paper, University of Trento and University of Perugia.

Davidović, Milena (1986) 'Nezaposlenost i društvena nejednakost u Jugoslaviji', *Gledišta*, 27(7–8):3–35.

Demirović, Alex (1996) 'NGOs: Social Movements in Global Order?', paper presented at American Sociological Association Conference, New York.

Denich, Bette (1994) 'Dismembering Yugoslavia: Nationalist Ideologies and the Symbolic Revival of Genocide', *American Ethnologist*, 21(2):367–90.

Denitch, Bogdan (1994) *Ethnic Nationalism. The Tragic Death of Yugoslavia*. Minneapolis and London: University of Minnesota Press.

DHA (1993) United Nations Revised Consolidated Inter-Agency Appeal for the Former Yugoslavia. Geneva: Department of Humanitarian Affairs, 8 October.

Dow, Sheila C. (1990), 'Post-Keynesianism as political economy: a methodological discussion', *Review of Political Economy*, 2(3):345–58.

Dragićević-Šešić, Milena (1992) 'Novokomponovana ratna kultura – kič patriotizam', in *Sociološki Pregled*, 26(1–4):97–107.

Duffield, Mark (1984) 'New Racism . . . New Realism: Two Sides of the Same Coin', *Radical Philosophy*, (37):29–34.

Duffield, Mark (1994a) 'An Account of Relief Operations in Bosnia', Relief and Rehabilitation Network, *Network Paper 3*, March. London: Overseas Development Institute.

Duffield, Mark (1994b) 'Complex Emergencies and the Crisis of Developmentalism.' *Institute of Development Studies Bulletin: Linking Relief and Development*, October, 25:37–45.

Duffield, Mark (1996) *Social Reconstruction in Bosnia and Croatia: An Exploratory Report for SIDA*. University of Birmingham: Centre for Urban and Regional Studies, November.

Đurek, Danijel (1981) 'Tehnologija borbe za dohodak', *Naše Teme*, 25 (12):1966–71.

Dyker, David A. (1990) *Yugoslavia. Socialism, Development and Debt*. London and New York: Routledge.

Eatwell, John, Michael Ellman, Mats Karlsson, Mario Nuti, and Judith Shapiro (1995) *Transformation and Integration: Shaping the future of central and eastern Europe*. London: Institute for Public Policy Research (IPPR).

ECE (1995) *Economic Survey of Europe in 1994–1995*. New York: United Nations.

Edkins, Jenny (1996) 'Legality With a Vengeance: Famines and Humanitarian Relief in 'Complex Emergencies'. *Millennium* 25(3):547–76.

Edwards, Michael (1993) 'How Relevant Is Development Studies?', pp. 77–92 in Frans J. Schuurman (ed.), *Beyond the Impasse: New Directions in Development Theory*. London: Zed Books.

Eggertsson, Thráinn (1990) *Economic Behavior and Institutions*. Cambridge: Cambridge University Press.

EIPF (1997) *Gospodarska Gibanja*, May:283.

Ekonomska Politika (1989) 'Tekstilna industrija: Više od štrajka', No. 1926:15–17.

Enzensberger, Hans Magnus (1993) *Aussichten aus den Bürgerkrieg*. Frankfurt am Main: Suhrkamp.

Enzensberger, H.M. (1994) *Civil Wars: From L. A. to Bosnia*. New Press.

European Forum (1995) *Status on Women in Eastern and Central Europe: Platform of the European Forum Working Group*. Brussels: European Forum for Democracy and Solidarity.

European Union (1997) 'EU's Real Target to Move East: 2002. Even that Date is Optimistic, Not for All Candidates', *International Herald Tribune*, 23 January.

Faber, Mient Jan (1996) *The Balkans. A Religious Backyard of Europe*. Ravenna: Longo Editore.

Fabinc, Ivo (1992) 'Slovenia's Position in the World – the Message from the Past', *Development and International Cooperation*, 8 (14–15):23–29.

Fallon, Padaić and David Shirreff (1982) 'The Betrayal of East Europe', *Euromoney*, September: 19–37.

Féher, Ferenc, Agnes Heller, and György Markus (1983[1979]) *Dictatorship over Needs. An Analysis of Soviet Societies*. London: Blackwell.

Ferris, Elizabeth G. (1996) 'Refugees: New Approaches to Traditional Solutions.' Paper presented at: Conference on: People of Concern, Geneva: United Nations High Commission for Refugees, 21–24 November.

Fischer, Stanley (1994) 'Russia and the Soviet Union Then and Now', in Olivier Jean Blanchard, Kenneth A. Froot and Jeffrey D. Sachs (eds), *The Transition in Eastern Europe*, 1. Chicago: University of Chicago Press, 221–52.

Fishman, Joshua (1980) 'Social theory and ethnography', in Peter Sugar (ed.), *Ethnic Diversity and conflict in Eastern Europe*. Santa Barbara: ABC-Clio.

Forum of Tuzla Citizens (1995) Investment in Democracy: The Parliament of BiH. Tuzla, December.

Foxely, Alejandro (1983) Latin American Experiments in Neoconservative Economics. Berkeley: University of California Press.

Frank, Andre Gunder (1992) 'Nothing New in the East', *Social Justice*, 19 (1):34–61.

Freedman, Lawrence (1995) 'Bosnia: Does Peace Support Make Any Sense?', *Nato Review*, 43(6):19–23.

Friedman, Jonathan (1988) 'Cultural Logics of the Global System: A Sketch', *Theory, Culture, and Society*, 5:447–60.

Friedman, Jonathan (1992) 'The past in the future: history and the politics of identity', *American Anthropologist*, 94(4):37–859.

Fukuyama, Francis (1992) *The End of History and the Last Man*. London and New York: Penguin.

Gellner, Ernest (1983) *Nations and Nationalism*. Oxford: Blackwell.

Gellner, Ernest (1992a) 'Nationalism in the vacuum', in A.J. Motyl (ed.) *Thinking Theoretically about Soviet Nationalities*. New York: Columbia University Press : 243–54.

Gellner, Ernest (1992b) *Postmodernism, Reason and Religion*. London and New York: Routledge.

Gellner, Ernest (1993) 'What Do we Need now? Social Anthropology and Its New Global Context', *Anthropology*, no. 5:2–4.

Gerner, Kristian (1991) *Central Europas återkomst*. Stockholm: Norstedts.

Geroski, Branko (1996) 'Macedonian Stock Exchange', *OMRI Digest*, no. 65, part 1, 1 April.

Giddens, A. (1985) *The Nation-State and Violence*. Berkeley and Los Angeles: University of California Press.

Gill, S. (1995) 'Theorizing the Interregnum', in B. Hettne (ed.) *International Political Economy. Understanding Global Disorder*. London and New Jersey: Zed Books.

Gilpin, R. (1987) *The Political Economy of International Relations*. Princeton: Princeton University Press.

Giner, Salvador (1985) 'Political Economy, Legitimation and the State in Southern Europe', in Ray Hudson and Jim Lewis (eds) *Uneven Development in Southern Europe*. London and New York: Methuen.

Glasman, Maurice (1994) 'The Great Deformation: Polanyi, Poland and the Terrors of Planned Spontaneity', *New Left Review*, no. 205:59–86.

Glenny, Misha (1990*) The Rebirth of History. Eastern Europe in the Age of Democracy*. London: Penguin.

Glenny, Misha (1993) *The Fall of Yugoslavia*. Harmondsworth: Penguin.

Glenny, Misha (1994) 'The Return of the Great Powers', *New Left Review*, no. 205:125–30.

Gomes, Ciro and R.M. Unger (1996) 'The Next Step: A Practical Alternative to Neoliberalism, the Roundtable on 'Alternative to the Neo-Liberal Model of Development', March 1996, Global Studies Research Program, University of Wisconsin-Madison, Slovene translation, in *2000 Dvatisoc*, 92:5–51.

Gómez de Estrada, Ofelia and Rhoda Reddock (1987) 'New Trends in the Internationalisation of Production: Implications for Female Workers', in Boyd, E. Rosalind *et al.* (eds), *International Labour and the Third World – The Making of a New Working Class*. Aldershot: Avebury.

Goulding, M. (1993) 'The Evolution of United Nations Peacekeeping', *International Affairs*, 69(3):451–64.

Gowan, Peter (1995) 'Neo-Liberal Theory and Practice for Eastern Europe,' *New Left Review*, no. 213.

Greek, Ragnhild, Ragni Lantz Ingelstam, and Brigitta Lorentzi (1995) 'Workshop Manual, Trial Edition', *Active Nonviolence for Human Rights, Democracy and Peace*. Peace Committee of the Swedish Ecumenical Women's Council.

Grenzebach, William (1988) *Germany's Informal Empire in South Eastern Europe*. Stuttgart: Franz Steiner.

Griffin, K. (1991) 'Foreign Aid After the Cold War', *Development and Change* 22:645–85.

Guerra, Stefano (1996) 'The Multi-Faceted Role of the ODIHR', *OSCE ODIHR Bulletin*, 4(2):10–20.

Gutman, Roy (1993) *A Witness to Genocide*. Shaftesbury: Element.

Habermas, Jürgen (1973) *Legitimationsprobleme im Spätkapitalismus*. Frankfurt: Suhrkamp Verlag.

Habermas, Jürgen (1981) 'Modernity versus Postmodernity', *New German Critique* 22:3–14.

Hankiss, Elemer (1990) *East European Alternatives*. Oxford: Oxford University Press.

Hardt, John P. (1996) 'A Report Card for Economies in Transition', in Reiner Weichhardt (ed.), *Status of Economic Reforms in Cooperation Partner Countries in the Mid-1990s: Opportunities, Constraints, Security Implications*. Bruxelles: NATO: 233–47.

Hayden, Robert M. (1992) 'Constitutional Nationalism in the Formerly Yugoslav Republics', *Slavic Review*, 51(4):654–73.
Hayden, Robert M. (1996) 'Schindler's Fate: Genocide, Ethnic Cleansing, and Population transfers', *Slavic Review*, 55(4):727–78.
Helsinki Watch (1992) *War Crimes in Bosnia-Hercegovina*. New York: Human Rights Watch.
Hettne, Björn (1990) *Development Theory and the Three Worlds*. London: Longman Development Studies.
Hettne, Björn (1997) 'The New Regionalism and the Balkans', in Jelica Minić (ed.) *EU Enlargement, Yugoslavia and the Balkans*. Belgrade: European Movement in Serbia, Institute of Economic Sciences, Ekonomska politika and Friedrich Ebert Foundation.
Higgins, R. (1993) 'The New United Nations and the Former Yugoslavia', *International Affairs*, 69(3):465–83.
Hirschman, Albert O. (1982) *Shifting Involvements: Private Interest and Public Action*. Oxford: Blackwell.
Hobsbawm, Eric (1994a) *Age of Extremes: The Short Twentieth Century 1914–1991*. London: Michael Joseph.
Hobsbawm, Eric (1994b) 'Barbarism: A User's Guide', *New Left Review*, no. 206:44–54.
Hobsbawm, Eric and Terence Ranger (eds) (1993[1983]) *The Invention of Tradition*. Cambridge University Press.
Hodgson, Geoffrey M. (1993) *Economics and Institutions. A Manifesto for a Modern Institutional Economics*. Oxford: Polity Press.
Hodgson, Geoffrey, W.J. Samuels and M.R. Tool (eds) (1994) *The Elgar Companion to Institutional and Evolutionary Economics, A–K*. Aldershot: Edward Elgar.
Hopkins, Terence K. and Immanuel Wallerstein (eds) (1996) *The Age of Transition: Trajectory of the World-System – 1945–2025*. London: Zed Books.
Horvat, Branko (1985) *Jugoslavensko Društvo u krizi*. Zagreb: Globus.
Huntington, Samuel P. (1993) 'The Clash of Civilizations?', *Foreign Affairs*, Summer: 23–49.
IFRCS (1995) *World Disasters Report*. Geneva: International Federation of Red Cross and Red Crescent Societies.
International Centre Against Censorship (1994) *Forging War: The Media in Serbia, Croatia and Bosnia-Hercegovina*, Article 19, Harvard.
Iwansson, Per (1996) 'Rehabilitation and Reconstruction of Housing in Bosnia-Herzegovina', discussion paper, Swedish International Development Agency.
Jacobsen, C.G. (1996) *The New World Order's Defining Crises: The Clash of Promise and Essence*. Aldershot: Dartmouth.
Jakobsen, Peter Viggo (1994) 'Multilateralism Matters But How? The Impact of Multilateralism on Great Power Policy Towards the Break-up of Yugoslavia', Working Paper RSC no. 18. Florence: European University Institute.
Jelavich, Charles (1990) *South Slav Nationalisms: Textbooks and Yugoslav Union before 1914*. Columbus: Ihio State University Press.
Jessop, Bob (1995) 'Regional Economic Blocs, Cross-Border Cooperation, and Local Economic Strategies in Postsocialism', *American Behavioural Scientist*, 38(5):674–710.
Joffe, Josef (1992) 'Bosnia: The Return of History', *Commentary*, 94(4):24–29.
Jowitt, Ken (1992) *New World Disorder. The Leninist Extinction*. Berkeley, Los Angeles and London: University of California Press.
Kaldor, Mary (1993) 'Yugoslavia and the New Nationalism', *New Left Review*, no. 197:96–112.

Kaldor, Mary and Vashee, Basker (eds) (1997) *Restructuring the Global Military Sector: Part I New Wars*. London: Cassell/Pinter.

Kaplan, Robert D. (1993) *Balkan Ghosts: A Journey Through History*. London: Macmillan.

Katunarić, *Vjeran* (1988) *Dioba društva. Socijalna fragmentacija u američkom, sovjetskom i jugoslavenskom društvu*. Zagreb, Sociološko Društvo Hrvatske.

Katunarić, Vjeran (1992) 'Multi-ethnic Yugoslavia and political change with particular reference to Croatia', *Peuples Méditerranéens*, no. 61:123–43.

Katunarić, Vjeran (1994) *Bogovi, elite, narodi* Zagreb: Antibarbarus.

Keen, David (1993) 'Image or Impact'? (mimeo), University of Bergen.

Kennan, F. (ed.) (1993) 'Introduction: The Balkan Crisis 1913 to 1939', *The Other Balkan Wars*. Washington, DC: Carnegie Endowment.

Kennedy, Paul (1993) *Preparing For the Twenty-First Century*. New York: Random House.

Keohane, R.O. and J.S. Nye (1989) *Power and Interdependence*. New York: HarperCollins.

Kohl, H. (1997) 'Kohl Speaks to Havel of Integration and Identity', *International Herald Tribune*, 23 January.

Kidrić, Boris (1952) 'Govor na VI kongresu KPJ', in *Borba Komunista Jugoslavije za socijalističku demokratiju (VI kongres KPJ/SKJ)* Belgrade: Kultura.

Kidrić, Boris (1969) 'O nekim principijelnim pitanjima naše privrede', in Boris Kidrić, *Sabrana dela knjiga* III. Belgrade: Kultura.

Koch-Weser, Caio (1996) 'Quotation of the Month: "Continued Partnership with the People"', *Transition*, 7(11–12):10–11.

Kornai, Janos (1994) 'Transformation Recession-Main Causes', *Journal of Comparative Economics*, 19(1), August.

Korošić, Marijan (1988) *Jugoslavenska kriza*. Zagreb: Naprijed.

Kostić, Cvetko (1955) *Seljaci industrijski radnici*. Belgrade: Rad.

Kovač, Oskar (1996) *Yugoslavia and the EU*. Belgrade: Institute of Economic Sciences.

Kozul-Wright, Richard and Paul Rayment (1997) 'The Institutional Hiatus in Economies in Transition and Its Policy Consequences' *Cambridge Journal of Economics*, 21:641–61.

Kraft, Evan (1995) 'Stabilizing Inflation in Slovenia, Croatia, and Macedonia: How Independence Has Affected Macroeconomic Policy Outcomes', *Europe–Asia Studies*, 47(3).

Kumar, Andrej (1997) 'Accession to the EU – Problems and Achievements', in Jelica Minić (ed.) *EU Enlargement, Yugoslavia and the Balkans*. Belgrade: European Movement in Serbia, Institute of Economic Sciences, Ekonomska politika and Friedrich Ebert Foundation.

Lal, Deepak (1983) *The Poverty of Development Economics*, Hobart Paperback 16. London: Institute of Economic Affairs.

Lampe, John R. (1989) 'Imperial Borderlands or Capitalist Periphery? Redefining Balkan Backwardness, 1520–1914', in Chirot, Daniel (ed.) *The Origins of Backwardness in Eastern Europe: Economics and Politics from the Middle Ages until the Early Twentieth Century*. Berkeley, Los Angeles and Oxford: University of California Press.

Lane, D. (1992) *Soviet Society Under Perestroika*. London: Routledge.

Liepitz, Alain (1987) *Mirages and Miracles: The Crisis of Global Fordism*. Thetford: The Thetford Press.

Likić-Brborić, Branka (1997) 'Towards Alternative Approaches to -Transition', in *Enterprise in Transition. Second International Conference on Enterprise in*

Transition Split-Brela. May 22–24: Proceedings, Split and Wien: Faculty of Economics, University of Split and DAAM International.

Lipton, David and Jeffrey Sachs (1990) *Creating A Market Economy in Eastern Europe: The Case of Poland*, Brookings Papers on Economic Activity 1. Washington, DC: Brookings Institution.

Lipton, David and Jeffrey Sachs (1991) 'Privatization in Eastern Europe: The Case of Poland', in Bohm, Andreja and Vladimir G. Kreacic (eds), *Privatization in Eastern Europe*. Ljubljana: ICPE:24–57.

Little, Ian M.D. (1982) *Economic Development: Theory, Policies and International Relations*. New York: Basic Books.

Livada, Svetozar (1988) 'Socijalno-demografske promjene u selu i poljoprivredi', *Sociologija Sela* no. 99–100:35–48.

Lodge, G. (1990) *Comparative Business-Government Relations*. Englewood Cliffs, NJ: Prentice-Hall.

Lucarelli, Sonia (1995) *The European Response to the Yugoslav Crisis: Story of Two-Level Constraint*, Working Paper RSC no. 37. Florence: European University Institute.

Lydall, Harold (1989) *Yugoslavia in Crisis*. Oxford: Claredon Press.

Maffesoli, Michel (1991) *Les Temps des tribus: le déclin de l'individualisme dans les sociétés de masse*. Paris: Librairie Générale Française.

Magnusson, Kjell (1988) 'Jugoslavien: Inför centralkommittéens möte', *Nordisk Øst-Forum*, no. 3–4:83–6.

Malcolm, Noel (1994) *Bosnia. A Short History*. London: Macmillan.

Marglin, Stephen A. and Juliet B. Schor (1990) *The Golden Age of Capitalism*. Oxford: Clarendon Press.

Marković, Luka (1979) *Klasna borba i koncepcije razvoja*. Zagreb: Naprijed.

Marković, Petar (1974) *Migracije i promene agrarne strukture*. Zagreb: Zadružna Štampa.

Meillassoux, Claude (1981) *Maidens, Meals, and Money: Capitalism and the Domestic Economy*. Cambridge University Press.

Memorandum SANU (1989) 'Memorandum SANU Grupa akademika Srpske akademije nauka i umetnosti o aktuelnim društvenim pitanjima u našoj zemlji', *Naše Teme*, 33(1–2):128–63.

Mencinger, Jože (1991) 'From a Capitalist to a Capitalist Economy?', in James Simmie and Jože Dekleva (eds), *Yugoslavia in Turmoil: After Self-management*, London and New York: Pinter, 71–87.

Mencinger, Jože (1992) 'Decentralised versus Centralised Privatization: Creation of the Starting Conditions', in *Privatization: An International Symposium*. London: Centre for Research into Communist Economies, 23–37.

Mencinger, Jože (1996) 'Privatization Experiences in Slovenia', *Annals of Public and Cooperative Economics*, 67(3):415–8.

Meštrović, Stjepan G. (1994) *The Balkanization of the West. The Confluence of Postmodernism and Postcommunism*. London and New York: Routledge.

Mihajlović, Kosta (1981) *Ekonomska stvarnost Jugoslavije*, Belgrade: Prosveta.

Miljević, Milan and Nikola Poplašen (1991) 'Politička kultura i međunacionalni odnosi', in Baćević, Ljiljana et al., *Jugoslavija na kriznoj prekretnici*. Belgrade: Institute of Social Sciences.

Milošević, Slobodan (1989) *Godine raspleta*, Belgrade: Beogradski izdavački Zavod.

Minc, Alain (1993) *Le Nouveau moyen age*. Paris: Gallimard.

Minić, Jelica (1996) 'A Regional Framework for Peace and Development in the Balkans', research paper. Belgrade: Institute of Economic Sciences.

Minić, Jelica (1997) 'Post-Dayton Economy – is the European Model of Reconstruction Possible for the Balkans?', in Minić, Jelica (ed.), *EU Enlargement, Yugoslavia and the Balkans*. Belgrade: European Movement in Serbia, Institute of Economic Sciences, Ekonomska politika and Friedrich Ebert Foundation.

Mitrany, David (1951) *Marx Against the Peasant: A Study in Social Dogmatism*. University of North Carolina Press.

Moghadam, Valentine M. (ed.) (1992) *Privatization and Democratization in Central and Eastern Europe and the Soviet Union: The Gender Dimension*. Helsinki: WIDER (World Institute for Development Economics Research of the United Nations).

Mossberg, Bjorn, Annette Wong Jere and Johnny Åstrand (1994) *Experience, Competence and Sustainability: A Follow-up of Swedish Humanitarian Aid to Croatia and Bosnia Herzegovina*. Lund: Lund University Center for Habitat Studies.

Mouzelis, Nicos P. (1978) 'Greek and Bulgarian Peasants: Aspects of their Socio-Political Situation during the Inter-War Period', in Mouzelis, Nicos: *Modern Greece. Facets of Underdevelopment*. London and Basingstoke, Macmillan.

Mouzelis, Nicos P. (1986) *Politics in the Semi-Periphery: Early Parliamentarism and Late Industrialisation in the Balkans and Latin America*. London: Macmillan.

Murrell, Peter (1995) 'The Transition According to Cambridge, Mass.', *Journal of Economic Literature*, XXXIII (March):164–178.

Müller, Klaus (1995) 'From post-communism to post-modernity? Economy and society in Eastern European transformations', in Grancelli, Bruno (ed.), *Social Change and Modernization: Lessons from Eastern Europe*. Berlin and New York: Walter de Gruyter.

Nairn, T. (1977) *The Break-up of Britain*. London: New Left Books.

Nelson, Joan (1986) 'The Diplomacy of Policy Based Lending', in Richard E. Feinberg (ed.), *Between Two Worlds: The World Bank's Next Decade*. New Brunswick, NJ: Transaction Books.

Norgaard, R.B. (1994) *Development Betrayed: The End of Progress and a Coevolutionary Revisioning of the Future*. London: Routledge.

Nuti, Mario and Richard Portes (1993) 'Central Europe: The Way Forward', in Richard Portes (ed.), *Economic Transformation in Central Europe: A Progress Report*. London: Centre For Economic Policy Research for the European Communities.

O'Brien, Philip (1984) 'Authoritarianism and Monetarism in Chile', *Socialist Review*, September–October: 45–79.

Ocić, Časlav (1983) *Integracioni i dezintegracioni procesi u privredi Jugoslavije*. Belgrade: the Central Committee of the League of Communists in Serbia.

OECD (1991) The Transition to a Market Economy. Paris: OECD.

OECD (1997) *Economic Survey of Slovenia 1996–1997*. Paris: OECD.

Okey, Robin (1992) 'State, church and nation in the Serbo-Croat speaking lands of the Habsburg Monarchy, 1950–1914', in Donal A. Kerr (ed.), *Religion, State, and Ethnic Groups. Comparative Studies on Governments and Non-Dominant Ethnic Groups in Europe, 1950–1940*. Dartmouth: New York University Press, 51–78.

Oliveira-Roca, Maria (1984) 'Tipovi migracije radnika u Jugoslaviji', *Sociologija Sela*, no. 83–86:3–16.

Oliveira-Roca, Maria (1988) 'Cirkulacija aktivnog stanovništva sela', *Sociologija Sela*, no. 99–100:131–42.

Oman, C. (1994) *Globalisation and Regionalisation: The Challenge for Developing Countries*. OECD Development Centre.

Panitch, Leo and Ralph Miliband (1992) 'The New World Order and the Socialist Agenda', *The Socialist Register 1992*: 1–25.

Pantić, Dragomir (1991) 'Nacionalna distanca građana Jugoslavije', in Ljiljana Baćević, *et al.* (eds) *Jugoslavija na kriznoj prekretnici*. Belgrade: Institute of Social Sciences.

Pearson, Raymond (1995) 'Empire, war and the nation-state in East Central Europe', in Paul Latawski (ed.), *Contemporary Nationalism in East Central Europe*. Basingstoke and London: St Martins Press, 25–40.

Perczynski, Maciej, Jan Kregel and Egon Matzner (eds) (1994) *After the Market Shock: Central and East-European Economies in Transition*. Aldershot, Brookfield USA, Singapore, Sidney: Dartmouth.

Peterson, Abby (1994) 'Racist and antiracist movements in postmodern societies: between universalism and particularism', paper prepared for: XIII World Congress of Sociology, Bielefeld, July 1994 (draft).

Petrin, Tea (1995) *Industrial Policy Supporting Economic Transition in Central-Eastern Europe: Lessons from Slovenia*, policy Papers in International Affairs, no. 43. Berkeley: Institute of International Studies, University of California.

Piccone, Paul (1990) 'Paradoxes of Perestroika', *Telos*, no. 84:3–32.

'Platform for the Preparation of Positions and Decisions of the Tenth Congress of the LCY', *Socialist Thought and Practice*, no. 53, 1973:3–178.

Pleskovic, Boris and Jeffrey Sachs, (1994) 'Political Independence and Economic Reform in Slovenia', in O.J. Blanchard, K.A. Froot and J.D. Sachs (eds), *The Transition in Eastern Europe*, 1. Chicago and London: The University of Chicago Press:191–220.

Plestina, Diana (1992) *Regional Development in Communist Yugoslavia: Success, Failure and Consequences*. Boulder, San Francisco, Oxford: Westview Press.

Podrebarac, Vladimir (ed.) (1985) *Socijalistički samoupravni preobražaj odgoja i obrazovanja u SR Hrvatskoj 1947–1984*. Zagreb: Školske novine.

Polanyi, Karl (1957[1944]) *The Great Transformation: The Political and Economic Origins of Our Time*. Boston: Beacon Press.

Poulantzas, Nicos (1975) *La Crise des dictatures*. Paris: Seuil.

Poznanski, Kazimierz Z. (1995) 'Dilemmas of Privatization in Eastern Europe and Russia', *Emergo*, 2(2):61–76.

Prasnikar, Janez and Jan Svejnar (1993) 'Workers' Participation in Management versus Social Ownership and Government Policies: Yugoslav Lessons for Transforming Socialist Economies', in A.B. Atkinson (ed.), *Alternatives to Capitalism: The Economics of Partnership*, proceedings of a conference held in honour of James Meade by International Economic Association at Windsor, England. New York: Saint Martin's Press in association with the International Economic Association.

Puljiz, Vlado (1977) *Eksodus poljoprivrednika*. Zagreb: University of Zagreb.

Puljiz, Vlado (1987) 'Ruralno-sociološka istraživanja i glavni trendovi promjena u našem selu', *Sociologija Sela*, 25:9–18.

Puljiz, Vlado (1988) 'Seljaštvo u Jugoslaviji', *Sociologija Sela*, no. 99–100:5–24.

Pupavac, Vanessa (1997) 'Theories of Conflict and Children's Rights', paper, Second Convention of the European Association for the Advancement of Social Sciences, Conflict and Cooperation, University of Cyprus, Nicosia, 19–23 March.

Putnam, Robert D. (1993) *Making Democracy Work: Civic Traditions in Italy*. Princeton University Press.

Ramet, Sabrina P. (1991) *Social Currents in Eastern Europe: The Sources and Meaning of the Great Transformation*. Durham, NC: Duke University Press.

Ramet, Sabrina P. (1992) *Nationalism and Federalism in Yugoslavia, 1962–1991*. Bloomington and Indianapolis: Indiana University Press.

Ramos, Joseph (1986) *Neoconservative Economics in the Southern Cone of Latin America 1973–1983*. Baltimore: Johns Hopkins University Press.

Rashish, Peter S. (ed.) (1995) *Building Blocks for a Transatlantic Economic Area, Final Report of the European Institute, 5th Annual Seminar on Trade and Investment*. Washington, DC: European Institute.

Räthzel, Nora (1997) *Gegenbilder deutscher Nation. Nationale Identitat durch Konstruktionen des Anderen*. Opladen: Leske und Budrich.

Reichel, Sarah (1996) *The European Administration of Mostar: Objectives and Achievements July 1994–July 1996*. EU Mostar, December.

Reno, William (1995) 'Reinvention of an African Patrimonial State: Charles Taylor's Liberia', *Third World Quarterly*, 16(1):109–20.

Richards, Paul (1995) Mimeo *Fighting For the Rain Forest: Youth, Insurgency and Environment in Sierra Leone*. University College London: Department of Anthropology.

Richmond, A.H. (1994) *Global Apartheid: Refugees, Racism, and the New World Order*. Toronto, New York, Oxford: Oxford University Press.

Rosenau, J. (1995) 'Distant Proximities: The Dynamics and Dialectics of Globalization', in B. Hettne (ed.) *International Political Economy. Understanding Global Disorder*. London and New Jersey: Zed Books.

Roskin, Michael G. (1991) *The Rebirth of Eastern Europe*. Englewood Cliffs, NJ: Prentice Hall.

Rupesinghe, Kumar (1996) 'Governance and Conflict Resolution in Multi-Ethnic Societies', pp. 10–31, in Kumar Rupesinghe and Valery A. Tishkov (eds), *Ethnicity and Power in the Contemporary World*. Tokyo: United Nations University.

Sachs, Jeffrey (1990) 'What is to be done?', *The Economist*, 13 January.

Sadowski, Yahya (1991) *Political Vegetables?: Businessman and Bureaucrat in the Development of Egyptian Agriculture*. Washington DC: Brookings Institution.

Salay, Jürgen (1992) 'An Economic Survey of Slovenia and Croatia', EFTA Occasional paper no. 42. Geneva: EFTA.

Salecl, Renata (1994) 'The Crisis of Identity and the Struggle for New Hegemony in the Former Yugoslavia', in Ernesto Laclau (ed.), *The Making of Political Identities*. London and New York: Verso.

Salvadori, Massimo (1963) *The American Economic System*. Indianapolis, New York: Bobbs-Merrill.

Samary, Catherine (1995) *Yugoslavia Dismembered*. New York: Monthly Review.

Sampson, Steven (1985) 'The Informal Sector in Eastern Europe', *Telos*, no. 66 (6): 44–66.

Samudavanija, C-A. (1991) 'The Three-Dimensional State', in J. Manor (ed.), *Rethinking Third World Politics*. London and New York: Longman.

Samuels, Warren J. (1995) 'The Present State of Institutional Economics', *Cambridge Journal of Economics*, 19:569–90.

Schierup, Carl-Ulrik (1990) *Migration, Socialism, and the International Division of Labour: the Yugoslavian Experience*. Aldershot: Avebury.

Schierup, Carl-Ulrik (1992) 'Quasi-proletarians and Patriarchal Bureaucracy. Aspects of Yugoslavia's Reperipheralisation', *Soviet Studies*, 44(1):79–99.

Schierup, Carl-Ulrik (1993) 'Prelude to the Inferno. Economic Disintegration and Political Fragmentation of Socialist Yugoslavia', *Migration*, no. 3:5–40.

Schierup, Carl-Ulrik (1995a) 'Eurobalkanism: Ethnic Cleansing, Nationalism and the post-Cold War Order', in Bianchini, Stefano and Paul Shoup (eds), *The Yugoslav war, Europe and the Balkans: How to Achieve Security*. Ravenna: Longo Editore: 31–44.

Schierup, Carl-Ulrik (1995b) 'The Spectre of Balkanism', *Europe*, no. 3:10–11.

Schierup, Carl-Ulrik (1995c) 'A European Dilemma: Myrdal, The American Creed, and EU Europe', *International Sociology*, 10 (4):347–67.

Schierup, Carl-Ulrik (1998a) 'From Fraternity to Fratricide: Nationalism, Globalism and the Fall of Yugoslavia', forthcoming in volume on nationalism, ethnic relations and social change in the Balkans edited by Stefano Bianchini. Ravenna: Longo Editore.

Schierup, Carl-Ulrik (1998b) 'Ethno-nationalism, Bureaucracy, and the Poverty of Reform Policies: Background to the Obstruction of Yugoslavia's Post-Communist Transformation', forthcoming in *Migration*.

Schrenk, Martin (1996) 'Eatwell, John, Michael Ellman, Mats Karlsson, Mario Nuti, and Judith Shapiro (eds. 1995) Transformation and Integration: Shaping the future of central and eastern Europe', *Books of the Month* 7:1.

Schuurman, Frans J. (1993) 'Introduction: Development Theory in the 1990s', pp. 1–48 in Frans J. Schuurman (ed.), *Beyond the Impasse*. London: Zed Books.

Scott, Richard W. (1995) 'Introduction: Institutional Theory and Organizations' in W. Richard and Sören Christensen (eds), *The Institutional Construction of Organizations. International and Longitudinal Studies*. Thousand Oaks, London, New Delhi: Sage, xi–xxiii.

SECI (Southeast European Cooperative Initiative) (1997) 'Southeast European Cooperative Initiative', paper presented in Sarajevo, 7 July.

Sheahan, John (1980) 'Market Oriented Economic Policies and Political Repression in Latin America', *Economic Development and Cultural Change*, 28(2):267–92.

Silverman, Max (1992) *Deconstructing the Nation: Immigration, Racism and Citizenship in Modern France*. London: Routledge.

Simoneti, Marko (1994) 'Privatizacija podjetij in razvoj financnega sistema v Sloveniji', working paper. Ljubljana: CEEPN (Central and Eastern European Privatization Network).

Sirć, Ljubo (1997) *Da li je kritika samoupravljanja jos uvijek aktuelna?* Belgrade, London: Institut Ekonomskih Nauka and CRCE (Center for Research on Communist Economies).

Skocpol, T. (1979) *States and Social Revolutions: A Comparative Analysis of France, Russia, and China*. Cambridge University Press.

Skocpol, Theda (1985) *Bringing the State Back In*. Cambridge University Press.

Smelev, Vladimir and Nikolai Popov (1987) *The Turning Point*. New York: Doubleday.

Smith, Anthony D. (1971) *Theories of Nationalism*. London: Duckworth.

Smith, Anthony, D. (1993) 'The Ethnic Sources of Nationalism', *Survival* 35(1): 48–62.

Sofianou, Evanthia (1995) 'Post-Modernism and the Notion of Rationality in Economics', *Cambridge Journal of Economics*, 19:373–389.

Sofos, Spyros A. (1996) 'Inter-ethnic Violence and Gendered Constructions of Ethnicity in Former Yugoslavia', *Social Identities*, 2(1):73–91.

Solimano, Andres (1994) 'Introduction and Synthesis', in Andres Solimano, Osvaldo Sunkel and Mario I. Blejer (eds), *Rebuilding Capitalism: Alternative Roads After Socialism and Dirigisme*. Ann Arbor: University of Michigan Press.

Soros, George (1997) 'The Capitalist Threat', *Atlantic Monthly*, 279(2):14–58.

Stark, David (1992) 'Path Dependence and Privatization Strategies in East Central Europe', *East European Politics and Societies*, 6 (1):17–54.

Statistical Yearbook of SFR Yugoslavia (1991) Belgrade.

Stavrianos, L.S. (1981) *Global Rift. The Third World Comes of Age*. New York: William Morrow.

Štiblar, Franjo (1993) 'The Rise and Fall of Yugoslavia: An Economic History View' (manuscript).

Strassman, Diana (1996) 'How Economists Shape Their Tales', *Challenge*, January–February:13–19.

Strpić, Dag (1988) 'Obrazovanje, tehnološki i društveni razvoj i društvena infrastruktura', *Naše Teme*, 1–2, 32:24–42.

Stubbs, Paul (1995) 'Nationalisms, Globalisation and Civil Society in Croatia and Slovenia', paper, Second European Conference of Sociology: 'European Societies: Fusion or Fission?', Budapest, 30 August–2 September.

Stubbs, Paul (1996) 'Social Reconstruction and Social Development in Croatia and Slovenia: The Role of the NGO Sector', Research Report R6274. London: Overseas Development Administration, ESCOR.

Suhrke, Astri (1993) 'A crisis diminished: refugees in the developing world', *International Journal*, Spring 1993:215–39.

Suhrke, Astri (1994) 'Towards a Comprehensive Refugee Policy: Conflict and Refugees in the Post-Cold War World', pp. 13–38 in W.R. Bohning and M.L. Schloeter-Paredes (eds), *Aid in Place of Migration?* Geneva: International Labour Office.

Summerfield, Derek (1996) 'The Impact of War and Atrocity on Civilian Populations: Basic Principles for NGO Interventions and a Critique of Psychosocial Trauma Projects', pp. 1–40 in *Relief and Rehabilitation Network Paper*. London: Overseas Development Institute.

Summers, Lawrence H. (1991) 'Keynote Address: Knowledge For Effective Action', *Proceedings of the World Bank Annual Conference on Development Economics 1991*. Washington, DC: World Bank.

Suny, Ronald Grigor (1993) *The Revenge of the Past. Nationalism, Revolution, and the Collapse of the Soviet Union*. Stanford University Press.

Szporluk, R. (1988) *Communism and Nationalism: Karl Marx Versus Friedrich List*. New York: Oxford University Press.

Tabak, Faruk (1996) 'The World Labour Force', pp. 87–116 in Terence K. Hopkins and Immanuel Wallerstein (eds), *The Age of Transition: Trajectory of the World-System, 1945–2025*. London: Zed Books.

Tägil, Sven (ed.) (1992) *Europa – historiens återkomst*. Hedemora: Gidlunds.

Taguieff, Pierre-André (1991) *Face au racisme 1–2*. Paris: Éditions la Découverte.

Taylor, Lance (1987) 'IMF Conditionality: Incomplete Theory, Policy Malpractice' in Robert J. Myers (ed.), *The Political Morality of the International Monetary Fund*. New Brunswick: Transaction Books.

Taylor, Lance (1988) *Varieties of Stabilization Experience*. Oxford University Press.

Thurow, Lester (1992) *Head to Head: The Coming Economic Battle Among Japan, Europe, and America*. New York: William Morrow.

Tilly, Charles (1993) 'Futures of European States', *Social Research* 59(4):705–17.

Tishkov, Valery (1997) *Ethnicity, Nationalism and Conflict in and After the Soviet Union: The Mind Aflame*. London: Sage.

Tomasevich, Jozo (1955) *Peasants, Politics and Economic Change in Yugoslavia*. Stanford and London: Stanford University Press.

Toye John F. (1987) *Dilemmas of Development*. Oxford: Blackwell.

UNCTC (United Nations Centre for Transnational Corporations) (1991) *World Investment Report 1991: The Triad in Foreign Direct Investment*. New York: UN Centre on Transnational Corporations.

UNDP (United Nations Development Programme) (1996a) *Human Development Report 1996*. New York: Oxford University Press of United Nations Development Programme.

UNDP (United Nations Development Programme) (1996b) *Workshop on Reconstruction, Reform and Economic Management in Bosnia and Herzegovina*. Vienna: Vienna Institute for Comparative Economic Studies.

UNHCR (United Nations High Commissioner for Refugees) (1995) *The State of the World's Refugees: In Search of Solutions*. Oxford: Oxford University Press for United Nations High Commission for Refugees.

United Nations (1992) General Assembly, Security Council, Document A/47/666, S/24809, 17 November.

Uvalić, Milica (1992) 'Yugoslavia: The Economic Costs of Disintegration', *EUI Working Paper* EPU No. 92/17. Florence: European University Institute.

Uvalić, Milica (1993) 'The Disintegration of Yugoslavia: Its Costs and Benefits', *Communist Economies and Economic Transformation*, 5(3):273–93.

Uvalić, Milica (1994) *Privatization in Disintegrating East European States: The Case of Former Yugoslavia*, Working Papers RSC No. 94/11. Florence: European University Institute.

Veit, John (1996) 'Bosnia: A Real Drug War', *High Times* March.

Vejvoda, Ivan and David Dyker (eds) (1996) *Yugoslavia and After: A Study in Fragmentation, Destruction and Rebirth*. London and New York: Longman.

Verba, S. (1971) 'Sequences and Development', in L. Binder, J. Coleman, J. LaPalombra, L.W. Pye, S. Verba and M. Weiher, *Crisis and Sequences of Political Development*. Princeton University Press.

Vodopivec, Milan (1996) 'The Slovenian Labor Market in Transition: Evidence from Microdata', *Development and International Cooperation* XII(22):89–151.

Voutira, Eftihia and Shaun A.W. Brown (1995) 'Conflict Resolution: A Review of Some Non-Governmental Practices – "A Cautionary Tale"', *Studies on Emergencies and Disaster Relief – Report no. 4*. University of Oxford: Refugee Studies Programme, Queen Elizabeth House.

Wade, Robert (1989) *Governing the Market*. Berkeley: University of California Press.

Wade, Robert (1992) 'East Asia's Economic Success: Conflicting Perspectives, Partial Insights, Shaky Evidence', *World Politics*, 44(4):270–320.

Wade, Robert (1993) 'Managing Trade: Taiwan and South Korea as a Challenge to Economics and Political Science', *Comparative Politics*, 25(2):127–45.

Wade, Robert (1996) 'Japan, the World Bank, and the Art of Paradigm Maintenance: The East Asian Miracle in Political Perspective', *New Left Review*, no. 217, May–June issue.

Wallerstein, Immanuel (1994) 'The Agonies of Liberalism: What Hope progress?', *New Left Review*, no. 204:3–17.

Walton, John and David Seddon (1994) *Free Markets and Food Riots*. Oxford: Blackwell.

Wandycz, Piotr S. (1992) *The Price of Freedom: A History of East Central Europe from the Middle Ages to the Present*. London and New York: Routledge.

Weber, M. (1981) *General Economic History*. New Brunswick: Transaction Books.

Weiss, Thomas G. (1996) 'Humanitarian Action in War Zones: Recent Experience and Future Research', paper, Symposium on Humanitarian Intervention, The Hague: Institute of Social Studies, 23 February.

Wells Paul (1991) 'Keynes's General Theory Critique of the Neo-classical Theories of Employment an Aggregate Demand', *Review of Social Economy*, 49(3), Fall.

West, Rebecca (1993[1942]) *Black Lamb and Grey Falcon*. London: Canongate.

Wilber, Charles and Kenneth P. Jameson (1984) 'Paradigms of Economic Development and Beyond' in Charles K. Wilber (ed.), *The Political Economy of Development and Underdevelopment*. New York: Random House: 1–26.

Williamson, John (1991) *Economic Opening of Eastern Europe: Three Lessons from*

216   *References*

the Yugoslav Experience. Washington, DC: Institute for International Economics.

Williamson, John (1996) 'The Washington Consensus Revisited', paper, conference on: Development Thinking and Practice, organised by the Inter-American Development Bank in Washington, 3–5 September.

Winiecki, Jan (1992) 'The Political Economy of Privatization', in Horst Siebert (ed.), *Privatization: Symposium in Honour of Herbert Giersch*. Tübingen: J.C.B. Mohr (Paul Siebeck).

Woodward, Susan (1986) 'Orthodoxy and Solidarity: Competing Claims and International Adjustment in Yugoslavia' in Ellen Comisso and Laura Tyson (eds), *Power, Purpose and Collective Choice*. Ithaca: Cornell University Press.

Woodward, Susan L. (1995a) *Socialist Unemployment: The Political Economy of Yugoslavia 1945–1990*. Princeton University Press.

Woodward, Susan L. (1995b) *Balkan Tragedy. Chaos and Dissolution after the Cold War*. Washington, DC: Brookings Institution.

World Bank (1991) *World Development Report* Washington, DC: World Bank.

World Bank (1995) 'Bosnia and Herzegovina: Economic Issues and Priorities', discussion paper, Central European Department of the World Bank.

World Bank (1996a) 'Bosnia-Herzegovina – The Priority Reconstruction Program: From Emergency to Sustainability', paper prepared by the European Commission and the Central Europe Department of the World Bank, 1, November.

World Bank (1996b) *The World Bank Participation Sourcebook*. Washington, DC: World Bank.

World Bank (1996c) 'Bosnia and Herzegovina: Towards Economic Recovery', Discussion Paper no. 2, prepared by the World Bank, the EC and the EBRD for the Second Donors' Conference, 2 April. Washington, DC: World Bank.

Wyzan, Michael L. (1994) 'Macedonia', in Michael Wyzan (ed.), *First Steps to Economic Independence in the Post-Communist World*. Westport: Praeger.

Young, Boris (1992) 'With Axes in their Eyes: Rentierism and Market Reform in Yugoslavia', *Studies in Comparative Communism*. xxv(3):274–286.

Yugoslav Survey (1990) 'Speech Presented by Ante Markovic on Results Achieved and Further Measures to Implement the Economic Reform Programme', xxi(2).

Yugoslav Survey (1995) 'Causes of the Black Economy and Factors Promoting its Expansion', xxvi(1).

Zapp, Kenneth (1993) 'The Economic Consequences of National Independence: The Case of Slovenia', *International Journal of Politics, Culture and Society* 7(1): 57–74.

Zarkovic-Bookman, Milica (1994) *Economic Decline and Nationalism in the Balkans*. New York: St Martin's Press.

Zarkovic-Bookman, Milica (1997) *The Demographic Struggle for Power: The Political Economy of Demographic Engineering in the Modern World*. London: Frank Cass.

Zaslavsky, Victor (1982) *The Neo-Stalinist State: Class, Ethnicity and Consensus in Soviet Society*. Armonk: M.E. Sharpe.

Županov, Josip (1969) *Samoupravljanje i društvena moć*. Zagreb: Naše Teme.

Županov, Josip (1977) *Sociologija i samoupravljanje* Zagreb: Školska knjiga.

Županov, Josip (1981) 'Aktualni društveni trenutak', *Naše Teme* 25(12):1945–56.

Županov, Josip (1983a) 'Tržište rada i samoupravni socijalizam', *Naše Teme* 27(3).

Županov, Josip (1983b) 'Znanje, društveni sistem i "klasni interes"', *Naše Teme* 7–8:1048–54.

Županov, Josip (1985) 'Radnićka klasa i društvena stabilnost', *Kulturni radnik*, no. 5:1–20.

Index

Adam, Heribert, 74, 75
Adamović, Ljubiša, 200
Adams, Nassasu, A., 119
Adanir, Fikret, 59
administration, fragmented in
    Balkans, 18
Adriatic tourist industry, 160
Afghanistan invaded by Soviet
    Union, 153
Afghanistan, 57
Africa, 119
    Horn of, 57
African National Congress (ANC),
    69
Aggarval, V., 90
aggregation of Eastern European
    countries for economic
    integration, 78
    see also free-trade clusters
agriculture, restored importance of,
    during economic crisis (1980s),
    51
    see also peasantry
aid agencies in live conflicts, 124
aid, humanitarian
    agencies, access for, 130
    diversion of, 130
    division of labour in, 129
    end of phase of, 144
    fusion with military protection, 129
    increase in costs of, 125
    lack of end-use monitoring of, 130
    needs assessments by warring
        parties, 130
    role during cold war, 118
    and security, 20–1, 118–46
    undermining local political
        opposition, 144
    as Western response to collapse
        of Yugoslavia, 124
Albania, 6, 16, 93
    rebellion in (1997), 7
    social revolution in, 35

'Albanisation', 17
Albrow, Martin, 34
Alma Ata (second founding
    meeting of CIS), 70
Amin, Samir, 19, 26–7, 81
Amsden, Alice, H., 147, 149, 151
Andersson, Benedict, 4, 27
Andorra, 81
Angola, 57
apartheid system, 75–6
Arendt, Hannah, 14
Argentina, 149
Armenia, 70
arms trade in Bosnia-Herzegovina, 19
Arrighi, G., 119
Asia, *see* East Asia
Asian High Performance Economies
    (HPAE), 147
    setting 'wrong' prices, 149, 169
Associated Labour Act (1976), 185
'asymmetrical client-state', 71–4
    description of, 73
Attali, Jacque, 197
austerity measures and exports, 53
    see also neo-liberal economic
        model
'authoritarian ethnocracies' of
    Balkans and Transcaucasia, 15
authoritarians, return of, 7–8
autocratic tendencies in Balkans
    and Transcaucasia, 64
autonomy, national and regional, 1
Avramović, Dragoslav, 163, 164
Azerbaijan, 70, 72

Bačković, Enver, 94
back-to-roots movements, 1
Bahro, Rudolf, 34
Balkan Conference on Stability and
    Cooperation in South-Eastern
    Europe, 195
Balkanisation, *see* multi-ethnic state
'Balkanism', 12